Jusepe de Ribera español

JUSEPE DE RIBERA

lo Spagnoletto

1591-1652

Edited by Craig Felton
and William B. Jordan

Kimbell Art Museum

Fort Worth, 1982

Distributed by
Washington University Press, Seattle and London

This catalogue is published on the occasion of an exhibition
at the Kimbell Art Museum, Fort Worth
December 4, 1982-February 6, 1983

Copyright 1982
by the Kimbell Art Museum
Library of Congress Card Number 82-84144
ISBN (Cloth) 0-912804-09-2
      (Paper) 0-912804-10-6
Printed in U.S.A.

Design: James A. Ledbetter

COVER
Saint Jerome and the Angel of Judgment, 1626
Museo e Gallerie Nazionali di Capodimonte, Naples
Catalogue number 7

FRONTISPIECE
Saint Matthew (detail), 1632
Kimbell Art Museum
Catalogue number 13

CONTENTS

LENDERS TO THE EXHIBITION

Cambridge (Massachusetts), The Fogg Art Museum, Harvard University (cat. no. 32)

Cleveland, Cleveland Museum of Art (cat. no. 29)

Columbia (South Carolina), Columbia Museums of Art and Science (cat. no. 22)

Dallas, Meadows Museum, Southern Methodist University (cat. no. 24)

Fort Worth, Kimbell Art Museum (cat. no. 13)

Greenville (South Carolina), Bob Jones University Collection of Sacred Art (cat. no. 28)

Hartford, Wadsworth Atheneum (cat. nos. 3, 17)

Indianapolis, Indianapolis Museum of Art (cat. no. 18)

London, Mr. and Mrs. R. E. A. Drey (cat. no. 20)

London, The National Gallery (cat. no. 27)

London, Trafalgar Galleries (cat. no. 30)

London, The Wellington Museum, Apsley House (cat. no. 37)

Madrid, Museo del Prado (cat. nos. 8, 9, 10, 21)

Madrid, Real Academia de Bellas Artes de San Fernando (cat. no. 34)

Mexico City, Collection Franz Mayer (cat. no. 22)

Milan, Archbishop's Palace (cat. no. 15)

Milan, Museo Poldi-Pezzoli (cat. no. 25)

New York, The Metropolitan Museum of Art (cat. no. 36)

Naples, Museo Civico Gaetano Filangieri (cat. no. 39)

Naples, Museo e Gallerie Nazionali di Capodimonte (cat. nos. 6, 7, 38)

Naples, Palazzo Reale (cat. no. 14)

Oberlin (Ohio), Allen Memorial Art Museum, Oberlin College (cat. no. 12)

Osuna, Museo Parroquial de Osuna, Colegiata de Osuna (cat. no. 4)

Paris, Musée du Louvre (cat. no. 33)

Pasadena, Mr. and Mrs. R. Stanton Avery (cat. no. 19)

Pasadena, The Norton Simon Foundation (cat. no. 1)

Philadelphia, Philadelphia Museum of Art (cat. no. 35)

Raleigh (North Carolina), Collection of the North Carolina Museum of Art (cat. no. 31)

Rome, Galleria Corsini (cat. no. 23)

Salisbury (Wiltshire), Collection of the Earl of Pembroke at Wilton House (cat. no. 16)

Strasbourg, Musée des Beaux-Arts, Château des Rohan (cat. no. 5)

Toledo (Ohio), The Toledo Museum of Art (cat. no. 26)

Toledo, Museo Fundación Duque de Lerma, Hospital de Tavera (cat. no. 11)

PREFACE

Exhibitions play a vital role in the life of a museum. They introduce to audiences new areas of art and help to maintain public interest in the permanent collection. Furthermore, exhibitions have the potential of making significant contributions to scholarship and to the diffusion of knowledge.

The principal reason for investing time and energy into the organization of an international loan exhibition like this one devoted to Jusepe de Ribera is its contribution to knowledge. Ribera's paintings offered a unique opportunity as an exhibition topic. An artist of great originality and expressive range, his oeuvre of paintings — mostly of religious and mythological subjects — had a profound impact upon the development of European art. Since this is the first time Ribera has been made the subject of a comprehensive exhibition of paintings, the works on view, as well as the accompanying monographic publication, will attempt to establish a clearer understanding of the artist's place in Western art. From the large number of major works, gathered together with some little known or widely dispersed examples, it is hoped that the museum visitor will be able to examine and evaluate at first hand the artist's imaginative eye and technical skills. Since the tenebrist subtleties and the refined brushwork of Ribera's paintings have heretofore eluded photographers, this opportunity should prove invaluable to students and scholars, and will undoubtedly contribute to the final resolution of some previous questions about stylistic sources, authorship, and dating.

The exhibition has been organized under the direction of Dr. William B. Jordan, Deputy Director of the Kimbell Art Museum, and Dr. Craig Felton, Assistant Director. Our gratitude extends to them as well as to the distinguished international team of scholars who contributed essays to the catalogue: Professor Sir Ellis Waterhouse of Oxford; Professor Jonathan Brown of the Institute of Fine Arts, New York University; and Professor Rosario Villari of the Instituto di Storia Moderna, University of Rome. We also wish to record our very considerable thanks to the many lenders — both private individuals as well as institutions — whose enthusiasm for, and commitment to, the project have enabled us to assemble such a complete representation of Ribera's work. In particular, we wish to acknowledge the generous cooperation and assistance of: Professor Raffaello Causa and his deputy, Professor Nicola Spinosa, of the Museo e Gallerie Nazionali di Capodimonte, Naples; Sr. D. Federico Sopeña and Dr. Manuela B. Mena Marqués of the Museo del Prado, Madrid; M. Pierre Rosenberg of the Musées de France, Paris; Sir Michael Levy of the National Gallery, London; and Sir John Pope-Hennessy and Mr. John Brealey of the Metropolitan Museum of Art, New York. The exhibition's contribution to our knowledge of the subject will, we trust, justify their confidence in the undertaking.

Edmund P. Pillsbury
Director

ACKNOWLEDGEMENTS

There are many friends and colleagues who have offered us their expertise and advice. We wish to express our special gratitude to Professors Sir Ellis Waterhouse, Michael Stoughton, and Jonathan Brown.

We are also deeply indebted to Professor Alfonso E. Pérez Sánchez, Professor Nicola Spinosa, Mlle. Jeannine Baticle, Professor J. H. Elliott, Professor R. Ward Bissell, Professor Marcus Burke, Mrs. Ann Tzeutschler Lurie, Professor Donald Posner, Professor Richard E. Spear, Dr. John T. Spike, and Professor Harold E. Wethey, as well as to Mr. Patrick Matthiesen, Dr. D. Stephen Pepper, and Professor Richard B. Trousdell.

We have also received valuable research assistance from, among others, Miss Helen Sanger of The Frick Art Reference Library, Mr. Robert Riggs Kerr of The Pierpont Morgan Library, Mrs. Karen Harvey and Mrs. Taeko Brooks of The Hillyer Art Library, Smith College, and Mrs. Edith Ostrowsky of The Map Division, The New York Public Library.

Copyediting of the manuscript was carried out by Betsy Colquitt with her usual care and sensitivity. The catalogue design is owed to James A. Ledbetter who has demonstrated his characteristic restraint and good taste.

We owe a final debt of gratitude to the entire museum staff for their patience and dedication. In particular, we wish to acknowledge the assistance of Edmund Pillsbury, who initiated the undertaking and oversaw many of the administrative details, and that of Foster Clayton, Karen King, Perry Huston and the conservation staff, Ruth Ann Rugg, Adrian Martinez, and E. B. Brown and the building staff.

CF and WBJ

FOREWORD

Jusepe de Ribera, called lo Spagnoletto (1591-1652), lived and worked most
of his life in Naples when that city and a sizable part of modern-day Italy
belonged to Spain. He is therefore an artist who has been claimed by posterity
in both countries, but an artist, once renowned, whose accomplishments far
exceed the level of recognition he has enjoyed outside of Italy or Spain in the
twentieth century. It was exactly thirty years ago that the last, indeed the only,
major book in English was published on Ribera's life and art. No major
monographic exhibition of his paintings has ever been held anywhere, yet few
art historians would argue with the assessment that he was the greatest painter
of the Neapolitan Baroque and one of the giants of seventeenth-century
naturalism. That an artist could be at once Neapolitan and profoundly
Spanish sounds like a contradiction, but in Ribera's time to be a citizen of
Naples did not preclude being a Spainard. That the stylistic roots of his art
were unquestionably Italian did not mean that it could not also express
something of the essence of Spanish culture in his time.

Ribera's naturalism and his individual artistic viewpoint are apparent from
his earliest paintings, a period of his work that was scarcely known fifteen
years ago. The heritage of theological reform, expressed by some artists of
the late sixteenth century, was developed much further by Ribera, who gave
compelling psychological characterization to the images of Christian heroes
and martyrs. His own form of naturalism, which is more strikingly physical
than that of any of his contemporaries, is also, paradoxically, more moving
in its spiritual intensity. Ribera's narrative scenes are infused with the
immediacy of actual events. His devotional images of saints are charged with
the directness and conviction of portraits from life. He also put classical
antiquity into the modern artistic idiom. His gods and goddesses do not
descend from some ideal Parnassus but are as tangible and real as are his
Christian saints.

While this exhibition brings together some of Ribera's most famous works,
as well as some that have seldom been seen publicly anywhere, it does not
pretend to document every phase of the artist's career — an ambition that
falls outside the scope of the project and awaits the full-scale retrospective
that will no doubt be organized in Europe on the occasion of the 400th
anniversary of the artist's birth in 1991. It has been our aim rather to
investigate a range of particular historical and stylistic questions posed by
these selected works and thereby to lay a foundation for a more profound
appreciation and understanding of the artist's achievement.

William B. Jordan

Catalogue Number 1
Sense of Touch, ca. 1615-1616
The Norton Simon Foundation, Pasadena

Catalogue Number 3
Sense of Taste, ca. 1615-1616
Wadsworth Atheneum, Hartford

Catalogue Number 5
Saint Peter and Saint Paul, ca. 1618-1620
Musée des Beaux-Arts, Strasbourg

Catalogue Number 6
The Drunken Silenus, 1626
Museo e Gallerie Nazionali di Capodimonte, Naples

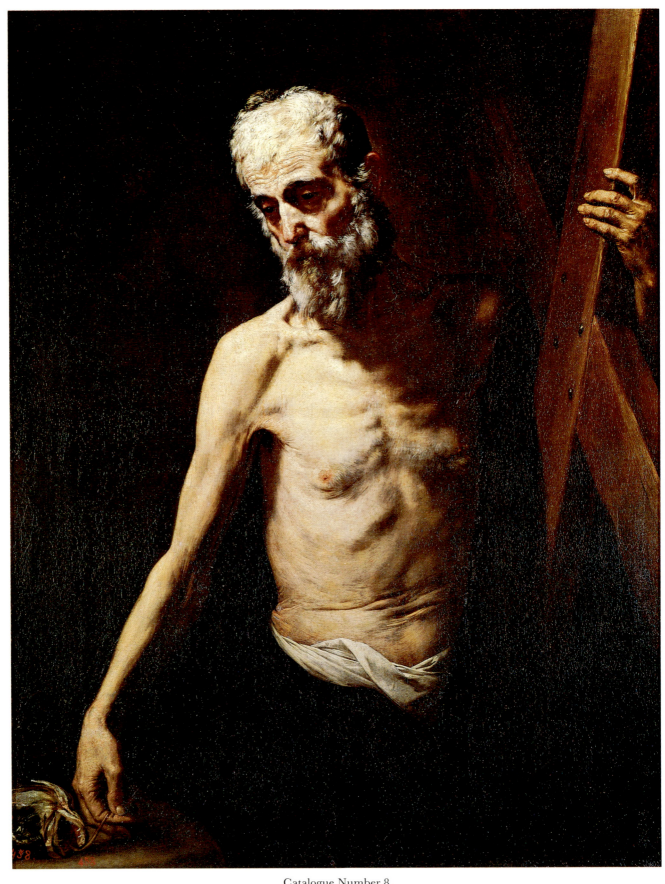

Catalogue Number 8
Saint Andrew with His Cross, ca. 1630-1632
Museo del Prado, Madrid

Catalogue Number 11
Magdalena Ventura with Her Husband and Son, 1631
Museo Fundación Duque de Lerma, Hospital de Tavera, Toledo

Catalogue Number 14
God the Father, ca. 1632-1635
Palazzo Reale, Naples

Catalogue Number 16
Democritus, ca. 1635-1637
From the Collection of the Earl of Pembroke at Wilton House

Catalogue Number 17
A Philosopher (? Protagoras), 1637
Wadsworth Atheneum, Hartford

Catalogue Number 18
A Philosopher (? Aristotle), 1637
Indianapolis Museum of Art

Catalogue Number 19
A Philosopher (? Plato), 1637
Mr. and Mrs. R. Stanton Avery

Catalogue Number 20
Girl with a Tambourine, 1637
Mr. and Mrs. R. E. A. Drey

Catalogue Number 21
Saint Christopher with the Christ Child, 1637
Museo del Prado, Madrid

Catalogue Number 22
Virgin of the Immaculate Conception, 1637
Columbia Museums of Art and Science

Catalogue Number 24
Knight of Santiago, mid-1630s
Meadows Museum, Southern Methodist University, Dallas

Catalogue Number 25
Portrait of a Jesuit, 1638
Museo Poldi-Pezzoli, Milan

Catalogue Number 26
Portrait of a Musician, 1638
The Toledo Museum of Art

Catalogue Number 27
Jacob with the Flock of Laban, 1638
The National Gallery, London

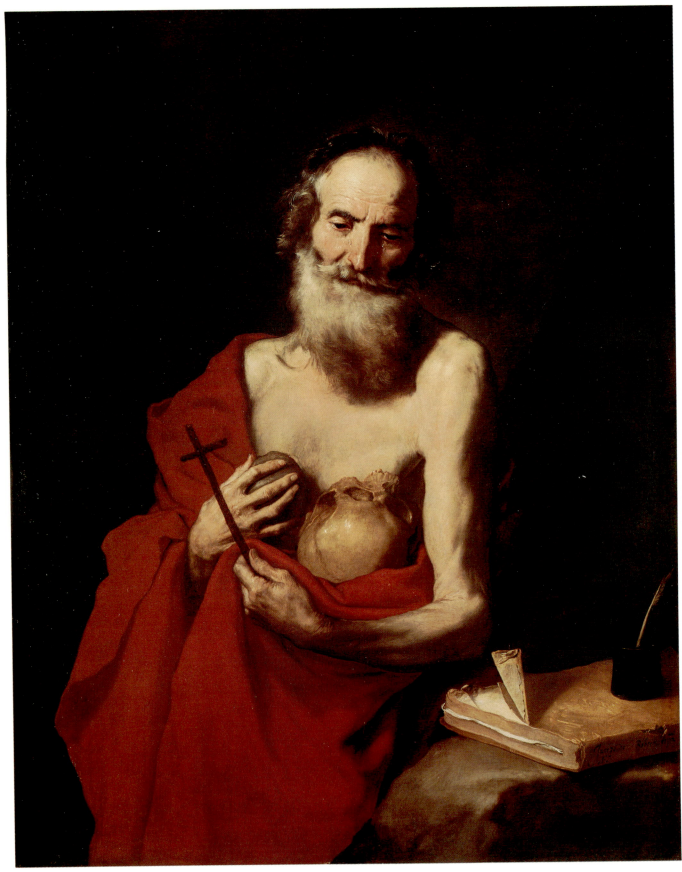

Catalogue Number 29
Saint Jerome, ca. 1638-1640
Cleveland Museum of Art

Catalogue Number 30
The Martyrdom of Saint Bartholomew, ca. 1638-1640
Trafalgar Galleries, London

Catalogue Number 33
The Clubfooted Boy, 1642
Musée du Louvre, Paris

Catalogue Number 36
The Mystical Marriage of Saint Catherine of Alexandria, 1648
The Metropolitan Museum of Art, New York

Catalogue Number 38
Saint Sebastian, 1651
Museo e Gallerie Nazionali di Capodimonte, Naples

CHRONOLOGY

February 17, 1591	Jusepe de Ribera, the second of three sons of Simón de Ribera, a shoemaker from Rusafa (Valencia), and Margarita Cuco, is baptized in the church of Santa Tecla in Játiva, Spain.
1601-1607	Presumed apprenticeship in Valencia.
1607-1614	Ribera's arrival in Naples.
Autumn 1606-July 1607	Caravaggio resident in Naples.
September, October 1609-late July 1610	Caravaggio again in Naples.
1614-1615	Trip to Parma where Ribera worked for Farnese and was praised by Ludovico Carracci as ''that Spanish painter who follows the school of Caravaggio and was with Signor Mario Farnese;'' letter of December 11, 1618.
April 1615	Recorded in the *Status Animarum* of Santa Maria del Popolo, Rome, as resident of via Margutta.
March 1616	Recorded again, having moved to the opposite side of the street.
May 7, 1616	Payment of dues of 12 *scudi* to the Accademia di San Luca, Rome.
1615-1616	Painted *Five Senses* (cat. nos. 1,2,3) (Mancini).
September 15, 1616	Marriage in Naples to Caterina Azzolino y India, daughter of the painter Gian Bernardino Azzolino.
1616-1620	Four *Saints* painted for the Collegiate Church in Osuna, Spain, ancestral home of the Duke of Osuna, Don Pedro Téllez Girón, Viceroy of Naples (see cat. no. 4).
1621	Etches *Saint Jerome Hearing the Trumpet of the Last Judgment* (fig. 53), a second version (fig. 57), and *The Penitence of Saint Peter* (fig. 55).
1622	Etches *Studies of Ears* (fig. 59), *Eyes* (fig. 60), *Nose and Mouth* (fig. 61); *Small Grotesque Head* (fig. 65); and probably *Large Grotesque Head* (fig. 62).

1622	Witnesses sister-in-law's dowry contract which states that Ribera owned a large house in Naples and a country estate by 1620.
1624	Etches *Martyrdom of Saint Bartholomew* (fig. 67) and probably *Saint Jerome Reading* (fig. 68).
1625	Spanish painter Jusepe Martínez visits Ribera in Naples.
January 29, 1626	Appointment to the Order of Christ of Portugal by Pope Urban VIII Barberini.
1626	*Drunken Silenus* (cat. no. 6) painted for Gaspar Roomer; paints two versions of *Saint Jerome and the Angel of Judgment* (cat. no. 7 and fig. 124).
May 3, 1626	Ribera and Caracciolo witness the marriage of Juan Dò, Ribera's studio assistant.
1627	Birth of first of six children to Caterina and Jusepe de Ribera.
1628	Paints *Martyrdom of Saint Andrew* (fig. 126); etches *Drunken Silenus* (fig. 70).
1629-1630	Velázquez visits the court in Naples.
August 17, 1629-May 9, 1631	Viceroyalty of Don Fernando Afán de Ribera, Duke of Alcalá, who probably influences Ribera to paint classical subjects (cat. nos. 9, 10); interested in natural oddities: *Bearded Woman* (cat. no. 11).
April 22, 1630	Prince Luis Moncada, son-in-law of the Duke of Alcalá, witnesses the baptism of Ribera's daughter, Margarita.
1631	Paints *Saint Roch* (fig. 148) and *Saint James Major* (fig. 149).
1632	Paints *Saint Matthew* (cat. no. 13), *Saint Paul* (fig. 137), *Tityus* (fig. 33) and *Ixion* (fig. 34).
1632-1635	Paints *The Holy Family Appearing to Saint Bruno and Other Saints* (fig. 139) and *God the Father* (cat. no. 14).

September 3, 1634	The Duke of Alcalá, the Viceroy of Sicily, commissions from Ribera "a painting of Our Lady showing great Anguish."
1635	Paints *Virgin of Immaculate Conception* (fig. 155) for the High Altar of the Convent Church of Las Agustinas Descalzas, Salamanca, a commission from the Count of Monterrey, Viceroy of Naples, 1631-1637.
1637	Paints a *Pietà* (fig. 25) for the Certosa di San Martino, Naples; paints *Venus Discovering the Dead Adonis* (cat. no. 23), *Apollo Flaying Marsyas* (figs. 165, 166) and *Saint Christopher and the Christ Child* (cat. no. 21).
1638	Receives contract from the Certosa di San Martino for *Moses* (fig. 27), *Elijah* (fig. 28), twelve Old Testament *Prophets* (figs. 29, 30), and the *Communion of the Apostles (Institution of the Holy Eucharist)* (fig. 49).
June 6, 1641	Receives contract from the Deputati of the Tesoro di San Gennaro for *The Escape of Saint Januarius from the Fiery Furnace* (fig. 42) which is not completed until 1646.
1642	Paints the *Clubfooted Boy* (cat. no. 33) for the Duke and Duchess of Medina de las Torres. The Duke (Don Ramiro Nuñez de Guzmán) was Viceroy of Naples 1637-1644; the Duchess was Princess of Stigliano.
1643	Paints *Baptism of Christ* (fig. 40).
July 8-9, 1647	Peasant uprising led by Masaniello (captured and executed July 16) quelled by Don Juan of Austria, illegitimate son of Philip IV, Admiral of the Spanish Fleet and Viceroy of Naples (October 1647-March 1648). Ribera family lives in Royal Palace during this period of unrest.
1647	Paints *Equestrian Portrait of Don Juan of Austria* (fig. 44); paints *Saint Simeon and the Christ Child* (fig. 45) for Don Antonio Ruffo of Messina.
1648	Paints *Mystical Marriage of Saint Catherine of Alexandria* (cat. no. 36); etches *Don Juan of Austria* (fig. 71).

1649-1650	Letters exchanged between Ribera and Ruffo for commission of a *Pietà* (now lost).
1650	Paints *Adoration of the Shepherds* (fig. 46).
June 20, 23 and September 6, 1651	Sends three letters to the prior of the Certosa di San Martino requesting money and lamenting death in Lecce of son-in-law, Giovanni Leonardo Sersale, Margarita's husband.
1651	Completes three paintings for the Certosa di San Martino: the *Communion of the Apostles* (fig. 49), *Saint Jerome* (fig. 47), and *Saint Sebastian* (cat. no. 38).
September 3, 1652	Jusepe de Ribera receives the last rites from a curate from the church of Santa Maria delle Neve at **Mergellina**, outside of Naples, near his country estate.

INTRODUCTION

Ellis Waterhouse

"Ribera was one of the great masters of Italian seventeenth-century painting" — this broadly stated judgment is a convenient oversimplification, perhaps rather like saying that "Henry James is one of the great masters of the English novel." Such a judgment may displease Spanish art historians and would presumably have exasperated Ribera himself, who was constantly adding to his signature that he was "Hispanus," or of Valencia, or even a native of Játiva ("Saetabensis"), and only occasionally added that he was a Roman Academician. If we knew more about the patrons for whom he worked, we might have some idea of the reasons which caused him to vary his signatures in this way. But it can hardly be denied that stylistically he was an Italian painter. He may have learned the rudiments of the practice of painting before he left Spain as a young man, and he probably always retained a memory of the kind of devotional paintings and sculptures to be seen in Spanish churches during his youth, but there is no echo of the Valencian School in his own paintings.

By the time he left Rome for Naples in 1616 — he was not yet thirty — he was already generally known as 'lo Spagnoletto.' This nickname was most probably given him by the foreign painters' colony in Rome, most of them Northerners, who called themselves *De Bentveugheln* and liked to give one another nicknames. It was probably due to the Spanish pretensions Ribera affected, and the diminutive form of the name was probably not affectionate but was perhaps due to his smallness of stature. The nickname proved convenient for Ribera after he had settled in Naples, because the name made clear that he was not a Neapolitan. The one indisputable point about Neapolitan art patronage in the earlier seventeeth century is that there was a prejudice against native Neapolitan painters.

The most prestigious commission likely to be available to a painter in Naples then was the decoration of the new Cappella del Tesoro di S. Gennaro in the Cathedral, and, on May 21, 1621, the Deputies of that Chapel passed a resolution that "the painting of the Chapel of the Glorious S. Gennaro and the necessary stuccoes ought not and cannot at any time in the future be given to a person who is a Neapolitan, or even a foreigner now living in Naples (except for what has already been given to Sr. Fabrizio Santafede) and this decision cannot be revoked for any conceivable reason." Perhaps the best way round such an engrained prejudice was to be a Spaniard, and thus neither a Neapolitan nor a "forastiero." It must be admitted, however, that in 1646, after the death of Domenichino, Ribera was commissioned to paint one of the altarpieces left undone (and Stanzione was given the other). Ribera painted his in the style of Domenichino and firmly put "Hispanus" after his signature.

During the seventeenth century, works by native Spanish painters were hardly known outside Spain, while Ribera's pictures were widely exported (particularly to the Low Countries), so that the name of 'Spagnoletto' became almost synonymous with the idea of Spanish painting for the outside world, and this designation is one of the reasons which has enabled the Spaniards to argue that he was a Spanish painter. The Spanish viceroys and the Spanish court obviously relished Ribera's art, and it is equally obvious that Ribera understood the taste of his Spanish patrons.

Probably the pictures he painted during his first ten years in Naples (1616-1626) were mainly intended for an audience in Spain. No pictures signed and dated before 1626 are known (though he did sign and date a few etchings in these years), but he told Jusepe Martínez, who visited him in 1625, that he was well paid for his works and sufficiently employed, and Martínez reports (in a book published in 1675) that Ribera already had in 1625 what is now called "an international reputation."

Although the commission is not documented, there seems no reason to doubt that Ribera was patronized by the Duke of Osuna, Viceroy from 1616 to 1620, and painted for him, about 1620, the group of unsigned pictures still in the Collegiate Church at Osuna. One of these is the *Saint Sebastian* of this exhibition (cat. no. 4), and it is instructive to compare this work with the *Saint Sebastian* of 1651 (cat.no. 38), one of Ribera's latest works, painted for the Certosa of San Martino. Although technically very different, the spiritual presentation of the saint is more or less identical in the two works. Both figures, treated naturalistically, are real young men preparing, almost with enjoyment, to undergo martyrdom. It can be argued that this depiction reflects a Spanish rather than an Italian taste. In the 1651 picture, the model, conceivably a Carthusian novice, seems to be experiencing the euphoria of martyrdom and an emotional ecstasy like that of Bernini's *Saint Teresa.*

There has, it seems to me, been some degree of misunderstanding about the character of Ribera's first, and Roman, style. Following Mancini's indications, written about 1620, this style has been considered "Caravaggesque." But the Hartford figure representing the *Sense of Taste* (cat. no. 3) is perhaps rather closer to Annibale Carracci's early *Bean Eater* (Rome, Galleria Colonna) than to Caravaggio, and my impression is that the more or less contemporary painter of whom Ribera was most conscious was Guido Reni. During the years 1615/1616 Guido was probably the "smartest" painter in Rome (when he took the trouble to be there), and we know from Mancini that Guido was both aware of Ribera and even thought rather well of his art. The Osuna *Saint Sebastian* is much closer to Guido than to the work of any other painter, and the Osuna *Crucifixion* also owes something to Guido and, like Guido's own rather earlier *Crucifixion of Saint Peter,* is an example of Bolognese classicism tempered by a knowledge of Caravaggio. That rather unexpected divagation from Ribera's normal subject matter, the *Flaying of Marsyas* (fig. 165) can perhaps also be explained by a desire to outdo Guido, who had already painted the same rather uncommon subject (in a picture now at Toulouse). Ribera in fact succeeds. Significantly perhaps, when the monks of San Martino were displeased with an altarpiece that Ribera had painted for them, they commissioned in its place an *Adoration of the Shepherds* from Guido Reni (see cat. no. 14). The stock account given by art historians that, during the 1630s and 1640s, the "Caravaggesque" *tenebroso* style of

Ribera was replaced in Neapolitan painting by Bolognese classicism is not really very perceptive. Such classical tendencies had always been present in the background of Ribera's style.

But it is worth wondering why, after ten years in Naples during which he signed no pictures, Ribera should have emerged from this "incognito" in 1626 with such an unexpected picture (and one of a type he is never known to have repeated) as the *Drunken Silenus* — an eccentricity to which he drew further attention by the splendid etching of 1628, a refined and improved variant, both of which he signed with exceptional fullness, as being by a Spaniard, a Valencian, and a native of Játiva, adding on the painting that he was "academicus Romanus," and on the etching that it was made in "Partenope." If we are right in thinking that the production of his first ten years in Naples nearly all went to Spain, then we can perhaps assume that Ribera was now looking for a new outlet. We are told by Palomino that the *Silenus* was painted for the Antwerp-born Gaspar Roomer, the richest man in Naples, and, apart from the viceroys, the only serious patron of the arts there in the 1620s.

Roomer, in addition to much more grandiose ventures as a financier and shipping magnate, had a flourishing import/export business in the works of contemporary painters, perhaps as a convenient form of ballast, and he specialized in the works of Northern painters working either in the Netherlands or in Italy (more especially in Rome). That by 1630 he already owned in Naples paintings by Van Dyck is known, and I would guess that, by 1626, he had imported at least one of those Bacchanalian scenes which were being produced by the young Van Dyck, Jordaens, or Rubens. The *Silenus* in the London National Gallery (no. 853), which is certainly a product of Rubens' studio, is a picture which may have belonged to another Flemish-Italian businessman (van Uffel) of the same type as Roomer; and I have little doubt that Ribera, who probably thought that his picture was intended for eventual export to the Netherlands, wanted to show that he could produce the same kind of picture, but in a considerably more classical manner and a less kermessy taste. Before the blue drapery oxidized, the *Drunken Silenus* must also have looked rather like a Guido Reni.

Another misunderstanding — that Ribera was essentially a painter of gruesome themes — has become almost canonical, largely owing to Byron's catchy lines:

Spagnoletto tainted
His brush with all the blood of all the sainted.

But it is well to remember that Byron wrote truthfully to John Murray: "I know nothing of painting — and I detest it — unless it reminds me of something I have seen or think it possible to see," and probably Byron's view of Ribera was not the general view of his generation. But Théophile Gautier was surely imitating Byron when he wrote, in a sonnet on that disagreeable *Prometheus* [sic] in the Prado:

Toi, cruel Ribera, plus dur que Jupiter,

Tu fais de ses flancs creux, d'affreuses entailles
Couler à flots de sang des cascades d'entrailles.

It has taken a long time to rid ourselves entirely of this romantic *cliché*. In fact penitence rather than martyrdom is Ribera's favorite activity for Saints, though it is to be feared that sincere penitence may seem a rather gruesome activity today!

The greatest number of Ribera's paintings, however — and a fantastic number of the works of his imitators — consists of half-length figures of elderly male persons, for whom it is not always easy to find a name. This phenomenon is common to many of the great European painters of the first half of the seventeenth century, and it may have been initiated in Spain with El Greco and his series of carefully differentiated Apostles known as *Apostolados*.

During the Renaissance, the Apostles had usually appeared either as undifferentiated types in a long predella, with a figure of Christ in the center, or in pictures of the *Last Supper,* a subject often treated dramatically and not well suited to display a variety of apostolic characters. Ribera, in his great last picture, the huge *Communion of the Apostles (Institution of the Holy Eucharist)* at San Martino (fig. 49), modified this convention by creating a variety of notable types, realistically studied from elderly models. He also seems to have produced *Apostolados,* though no series survives intact today. There is evidence that the young Velázquez may also have produced such a series. Rubens made his first *Apostolado* for a Spanish patron, the Duke of Lerma, and Van Dyck seems to have made at least two sets before 1620, one of which remained intact until the present century. Even a Protestant painter such as Rembrandt created ''Apostle'' types.

Van Dyck and Ribera both chose their models from the humbler walks of life, and Ribera expanded this practice to include patriarchs and prophets (such as those in the spandrels of the nave arcades in San Martino) and also figures which tend generically to be called ''Philosophers.'' Among his followers these sometimes almost degenerate into *genre,* and Luca Giordano in particular painted a considerable number of these ambiguous figures. It may be that a liking for classless, realistic figures of this kind was a Spanish predilection, and it occurs in Spanish Milan, as well as in Spanish Naples. The series of half-length figures — certainly of saints but not always identifiable, which Daniele Crespi painted for the church of Sta. Maria della Passione at Milan during the 1620s — shows a close affinity with Ribera.

A further extension of this taste, more recognizably Spanish, is the tendency for the realistic portrayal of downright oddities. The most famous examples are Velázquez's portraits of the dwarfs and jesters of the Spanish Court. It has often been suggested that Velázquez painted these for his own technical pleasure because he was unable to make technical experiments with commissioned portraits of royalty, but they seem in fact to have been just as much royal commissions as portraits of the royal family. But the prototypes of such pictures in the Spanish royal collections go back to the middle of the sixteenth century, when Antonio Moro, the creator of the Spanish royal portrait, painted *Pejerón* (Prado), the fool of the Count of Benavente, and also Cardinal Granvella's dwarf. In 1590 Sánchez Cotán, who was later to become a very devout Spanish Carthusian, painted the likeness of an elderly lady with a long beard *(La barbuda de Peñaranda)* which is a forerunner of Ribera's *Magdalena Ventura* (cat. no. 11). The motive for such pictures was certainly not vulgar curiosity but rather the wish to record one of God's marvelous and surprising creations.

One would like to know whether the same motive prevailed in the painting of what is surely Ribera's masterprice, *'Le Pied Bot'* (cat. no. 33) in the Louvre. This faithful and realistic image shows a figure we might quite possibly see in Naples today. The portrait reveals the quintessential Neapolitan *scugnizzo,* here unusually landscaped, and it has a radiant quality of life which suggests the feeling that God is justified in all his works, however distorted they may be. In the work of the Ostade or the Le Nain brothers (and of many other seventeenth-century painters), we have an uneasy feeling that the notion prevailed that the lower classes were really rather picturesque. It is my impression that such an idea is shamed out of existence by Ribera, and we would give much to know under what circumstances the picture came to be painted. Interestingly, it came to the Louvre in 1869 with the bequest of Dr. Louis La Caze, which included other major masterpieces depicting classless heroes — pictures which were very little esteemed at the time, such as Watteau's *Gilles* and a wonderful series of humble still lives by Chardin. It is perhaps fair to say that Ribera's finest achievements, rather than being specifically Spanish or Italian, have an international status in an ideal world of the imagination which has a sophisticated concern with human values.

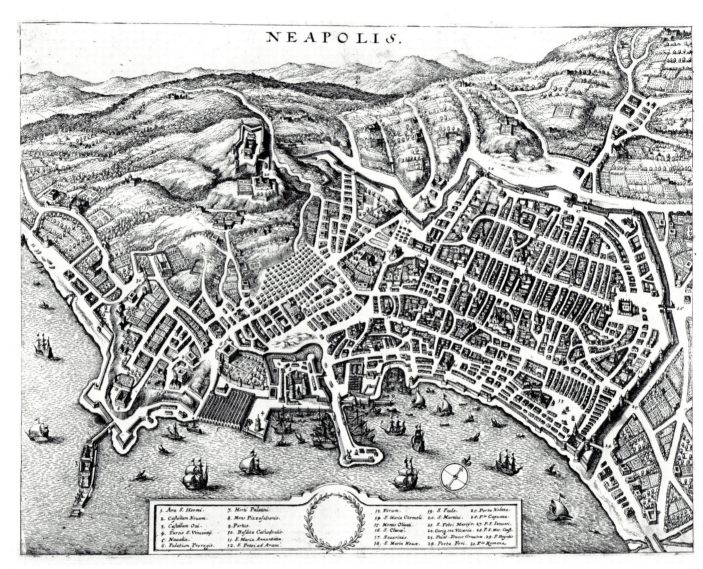

NEAPOLIS.

1. Arx S. Hermi.	7. Horti Palatini.		13. Forum.	19. S. Paulo.	25. Porta Nolana.
2. Castellum Nouum.	8. Mons Pizzafalconis.		14. S. Maria Carmeli.	20. S. Martini.	26. Pta Capuana.
3. Castellum Oui.	9. Portus.		15. Monte Oliueti.	21. S. Petri Martyr.	27. P.S. Ianuari.
4. Turzie S. Vincentij.	10. Basilica Cathedralis.		16. S. Clarae.	22. Curia seu Vicaria.	28. P.S. Mar. Cost.
5. Naualia.	11. S. Maria Annunhata.		17. Souerinis.	23. Palat. Ducis Grauina.	29. P. Regalis.
6. Palatium Proregis.	12. S. Petri ad Aram.		18. S. Maria Nouae.	24. Porta Fori.	30. Pta Romana.

Figure 1
Map of Naples, 1646, Courtesy of The Map
Division, The Research Libraries, The New York
Public Library

NAPLES IN THE TIME OF RIBERA
Rosario Villari

During the first half of the seventeenth century, Naples became the most crowded city in Europe. Its population, already very dense at the end of sixteenth century, increased to about 450,000 during the next fifty years. This exceptional concentration of the population in the capital, caused primarily by immigration from the surrounding countryside, reflected a social imbalance in the Kingdom of Naples. In other parts of Europe and Italy, the movement of manufactures and capital in the period following the end of the great economic expansion of the sixteenth century, had been away from the cities, where economic activity was hampered by guild regulations and official control and into the countryside and villages. In the Kingdom of Naples, on the other hand, the rigidity of baronial domination left little room for initiative in the countryside. The result of this was that a growing population continued to flow toward the capital city, while in the countryside the beginning of the period of crisis coincided with the greatest outbreak of banditry that southern Italy had ever known.

But Naples' population explosion was not caused solely by emigration from the countryside, and its results, at least in the initial stages, were not entirely negative. The Kingdom of Naples had passed under Spanish control in the fifteenth century, and since then the city of Naples had become an increasingly important commercial and financial center. Businessmen from Genoa, Tuscany, Lombardy, Flanders, Portugal, and Spain were attracted to Naples chiefly by the possibilities of tax farming, and of securing commercial and feudal rights in exchange for loans made to the Spanish Crown. The development of an administration and political apparatus — about a third of it, at the higher levels, consisting of Spaniards — also contributed to the growth of the city. Moreover, the immigrants from the provinces were not exclusively, and perhaps not even primarily, poverty-stricken peasants and starving vagabonds. "The wealthy are coming to live in Naples," reads a document from the second half of the sixteenth century; that this was at least partly true is demonstrated by the fact that the seven suburban areas that grew up outside the city walls were not miserable shanty-towns but new neighborhoods which resembled those already in existence. Like them they were residential centers bustling with commercial and artisan activity. At this time, the city still had a relatively strong industrial base. Apart from its principal industrial occupation, the manufacture of silk, the port and the arsenal generated intense activity, and there was a widespread network of artisan and commercial enterprises.

Despite overcrowding and its attendant problems, Naples in the seventeenth century nonetheless managed to sustain a balanced and orderly urban life. In character it remained firmly within the Italian and European civic tradition, with its population still organized on a corporate institutional basis. The city was divided into *ottine* or sections with their own headquarters and popular leaders. The nobility were grouped into *Seggi* or small assemblies and there were guilds and confraternities, together with police and welfare institutions. In politics and administration, in religion and culture, activity was great and constantly growing.

Figure 2
The Count of Lemos, 1610, from Parrino, *Teatro eroico de' Vicere di Napoli,* 1692

Figure 3
Artist Unknown. *Francisco de Quevedo,* ca. 1630, Instituto de Valencia de Don Juan, Madrid

Admittedly, even if the city succeeded in avoiding the kind of disintegration that was to overtake it in later times, Naples had been experiencing the symptoms of crisis since the last two decades of the sixteenth century. But while the countryside reacted above all with banditry, the city itself responded to the new difficulties with a notable enrichment of its intellectual life and an intensification of the political struggle. There are clear parallels between the history of Naples and that of Spain in the period covering the end of the sixteenth to the middle of the seventeenth century. Both were faced with social and political decline, and in both there was a corresponding ferment of ideas, proposals, and attempts at reform, along with a new literary and artistic flowering and a promise of new scientific inquiry. In this sense, Naples, like Spain, had a little "golden century" of its own. In the city, there was no lack of violent tension, but the outbreaks of violence, unlike those in the countryside, became intertwined with the cultural movement, and even at the beginning, had some political and idealistic content. Two famous episodes at the end of the sixteenth century can be considered as manifestations of an economic, political, and ideological crisis. One was the popular uprising of 1585, which had at least an indirect connection with Giambattista della Porta and Colantonio Stigliola and with the group of naturalists associated with the Natural History Museum of Ferrante. The other was the resistance of the Monastery of San Domenico to an attempt by the papal nuncio and the government to evict its monks. The Monastery of San Domenico was one of the main centers of intellectual life in the Kingdom of Naples: the famous philosopher, Giordano Bruno, spent all his formative years there; the visionary and political theorist Tommaso Campanella stayed there periodically in the decade before he was arrested for his attempt at rebellion; and one of Caravaggio's first paintings to be seen in Naples, the *Flagellation of Christ,* was placed in a chapel there.

These and other politico-cultural events of the time demonstrate that the little "golden century" of Naples was hardly one in which living conditions were easy. In reality it was an age full of contrasts, violence, and deep exasperation. But the viceroys who governed Naples for the King of Spain were not insensitive to, nor untouched by, the reforming winds beginning to blow through Neapolitan society and culture. An early example of this is provided by Enrique de Guzmán, Count of Olivares (the father of the future principal minister of Philip IV of Spain), who served as Viceroy of Naples from 1595 to 1599. His predecessor, the Count of Miranda, had reported adversely on the situation in Naples, and in particular on the crown's lack of authority and the excessive power of the nobility. Olivares tried to deal with these problems, but the reaction of the nobility led to his removal from office and his recall to Madrid. A Neapolitan writer, Giulio Cesare Capaccio, noted later: "If Philip II had not died, it is believed that Olivares would not have been removed so quickly from office, for he seems to me to have governed like a true Viceroy." This observation, made when Philip IV was on the Spanish throne, was probably intended not so much to exalt the figure of Philip II as to express the idea of a decline, of a loss of power and prestige by the Spanish Monarchy, under the government of his successor, Philip III (1598-1621). But in the first

Figure 4
The Duke of Osuna, 1616, from Parrino, *Teatro eroico de'*
Vicere di Napoli, 1692

two decades of the century, the main current of the Neapolitan reform movement, which expressed ideas and attitudes that were widespead among members of the city's middle class like Capaccio himself, tended to look to the Spanish crown to bring about reforms in the face of intense opposition by an autonomous nobility.

One of the successors of Olivares, Pedro Fernández de Castro, Count of Lemos (fig. 2), Viceroy of Naples from 1610 to 1616, succeeded in realizing a partial but important program of reform: but this was possible because his activities, which were concentrated on administrative and financial reformation, left the functions and power of the nobility untouched. In 1615, the year before Ribera's arrival in Naples, the Count of Lemos, continuing his reform program, issued orders for the reorganization of the university, taking as his model the statutes of the University of Salamanca in Spain. He also ordered the construction of a new university center (until that time, the *Studium* had been located in the Monastery of San Domenico). Lemos' initiative was part of a complex political scheme designed to promote and control cultural life and reform the administration, while at the same time reinforcing Spanish hegemony. His plans led to the intensification of exchanges with Spain and to an increased Spanish cultural presence in Naples, but it also had other consequences, not least for the Spaniards themselves. They had always been fascinated by Renaissance and post-Renaissance Italy. Now, as they tried to come to grips with the problems of their own country, some of them were influenced by the lively political debate under way in Naples. The most striking example of this is provided by the great Spanish writer, Francisco de Quevedo (fig. 3). As adviser to the Duke of Osuna (fig. 4) who governed Naples from 1616 to 1620, he was a participant in the last dramatic attempt made by a Spanish viceroy to collaborate with Neapolitan reformers in a common program of reform.

At that time the two greatest Neapolitan intellectuals, the philospher Tommaso Campanella and the economist Antonio Serra, were in prison. The same fate had befallen in earlier years one of the initiators of the reform movement, the historian Giovanni Antonio Summonte, who had been forced to submit to the burning of his *History of the Kingdom of Naples,* and its republication in a censored version. In spite of all this, the reform movement, which was divided into twenty-nine sections, with its center located in the Monastery of Sant'Agostino, continued to develop inside the framework of the administrative and political life of the populace. It also had a following among the founders and members of the Accademia degli Oziosi, a cultural institution of great importance which had come into existence with the help of the Viceroy Lemos.

The main objective of the reformers was equal representation of nobility and commoners in the government of the city. This looked like a limited objective, but in reality its realization would have had great repercussions on the political order of the entire Kingdom and on its relations with Spain. During his viceroyalty of 1616-1620, the Duke of Osuna adopted this program and tried to carry it out with support of a large popular movement led by the jurist Giulio

Figure 5
Duke of Medina de las Torres, 1637, from Parrino, *Teatro eroico de' Vicere di Napoli,* 1692

Figure 6
Micco Spadaro. *The Masaniello Uprising (1647),* Museo Nazionale di San Martino, Naples

Genoino. But his initiative was thwarted by the government in Madrid, and by extremely strong resistance in Naples itself. The Duke of Osuna, the target of violent accusations by the representatives of the nobility, was recalled to Spain, put on trial, and excluded from all political and governmental activities; Genoino was imprisoned in a fortress in northern Africa from which he was freed almost by accident twelve years later.

The failure of Osuna's reforming initiative and the fate of its promoters were the prelude to a change in the position and function of Naples within the Spanish dominions. The reform movement in Naples had been defeated. When Philip IV came to the throne of Spain in 1621, he and his ministers were preoccupied with Spain's domestic problems and with questions of imperial defense; and when they turned their attention to Naples, it was primarily as a potential supplier of men and money for Spain's wars against the Dutch and the French.

The enormous financial burden imposed on Naples in the 1620s and 1630s played havoc with its economy and its administration, especially during the viceroyalties of Ribera's patron, the Count of Monterrey (1631-1637) (fig. 167), and his successor, the Duke of Medina de las Torres (1637-1644) (fig. 5). ''I beg Your Majesty,'' wrote the latter to Philip IV, ''to consider that he is asking for even more money from this Kingdom than he is receiving from the silver mines of America.'' But even worse than the quantities demanded were the methods used to raise the money. Acquiescence was secured by the concession of substantial privileges to the feudal baronage and to a group of large-scale speculators. The anti-feudal policies pursued in the sixteenth century by Ferdinand the Catholic and the Emperor Charles V, and continued with difficulty by Philip II, were overturned and abandoned. When one of the most anarchical and unruly of the barons, Gian Girolamo Acquaviva, Count of Conversano, was arrested in Naples in 1643 for crimes committed in his fiefs in Apulia and for conspiring with French agents in Italy, the King took the trial into his own hands, and the Count came back from Spain with a pardon in his pocket and with a grant of new feudal prerogatives. ''The times are unfavorable for major administrative changes,'' commented the Duke of Medina de las Torres when faced with other similar events, ''but the system of government in this city is so unsatisfactory that, for its own benefit and tranquillity, Your Majesty should take the matter in hand.'' A few years later, in July 1647, the tensions that had accumulated over half a century and that had been aggravated by the heavy repercussions of the Thirty Years War gave rise to a revolutionary movement which spread out into the provinces from the capital. During the initial phase of this Neapolitan revolution of 1647-1648, the idea of the appeal to the sovereign, of the convergence between monarchical absolutism and popular reformism, was upheld once again by the aging Giulio Genoino, partly to reduce the trauma of a violent break with legality. But in reality a deep rupture had been created between Naples and the Spanish Crown. In various ways, through cautious references to the revolt of the Netherlands or to a presumed age-old republican tradition in Naples, the idea of independence from Spain had already

Figure 7
The Count of Oñate, 1648, from Parrino, *Teatro eroico de' Vicere di Napoli,* 1692

penetrated the popular movement. The course of the revolution, which lasted from July 1647 to April 1648 turned at an early stage toward open confrontation with Spain and the creation of an independent Republic. The myth of the ancient republican tradition, which had been developed some years earlier by the historian Francesco De Pietri and which had circulated among the learned as a mere piece of scholarly erudition, now became the subject of political propaganda and an argument in favor of independence: ''What participant in political debate can be so recklessly ignorant,'' wrote Giuseppe Donzelli in *Partenope liberata,* published during the course of the debate, ''as not to know that the city of Naples has been a free republic for three thousand years. . . and freedom is truly one of the noblest prerogatives of man, and such a sweet source of sustenance that by simply smelling it one can be nourished. It is not therefore surprising that it is avidly desired. . . and all the more so by those peoples who, fed on it for thousands of years, were then reduced to centuries of fasting.'' One indication of the distance now separating the people of Naples from the Spanish Monarchy was the unanimity of view that had emerged among intellectuals and artists about the revolt itself. A remarkable, and indeed unprecedented, manifestation of this unanimity is to be found in the depiction of the revolt in contemporary paintings. Two artists, Micco Spadaro in Naples, followed by Cerquozzi in Rome, did paintings showing the first stage of the revolution. Of the two, Spadaro's was the more penetrating, displaying a greater wealth of detail and more knowledge of the political and social problems involved (fig. 6).

The revolt came to an end in 1648 not because of the repression carried out by the barons in the provinces, nor because of the arrival of the Spanish army, but for reasons of a purely political and social nature. The first was the lack of connection and the difference in character between the revolts in the provinces and in the capital, together with the relative weakness of the social base of the movement as a whole; the other was the skill displayed by one of the last political figures of real stature in the service of the Spanish Hapsburgs, the Count of Oñate (fig. 7). On becoming viceroy of Naples (1648-1653) he succeeded in securing an agreement with the principal popular leaders and made himself the partial interpreter of the aspirations for reform. There was no basic change in the political and social situation, and indeed the plague of 1656 still further weakened the productive capacity of the Kingdom. But the cultural and political ferment of those fifty years remained a reference point for later generations, especially in the period between the attainment of independence in the earlier eighteenth century and the new republican experience of 1799.

THE PAINTINGS OF RIBERA

Craig Felton

Jusepe de Ribera—a Spaniard from the city of Valencia, member of the Accademia di San Luca in Rome, knight of the Order of Christ of Portugal, court painter to successive viceroys in the Kingdom of Naples—ranked among the most innovative and important artists of his day. His works were collected by King Philip IV, the grandees of Spain, and prominent religious institutions in Naples. The many contemporary copies and imitations of his paintings attest to his fame during his lifetime. Then almost from the moment of his death, the fame and the fortune he expected his art to provide his family diminished; subsequently, both the painter and his artistic legacy have often been misrepresented.

Of the major seventeenth-century Spanish painters—Velázquez, Zurbarán, Murillo, and Ribera—"lo Spagnoletto," as Ribera was called, remains the least known and studied. Although he signed most of his canvases "español," his first major biographer, Bernardo De Dominici, wrote mistakenly in 1742 that Ribera's birthplace was in Lecce, in the heel of the Italian peninsula.[1] An accurate outline of his biography was not gathered until the end of the nineteenth century, and the important documents establishing his presence in Rome in 1615 were discovered barely a decade ago. As yet, history remains silent about his artistic origins in Spain, about the date at which he left his native land, and about his training and career to his twenty-fifth year. With whom or in what studios in Italy he may have worked is unknown, and only a few paintings from his earliest years seem to have survived (see cat. nos. 1, 2, 3).

But if many facts about Ribera's life await discovery, the reasons for his, or any other artist's, settling in Naples in the seventeenth century are readily apparent. Naples, second largest city in Europe (only Paris was larger), experienced economic and political advantages unknown elsewhere. The capital of the Kingdom of Naples, the city was a rich and valued part of the Spanish royal domain. The governing officer, a viceroy appointed by the Crown, enjoyed Spain's most lucrative diplomatic post.[2] In Naples, the viceroys, invariably of Spain's oldest and noblest families, augmented their fortunes and directed large portions of their wealth and influence to enlarging both the King's art collection and their own. Frequently, viceroys succeeded to their posts in Naples after service as Spanish ambassadors to the Holy See in Rome, where they had the opportunity to become knowledgeable about modern currents in Italian painting. Such was the case with viceroys as early as the reign of Philip II (1556-1598), who admired and collected Venetian painting. By the reign of Philip IV (1621-1665) in the seventeenth century, the Roman appointment was a usual steppingstone to the more important Neapolitan office. Philip IV's prime minister, the Count-Duke of Olivares, secured diplomatic appointments for members of his family, such as the Count of Monterrey, and for his trusted officials. The personal allegiances of the prime minister encouraged his tolerance of the excesses of the Neapolitan court, and shipments of paintings from Italy to Madrid assured Olivares' favor with the Crown. In Madrid, Olivares was charged with building and decorating the Palace of the Buen Retiro, a project which continued during Ribera's maturity

Far enough removed from Spain to operate independently, Naples in the seventeenth century became the major commercial port in the Mediterranean. In keeping with its increasing importance, the city undertook extensive building programs—a new royal palace, churches, convents, and monasteries. Second only to Rome as the greatest center of art patronage in southern Europe, Naples had the unique advantage of a direct connection to the Spanish court. In Spain Philip IV's residences, as well as the elaborate houses of his grandees, had art collections rivaling those in Italy of the Barberini, Giustiniani, Borghese, Ludovisi, Farnese, and Pamphilj.

In 1625 when the Spaniard Jusepe Martínez traveled to Italy, he reported on his meeting with Ribera.[4] When Martínez inquired why Ribera remained in Naples, ''lo Spagnoletto'' answered that Spain piously mothered strangers, but to her own sons was a cruel stepmother. Ribera predicted that Spain would welcome him home as a great painter but within a year would ignore him. Yet Ribera's patrons included his countrymen in Naples as well as collectors in Spain. His adopted city provided obvious advantages for his career: he had two centers of patronage, and he was well situated to keep in touch with changing artistic fashions in Italy. He also had married in Naples and became owner of substantial properties there. As becomes clear from Professor Villari's essay in this volume, an explanation for Ribera's pointed insistence on his Spanish origin and allegiance was the urgent campaign of the viceroys to maintain a Spanish hegemony over an increasingly rebellious population. He was clearly the painter of the ruling elite.

• • •

The first modern study of the paintings of Ribera was written by August L. Mayer as a dissertation for the University of Leipzig in 1908. Thereafter Mayer, a pioneer in the scholarship of Spanish painting, published many articles on Ribera, and his monograph *Jusepe de Ribera,* which appeared in 1923, contained the first extensive checklist of the autograph and attributed paintings of the artist. Other significant studies published in the 1920s include articles by Elías Tormo y Monzó and his *Ribera* (1922) and George Pillements' *Ribera* (1929) with its important critical observations on the artist. The first substantial biography in English on Ribera is Elizabeth DuGué Trapier's book of 1952, which incorporates all data then known and evaluates the major works of Ribera's oeuvre. Many later writers such as Delphine Fitz Darby, José Milcua, Ulisse Prota-Giurleo, Carlos Sarthou Carreres, to mention only a few, have pursued individual problems of attribution, iconography, interpretation, and documentation.

Since 1966, when Roberto Longhi published a short but seminal article about Ribera's *Five Senses* (see cat. nos. 1, 2, 3), the artist's paintings have received increasing scholarly attention. Part of this interest has arisen from the efforts of Professor Raffaello Causa, Soprintendente per i Beni Artistici e Storici della Campania and Director of the Museo di Capodimonte, who publishes extensively on Neapolitan art and encourages scholarship on the subject. My dissertation for the University of Pittsburgh in 1971 entitled *Jusepe de Ribera, a*

Catalogue Raisonné and available through University Microfilms, Ann Arbor, attempted to bring together all the Ribera material known at the time and to sort out autograph works from the many hundreds of paintings attributed to Ribera. In 1978, Dr. Nicola Spinosa, Deputy Director of the Capodimonte Museum, published in the Rizzoli series, Classici dell'arte, another complete catalogue of Ribera's paintings, accompanied by an insightful essay by Dr. Alfonso E. Pérez Sánchez. With the benefit of Dr. Spinosa's excellent critical observations and the opportunity provided by this project to review the artist's paintings, many of my earlier opinions and conclusions have been revised.

Although Mayer also cited a few drawings attributed to Ribera in his 1923 monograph, this part of Ribera's oeuvre has been systematically explored only in recent years. The late Dr. Walter Vitzthum published articles during the 1960s in which he presented his discoveries of many of Ribera's drawings. His work culminated in the inclusion of a splendid group of Ribera drawings in an exhibition entitled *Cento disegni napoletani* held at the Uffizi in 1967. Studies by Professor Jonathan Brown have further advanced our knowledge of this phase of Ribera's art. Professor Brown also arranged the impressive exhibition of Ribera's drawings and etchings at The Art Museum, Princeton University, in 1973, and the exhibition catalogue is a major contribution in recent Ribera studies. Brown's continuing investigations have resulted in several articles, including the essay in this publication.

● ● ●

From the substantial Ribera scholarship now available, the main outline of the artist's life has been established with some clarity. Born in Játiva, a small mountain town south of Valencia, Ribera could claim Spanish nationality of which he remained proud throughout his life; nevertheless, he left his homeland in his youth, traveled to Italy to learn from the great works of the Renaissance, and never returned to Spain. A very likely port of entry for the young Spaniard was Naples. Presumably, he established himself there temporarily before going north to complete his studies and to further his skills. The artistic styles and influences most prized in Naples were Italian, with the predominant sources of inspiration coming from Rome. Various biographers relate that Ribera went to the north of Italy, settled briefly in Parma, and later lived briefly in Rome. Easter census records taken in Rome for the parish of Santa Maria del Popolo in 1615 and 1616 are the first documents pertaining to Ribera as an adult.[5] In April 1615, Ribera, then twenty-four, resided in quarters in the via Margutta. He shared a household with his brother Juan, with Giovanni Coraldo and Giovanni Calvo, both of Saragossa, and with Pietro Maria da Valerano Garzone, an Italian. The census of March 1616 lists the same household members, living by then on the opposite side of the same street. Other archival records indicate that on May 7, 1616, Ribera paid his dues to the Accademia di San Luca in Rome.[6] Then with surprising abruptness, he left Rome for Naples where ecclesiastical records document his marriage on September 15, 1616.

Documents pertaining to Ribera's youth are scant. The register in the church of Santa Tecla in Játiva records the marriage of the painter's parents, Simón Ribera, a shoemaker originally from the Valencian suburb of Rusafa, and Margarita Cuco, on January 17, 1588.[7] Their first son, Jerónimo, was baptized on October 1, 1588; Jusepe was baptized on February 17, 1591; and their last son, Juan, was baptized on May 12, 1593. Juan followed Jusepe to Italy and worked in his studio in Naples. In July 1597 Ribera's father married Angela Ferrandiz.[8]

Although little is known of Ribera's earliest years, he would have been apprenticed at the age of twelve or thirteen to a master artist who would have educated him and assigned such elementary tasks as grinding pigments and preparing canvases. Unverified in the Ribera biography is the suggestion that the young Jusepe was apprenticed in the studio of Francisco Ribalta (1565-1628), the preeiminent painter of Valencia. This notion was originally stated in Antonio Palomino's *El parnaso español pintoresco laureado,* published in Madrid in 1724.[9] In his biographies of artists Palomino states that Ribalta studied in Italy in the hope of making himself a suitor worthy to marry his master's daughter. By Palomino's account, Ribalta's study concentrated on the works of Raphael, Annibale Carracci, and Sebastiano del Piombo. Later in this treatise, however, Palomino contradicts himself on Ribalta's Italian journey. As Darby pointed out in 1938, Ribalta's teacher was Juan Fernández Navarrete, ''El Mudo,'' in Madrid, and Ribalta married Inéz Pelayo, who died in childbirth in 1601.[10] Because Ribera's name follows that of Ribalta in Palomino's manuscript, Darby hypothesized in her monograph *Francisco Ribalta and His School* that a page perhaps became misplaced and was inserted in the wrong sequence; no present evidence indicates that Ribalta left Spain during his youth. The story about the student artist traveling to Italy to perfect his skills and to earn his future bride is perhaps more appropriately assigned to the biography of Ribera. But as Darby further notes, the name of Ribera figures in no documents of Ribalta and his studio.

The persistence of the Ribalta-Ribera connection continues in twentieth-century literature on Ribera. For example, González Martí wrote in 1928 that Ribera entered Ribalta's studio in 1601, remained there until 1607, and after a violent argument with his master, left suddenly for Naples. The argument developed out of a flirtation involving Ribalta's daughter María Ana. On coming to Naples, Ribera was reunited with his father after a separation of about two years. González Martí provides no documentation supporting any of these details.

Ribalta's studio was Valencia's most prestigious, and its fame and its location near Játiva make plausible the young Ribera's learning there the rudiments of painting before his journey to Italy. In 1607, Ribera was sixteen; for an ambitious youth seeking an artistic career, this age was appropriate to leave Spain for the attractions of Italy.

Figure 9
Caravaggio. *Flagellation of Christ,* 1607, Museo e
Gallerie Nazionali di Capodimonte, Naples

Figure 8
Caravaggio, *Seven Works of Mercy,* 1607, Pio Monte
della Misericordia, Naples

If Ribera indeed arrived in Naples in 1607, the busy port city would have
offered the young artist many discoveries. The major artistic figure then in
Naples was Michelangelo Merisi da Caravaggio, who had left Rome on
May 31, 1606, as a fugitive from justice.

Caravaggio's arrival in Naples sometime in late September or early October
of 1606 must have caused great excitement because by October 6 he had
already accepted a commission from Nicolò Radolovich for a large painting
now lost of the Madonna and Child surrounded by a glory of angels and
adored by Saints Dominic and Francis on one side and Saints Nicolò and Vito
on the other.[11] For another major painting, *The Seven Works of Mercy* (fig. 8),
commissioned by the governors of the Pio Monte della Misericordia for the
principal altar of their church, Caravaggio received payment by January 9,
1607.[12] On May 11 and 29 of 1607, Caravaggio received payments on a
Flagellation of Christ (fig. 9), commissioned by the De Franchis (or De Franco)
family for their chapel in San Domenico Maggiore. A *Crucifixion of Saint Andrew*
was commissioned from Caravaggio in 1607 by Don Juan Alonso Pimental y
Herrera, 8th Count of Benevente, and Viceroy of Naples from 1603 to 1610.
Taken to Spain in July of 1610, the painting was acquired by the Cleveland
Museum of Art in 1976.[13] Presumably Caravaggio brought the *Madonna
of the Rosary,* now in the Kunsthistorisches Museum in Vienna, with him on
his journey from Rome to Naples. Thus, Naples between 1607 and 1610
offered several major Caravaggio paintings which Ribera could have seen.[14]

Figure 11
Carlo Sellitto. *Christ Saving Saint Peter from the Sea,*
ca. 1608, Santa Maria di Monteoliveto, Naples

The year 1607 proved also a turning point in Neapolitan painting. With Caravaggio's arrival, the predominant style almost immediately changed from an adherence to fashionable late mannerist Roman decorative painting to a direct adaptation of Caravaggio's naturalism, heightened by an even more intense chiaroscuro termed "tenebrism." Even when Roman-Bolognese classicism affected the next generation of Neapolitan painters, a certain Caravaggesque naturalism lingered.

Upon arriving in Naples, Ribera would have continued his training. Although no documents illuminate this stage of his career, it is tempting to surmise that Ribera studied with one of Caravaggio's adherents in Naples. The first native Neapolitan painter immediately responsive to Caravaggio's art was Giovanni Battista Caracciolo (1578-1635), whose *Immaculate Conception,* painted in 1607 for Santa Maria della Stella, demonstrates his awareness of Caravaggio's remarkable achievements.[15] Also among the earliest Neapolitan followers of Caravaggio is Carlo Sellitto (1580-1614), who received commissions in many important churches.[16] His *Christ Giving the Keys to Saint Peter* (fig. 10) and *Christ Saving Saint Peter from the Sea* (fig. 11), both painted about 1608 for the Cortone Chapel in Sant'Anna dei Lombardi, have technical similarities with the *Penitent Saint Peter* (fig. 120) painted by Ribera for the Collegiate Church of Osuna, ca. 1616-1618 (see cat. no. 4). If Ribera worked in Sellitto's studio in 1614, the latter's untimely death on October 1 of that year might account for Ribera's departure for the north of Italy.

Figure 10
Carlo Sellitto. *Christ Giving the Keys to Saint Peter,*
ca. 1608, Santa Maria di Monteoliveto, Naples

Figure 12
Ribera. *Martyrdom of Saint Bartholomew,* ca. 1616, H. Shickman Gallery, New York

Figure 13
Ribera. *Derision of Christ,* 1616-1618, Pinacoteca di Brera, Milan   (Alinari)

• • •

Until about fifteen years ago, the earliest known painting by Ribera was the *Drunken Silenus* (cat. no. 6), signed and dated 1626. Since then, the first works to be recognized from the previous decade are the paintings representing the *Five Senses* (cat. nos. 1, 2, 3), which are mentioned by Mancini.[17]

On Ribera's early career, the seventeenth-century commentator Francesco Scannelli is helpful.[18] Writing in 1657, five years after Ribera's death, Scannelli remarks of Ribera's early paintings:

> In Rome around this time [the second decade of the
> seventeenth century] rather mannered subjects painted by
> the artist called "lo Spagnoletto" imitated truth successfully,
> but were as yet weak in technique and invention. The
> paintings are nearby, especially in Rome; the best are in the
> Palace of Prince Giustiniani where there are several works.

A few surviving paintings fit Scannelli's description and may be placed among Ribera's early works, in the general period of the Osuna *Saints* (see cat. no. 4). A *Martyrdom of Saint Bartholomew* (fig. 12) in a private collection in New York may be identifiable with the earliest of these paintings.[19] Another autograph work surely belonging to these years is the *Derision of Christ* (fig. 13) now in the Brera. The subject demonstrates the rugged naturalism for which Caravaggio is famous; in fact, according to Bellori, Caravaggio also painted such a work (known only through a possible copy in Vienna) for the Marchese Vincenzo Giustiniani. Other versions of the subject by Manfredi, Valentin, and Orazio Gentileschi (fig. 14) explore this Caravaggesque idiom, and Ribera probably knew such works in Rome.[20] Although Ribera's *Derision* uses full-length figures, their immediacy and scale are similar to figures in works by Caravaggio's first-generation followers. The lighting formula, with bright passages and areas of heavy shadows merging into a uniformly dark background, is also consistent with paintings by the Caravaggisti in Rome during the second decade of the century. Ribera's figures strike theatrical poses derived from sixteenth-century sources, largely known through prints. The composition combines late mannerist design, Caravaggesque lighting, and an early seventeenth-century concern for visual accuracy and a faithful imitation of surface texture.

Following soon after these two paintings, which may have been produced in Rome, the four *Saints* at Osuna show new refinements in the handling of composition and of perspective.[21] Of this group, the *Penitent Saint Peter* is a subject and design which Ribera repeated with only slight modifications in an etching dated 1621 (fig. 55). The other three *Saints* (cat. no. 4 and figs. 118, 119) depict sculptural figures set in well-defined spaces or landscapes which expand to distant mountains and low horizon lines. In these paintings, the shading is consistent with observed reality, and various aspects of the composition such as the faces, hands, and still-life objects are executed in fluid brushstrokes and rich impasto to increase the sense of physical presence.

Figure 14
Orazio Gentileschi. *Crowning with Thorns,* 1616-1618,
Collection Lizza-Bassi, Varese (Alinari)

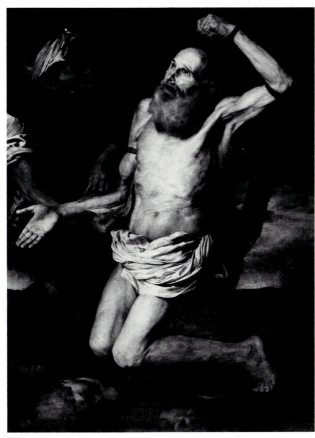

Figure 15
Ribera. *Saint Paul,* 1616-1618, Picture Gallery,
Church of the Gerolomini, Naples

Figure 16
Ribera. *Martyrdom of Saint Bartholomew,* 1616-1618,
Galleria Pallavicini, Rome

Figure 17
Ribera. *Martyrdom of Saint Lawrence,* 1620-1624, 1976
Art Market, London

Figure 18
Ribera. *Lamentation Over the Body of Christ,* 1622-1624,
Musée du Louvre, Paris

Figure 19
Ribera. *Preparation of Christ for the Cross,* 1622-1624,
Parish Church, Cogolludo

Shortly after arriving in Naples, Ribera painted three head-and-shoulder compositions of *Saint Peter, Saint Paul* (fig. 15), and *Saint James Major* for the church of the Gerolomini, a series which may once have included all of the Apostles. The heads of these figures have been realized with a dense, heavy impasto applied with a coarse brush similar to the technique used for the *Sense of Touch.* Another work, also in the Gerolomini but painted a few years later, is the *Saint Andrew with His Cross* (fig. 125), which demonstrates a mature understanding of a naturalistically realized figure modeled with a greater understanding of a uniform pattern from a soft, yet direct, light source.

Evidencing similar technical advances is the *Martyrdom of Saint Bartholomew* (fig. 16) now in the Galleria Pallavicini, Rome, in which the concentration of energy and of visual effect is increased by the dramatic requirements of the subject. From a similar time is the Strasbourg *Saint Peter and Saint Paul* (cat. no. 5). The faces and hands of these two figures are structured with textured surfaces following the natural contours of the anatomy, but the subtleties of modeling with softer patterns of light and shadow give a greater richness and strength to the characterizations. These stylistic features also appear in the *Martyrdom of Saint Lawrence* (fig. 17), painted about 1620-1624, a mature composition which uses elements that Ribera attempted to understand and employ in his earlier, less accomplished paintings. Modifying the poses of such figures as those in the Brera *Christ* and the Osuna *Saint Sebastian* (cat. no. 4), and expanding the spatial depth of the composition, Ribera produced in this work the most mature design of his paintings to date. The popular success of the *Martyrdom of Saint Lawrence* is confirmed by the numerous contemporary copies of the composition (Vatican Pinacoteca, Cathedral of Taverna, Dresden Gemäldegalerie). This aggressive realism looks forward to the *Drunken Silenus* (cat. no. 6) of 1626, a work that summarizes the artist's early career.

Also from the early 1620s is the *Lamentation over the Body of Christ* (fig. 18), which shows greater variation in surface treatment and paint texture and a more integrated figural arrangement of the scene than earlier paintings. The actual subject, as in Caravaggio's famous prototype painted for the Oratorian fathers of Santa Maria in Vallicella in Rome, is the presentation of the body of Christ; however, Caravaggio's mourners dramatically express their emotions, while Ribera's figures, grieving and shocked, are stunned and silent.

The *Preparation of Christ for the Cross* (Cogolludo, Parish Church) (fig. 19) suggests Ribera's further advancements in design. Here a more complex group of figures occupies the pictorial space. Although the pose of Christ varies somewhat from that of the Osuna *Saint Sebastian,* the modeling of the figure is achieved through similar spotlit effects.

A slightly later version of the *Lamentation over the Dead Christ* (fig. 20) now in the National Gallery, London, employs a more traditional format for its subject. Maclaren and Braham postulate the painting as "from before 1626."[22] Such dating is reasonable, because the *Lamentation* is consistent in design with

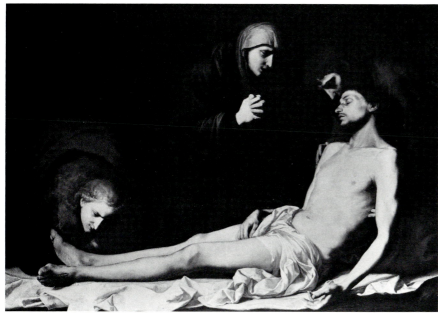

Figure 20
Ribera. *Lamentation over the Dead Christ,* ca. 1624-1626, National Gallery, London

Figure 21
Ribera. *Calvary,* ca. 1626, Collegiate Church, Osuna

Figure 22
Guido Reni. *Calvary,* 1616, Pinacoteca Nazionale, Bologna

Figure 23
Guido Reni. *Crucifixion of Saint Peter,* 1607, Pinacoteca
Vaticana, Rome   (Alinari)

other Ribera works dated to the period, and already reveals the full range of the artist's technical abilities, especially in the treatment of the flesh parts.

By the mid-1620s, with the help of his father-in-law, Gian Bernardino Azzolino, Ribera secured an important commission for the monumental *Saint Jerome and the Angel of Judgment* (cat. no. 7), painted for the Trinità della Monache and signed in 1626.[23] His large altarpiece, the *Holy Family Appearing to Saint Bruno and Other Saints* (fig. 139) with the *God the Father* (cat. no. 14), painted some years later, was also in the Church of the Trinità della Monache where Azzolino was one of the principal painters.

Sometime probably in 1626, the Dowager Duchess of Osuna, Doña Catalina Enríquez de Ribera, or a member of her family, commissioned from ''lo Spagnoletto'' a monumental *Calvary* (fig. 21) (336 x 230 cm) for the family chapel in the Collegiate Church at Osuna.[24] The simple grandeur and order of this work demonstrate a new awareness of classical art. Baroque rhetorical gestures or theatrical displays are absent. Energies and emotions of the figures are restrained, yet the drama of the Passion is evoked. In its organization and figure style the work recalls Il Cavalier d'Arpino's earlier treatment of the subject of ca. 1590 in the Certosa di San Martino, Naples. It has also been suggested that the head of Christ is derived from Guido Reni (fig. 22) and that Michelangelo served as the source for the torso and legs of Christ.[25]

Painted in 1628, the *Martyrdom of Saint Andrew* (fig. 126) in the National Museum, Budapest, is one of Ribera's most successful multi-figured compositions. The rich, varied paint surface and the virtuoso brushwork are the most accomplished to date. Although the design is intricate, the individual elements appear in a clearly organized space which delineates physical reality and evokes spiritual meaning without betraying the influences of either Caravaggio or Guido Reni who provided the source for individual details for the design of the principal figure. Ribera's figure of Saint Andrew calls to mind Guido Reni's *Crucifixion of Saint Peter* (fig. 23), commissioned in 1607 by Cardinal Pietro Aldobrandini.[26] Guido's painting has a studied balance and stillness which characterize many of Ribera's paintings throughout his career. Another important feature of Guido's early style which Ribera adapted is the manner of applying the paint.

Figure 25
Ribera. *Pietà,* 1637, New Sacristy, Church of the
Certosa di San Martino, Naples

Figure 26
Massimo Stanzione. *Pietà,* 1638, Church of the
Certosa di San Martino, Naples

Figure 27
Ribera. *Moses,* 1638, Church of the Certosa di San
Martino, Naples   (Alinari)

Figure 28
Ribera. *Elijah,* 1638, Church of the Certosa di San
Martino, Naples   (Alinari)

Figure 29
Ribera. *Noah,* 1638, Church of the Certosa di San
Martino, Naples   (Alinari)

Figure 30
Ribera. *Jonah,* 1638, Church of the Certosa di San
Martino, Naples   (Alinari)

Several Ribera paintings of the *Martyrdom of Saint Bartholomew* are dated to about this same time. The *Martyrdom* in the Cathedral of Nicosia, that in the Pitti Palace (fig. 24), and that in the Musée des Beaux-Arts in Grenoble are technically and stylistically related to the Budapest *Saint Andrew*. These ambitious works of the late 1620s, all large and intended for patrons of consequence, are unsigned. After 1630, Ribera carefully signed most of his paintings.

The decade of the 1630s saw the flowering of the artist's genius; and during this period he produced many of the outstanding works in this exhibition such as the *Saint Andrew* (cat. no. 8), the *Bearded Woman* (cat. no. 11), *God the Father* (cat. no. 14), the *Venus and Adonis* (cat. no. 23), and three portraits (cat. nos. 24, 25, 26). These works, discussed individually in the catalogue entries, display the full technical virtuosity and range of subject matter achieved by the artist. Ribera's patronage also increased during this period. He received commissions from the King of Spain and from the Viceroys, the Duke of Alcalá and the Count of Monterrey, two of the greatest patrons of Neapolitan art. He also worked for important ecclesiastical authorities, and in 1638 he was commissioned a series of paintings from the Certosa di San Martino (see cat. nos. 14 and 38).[27]

Ribera's first documented painting for the monks of the Certosa is a *Pietà* (fig. 25), signed and dated 1637, which was placed above the altar in the new sacristy. Massimo Stanzione also painted a *Pietà* (fig. 26) for the Certosa, which, although larger than Ribera's, lacks its dramatic intensity. Stanzione's work, done in 1638, was installed in the center of the back wall of the nave, between Ribera's half-length figures of *Moses* (fig. 27) and *Elijah* (fig. 28), both of which are signed and dated 1638.

To complete the nave decoration the monks also commissioned a series of twelve Old Testament *Prophets*. These canvases were set into the spandrels of the arches at the entrances to three chapels on each side of the nave (fig. 141). The great naturalism of the figures is in striking contrast to the decorative intarsia which surrounds them. Although names have been proposed for each, only the *Noah* (fig. 29) and the *Jonah* (fig. 30) are identified by their symbols of ark and whale. In addition to these paintings, the Certosa also commissioned two half-length pictures, a *Saint Jerome* (fig. 47) and a *Saint Sebastian* (cat. no. 38), and a large *Communion of the Apostles (Institution of the Holy Eucharist)* (fig. 49), all of which were not signed and dated until 1651.

During the early 1630s, Ribera began to use brighter, more luminous colors and softer, more open effects of light and atmosphere than in his earlier compositions. This change was a result of the preference for the more classical Bolognese style which had dominated decoration in Rome during the 1620s and then altered the course of Neapolitan taste following Domenichino's commission in 1631 to decorate the Cappella del Tesoro in the Cathedral of Naples.[28]

Figure 31
Ribera. *Liberation of Saint Peter,* 1639, Museo del Prado, Madrid

Figure 32
Ribera. *Martyrdom of Saint Philip,* 1639, Museo del Prado, Madrid

Figure 33
Ribera. *Tityus,* 1632, Museo del Prado, Madrid

Figure 34
Ribera. *Ixion,* 1632, Museo del Prado, Madrid

Two paintings dated 1639, *The Dream of Jacob* (fig. 171) and *The Liberation of Saint Peter* (fig. 31) (Prado 1117 and 1073), exhibit a greater spatial expansiveness than Ribera's earlier compositions. Moreover, the angel of the *Liberation,* one of the most beautiful figures in all of Ribera's art, radiates light from its richly colored garments and wings: pinks changing to magenta and mauve are juxtaposed against burnt orange, transparent ochres, and creamy yellows and white. Although Ribera's palette here reflects Bolognese art, this angel also seems to have a Venetian richness suggesting comparisons with Tintoretto and Veronese.

One of Ribera's most complex later designs is the powerful, light-filled *Martyrdom of Saint Philip* (fig. 32) (Prado 1101).[29] The massive body of the saint is positioned with the dynamics of Ribera's earlier martyrdoms, and the drama of the event surpasses almost all of his other multi-figured paintings. Since the robust figure of Saint Philip so closely resembles those giants *Tityus* (fig. 33) and *Ixion* (fig. 34) (Prado 1113, 1114), both painted in 1632, the date of this *Martyrdom* has sometimes been read as 1630; however, the lighter palette and expansive design support the reading of the date as 1639.

Four other paintings, in the Prado from the seventeenth-century collection of the Marquis de los Llanos, mark Ribera's change to a more restrained style and to more structurally controlled settings. All the pictures show the figures set in mid-ground with a dark cave, trees, or distant mountain views. According to Tormo, the *Saint John the Baptist* (fig. 35) (Prado 1108) and the *Mary Magdalen in Prayer* (fig. 36) (Prado 1103) symbolize youth, and the *Saint Bartholomew* (fig. 37) (Prado 1110) and the *Saint Mary of Egypt* (fig. 38) (Prado 1106) old age.[30] Although none of these four paintings is signed and dated, the *Saint Agnes in Prison* (fig. 39), now in Dresden and signed and dated 1641, shows marked similarity to the group. The Prado series can reasonably be assigned to the same time in Ribera's oeuvre.

Figure 35
Ribera. *Saint John the Baptist,* ca. 1640, Museo del
Prado, Madrid

Figure 36
Ribera. *Saint Mary Magdalen,* ca. 1640, Museo del
Prado, Madrid

Figure 37
Ribera. *Saint Bartholomew,* ca. 1640, Museo del Prado,
Madrid

Figure 38
Ribera. *Saint Mary of Egypt,* ca. 1640, Museo del
Prado, Madrid

Figure 39
Ribera. *Saint Agnes in Prison,* 1641, Gemäldegalerie,
Dresden

Figure 40
Ribera. *Baptism of Christ,* 1643, Musée des
Beaux-Arts, Nancy

One of the great masterpieces of Ribera's late years is the *Baptism of Chirst* (fig.
40) in Nancy, painted in 1643. In many ways, it is the summation of his
creative and technical abilities. No other of his paintings could so rightly be
called "Bolognese," but Ribera has surpassed his sources in the arrangement
of the classical figures which assert their physicality. The contrast to Bolognese
painting is made explicit when Ribera's painting is compared with Guido
Reni's *Baptism of Christ* (fig. 41) of 1621-1623, and the *Samson Victorious,*
1611-1612. Despite superficial resemblances of subject and figure type, the
strength and naturalistic integrity of Ribera's figures retain a direct visual
appeal which causes them to be immediately felt rather than intellectually
perceived.

In the first half of the seventeenth century, the most important project in
Naples was the decoration in the Cathedral of La Real Cappella del Tesoro di
San Gennaro.[31] The chapel was founded in 1527 to glorify the city's most
sacred relic, two vials of blood of Naples' patron, Saint Januarius (San
Gennaro), but decoration of the chapel did not begin for almost a century. The
commission for the large altarpiece on the right side of the Tesoro was awarded
to Ribera on June 6, 1641, following the death of Domenichino, who left the
project unfinished. The subject of Ribera's painting is *The Escape of Saint*

Figure 41
Guido Reni. *Baptism of Christ,* 1621-1623,
Kunsthistorisches Museum, Vienna

Figure 42
Ribera. *The Escape of Saint Januarius from the Fiery Furnace,* 1646, Cappella del Tesoro, Cathedral, Naples

Januarius from the Fiery Furnace (fig. 42). The commission specified that the work was to be done in oil on copper washed with silver; from the size of the gigantic copper sheet (320 x 200 cm), Ribera probably painted this work in the chapel itself.[32] This painting was completed in 1646. The figure used for the Saint, who emerges unharmed from the great blast of the furnace on the right of the painting, is the same as that found in the *Apotheosis of Saint Januarius* (fig. 161), now in Salamanca (see cat. no. 22). The seraphim in the upper right corner of the composition are easily recognizable as visual types used earlier by Ribera in such works as the *Holy Family Appearing to Saint Bruno and Other Saints* (see cat. no. 14) and the *Ecstasy of the Magdalen* (fig. 43).

The year 1647, which saw Ribera receive a payment as great as 1000 ducats for the Saint Januarius altarpiece,[33] was economically and politically devastating for Naples. The viceroys and their court, the many religious institutions with their extensive clergy, and artists such as Ribera lived in luxury, while the other extreme of society knew only poverty. Following the departure on May 6, 1644, of the Viceroy, the Duke of Medina de las Torres, the situation worsened. Medina's successor, Juan Alfonso Enríquez, Admiral of Castile, ruled only from May 14, 1644, until February 10, 1646, when he withdrew to Rome. Under the next Viceroy, Don Rodrigo Ponce de Léon,

Figure 43
Ribera. *Ecstasy of the Magdalen,* 1636, Real Academia de Bellas Artes de San Fernando, Madrid

Figure 44
Ribera. *Don Juan of Austria,* ca. 1647, Palacio Real, Madrid

Duke of Arcos (February 11, 1646-January 26,1648), the starving populace revolted. During the night of July 8-9, 1647, the uprising raged through Naples, and the Spanish troops fought to keep control of the Castello and the Royal Palace. Ribera and his family, along with many Spanish nobles, took refuge in the palace. Finally, Masaniello, the leader of the revolt, was captured, and on July 16, was executed.[34]

During these five turbulent months of 1647 in which Don Juan of Austria, illegitimate son of Philip IV, was in Naples to quell the revolt, Ribera painted a full-scale equestrian portrait of the Prince (fig. 44). This portrait is signed *Joseph de Ribera Español / Valentinus Civ. Academia Romana.* Ribera's final etching (fig. 71), dated 1648, derives from this painting. Far below the promontory where Don Juan sits astride his rearing mount, the Spanish fleet of which he was commander, is shown sailing into the Bay of Naples. The background panorama of the city includes the Castel Sant'Elmo on the waterfront and the Certosa di San Martino high on the distant hill.

In 1647, Ribera painted a *Saint Simeon and the Christ Child* (fig. 45), which was bought directly from the artist by Don Antonio Ruffo of Messina.[35] This important work, in an English private collection since about 1761, was sold in 1981. The superior condition of this painting affirms Ribera's enormous technical prowess. This work must have greatly pleased Ruffo, who subsequently commissioned several other paintings from Ribera. A *Pietà* was the subject of letters exchanged between Ribera and Ruffo in 1649 and 1650. The artist complained of a long and difficult illness which prevented his progress with this painting. By December 5, 1650, the *Pietà* was consigned to Don Antonio's brother Fra Don Fabrizio Ruffo, Prior of Bagnara, who had been responsible (along with his nephew Fra Francesco Maria Ruffo) for making payments to Ribera during the previous two years. This *Pietà* is now known only through copies.

Only one painting by Ribera is dated 1650, the large *Adoration of the Shepherds* (fig. 46), now in the Louvre. Of monumental scope, the painting offers great richness and variety of textured surfaces. The range of modeling of the shepherds and the Holy Family conforms to Ribera's practice during his late years. This sense of vivid naturalism is also found in the half-length figure of *Saint Mary of Egypt* (cat. no. 39), signed and dated in 1651.

Ribera used a similar design for the wonderfully expressive *Saint Jerome* (fig. 47) commissioned by the Certosa di San Martino perhaps in 1638 but not completed until 1651. Unlike the *Saint Mary of Egypt,* in which the surface has been brought to a level of high detail and finish, this painting exhibits a freedom of brushwork which gives it a fresh, sketch-like appearance. One of Ribera's last paintings, another *Saint Jerome* (fig. 48) now in the Prado, is signed and dated 1652. Though surely completed within months of the artist's death, the painting shows a virtuosity of brushwork. Perhaps the old Ribera realized that he lacked time to build his surfaces with multiple layers of paint and fine accents of retouching details; instead, he gave each stroke maximum

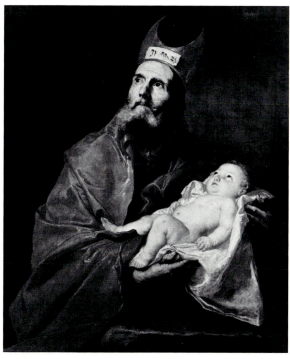

Figure 45
Ribera. *Saint Simeon and the Christ Child,* 1647,
ex-Collection Marquis of Bristol, Ickworth

Figure 46
Ribera. *Adoration of the Shepherds,* 1650, Musée du
Louvre, Paris

Figure 47
Ribera. *Saint Jerome,* 1651, Museo e Gallerie
Nazionali di Capodimonte, Naples

effectiveness—a tribute to the creative techniques developed over many years.

His final great commission, and the largest painting of his career, is the
Communion of the Apostles (Institution of the Holy Eucharist) (fig. 49), which is
placed at the back on the left side of the choir of the Certosa di San
Martino.[36] A part of the large commission awarded to Ribera in 1638, this
painting became the subject of a controversy between the artist and the monks,
which continued as a lawsuit filed by Ribera's heirs shortly after his death. The
final settlement was not made until July 9, 1655.[37]

Figure 48
Ribera. *Saint Jerome,* 1652, Museo del Prado, Madrid

The last rites for Jusepe de Ribera are recorded on September 3, 1652, in the small church of Santa Maria del Parto at Mergellina, a country town on the outskirts of Naples. A longer entry in the registry of deaths for the Parrocchia di San Giovanni reads:

> a 3 dì settembre 1652 - Giuseppe Rivera, marito di Cat[a]
> Azzolino, havita[nte] à mergoglino [Mergellina], ha ric.[to] li
> SS.[mi] Sac.[ti] dal cura[to] di S. M. della Neve, et sep.[to] à
> Merglino.[38]

This simple farewell to the life of the painter seems to anticipate the abrupt end of the "school" of naturalism he epitomized and led for some thirty years. Within four years, the Kingdom of Naples was devastated by the plague. Among those presumed to have died were Massimo Stanzione and the young Bernardo Cavallino, the most talented heir to the rich heritage of the previous half-century. The versatile Luca Giordano, trained in Ribera's studio, abandoned the forceful naturalism of his master for the fluid and painterly manner derived from the late frescoes of Pietro da Cortona. Giordano developed a facile style which soon advanced his career away from Naples and into the circles of the new generation of European patrons who favored the lighter, happier styles associated with the Rococo.

The innovations of Ribera languished, for the most part, until their revival at least in spirit by the "modern" generation of French painters who, tiring of the academic manner, reinvestigated light, form, color, and texture, and liberated the brush and the painted surface in new dynamics of composition and interpretation. Certainly, artists such as Delacroix knew Ribera's paintings from those examples in the Galerie Espagnole in Paris. When Ribera's canvases are evaluated in relation to those of other seventeenth-century artists, his stature grows.

Ribera's most significant technical innovation was his method of applying his paints. Throughout his long career, his skills with the brush advanced to such a level of proficiency that he was able to realize major sections of anatomical structure with single, long, sweeping strokes. His method of building up his composition was highly original. There are few working drawings for details of his figures or for many of his compositions, and likely, for the most part, he worked directly on his canvases, structuring his compositions as he progressed. In his earliest known paintings, the series of the *Five Senses,* he modeled the contours of the faces and hands with varying shades of dark pigment, progressing toward the lighter shades, and then, while the intermediate layers of paint were still wet, he brushed across the lightest values and the highlights. The coarsely bristled brush which he used for this final resolution of form gouged through several levels of paint, with each level exposed to surface visibility. The final image is an impasto that gives texture and definition to the forms. Interestingly, this unique technique owes a greater debt to Guido Reni's early works than to those of Caravaggio or any of his immediate followers in Rome.

As Ribera grew more adept at this manipulation of the paint surface, he varied his brushwork for the individual figures depending upon their position within the space of the composition. A fine example by which to demonstrate this versatility is found in one of his masterpieces, *The Mystical Marriage of Saint Catherine of Alexandria* in the Metropolitan Museum at Art (cat. no. 36). The extremes in the quality of paint application vary from the old Saint Anne, whose weathered face Ribera modeled with free, thin brushstrokes, to the young and beautiful Saint Catherine, whose rich enamel-like complexion the artist rendered with a thick impasto.

The mood, or emotional substance, of Ribera's paintings is also noteworthy. In an age aptly called Baroque, his compositions are not meritritious but are straightforward and direct. The simplest summation of Ribera's art would include among its characteristics a truth to nature, an understanding of humanity, and a visual affirmation of a profound spirituality. Perhaps as much as any painter of his age, he incorporated within his art the opposing poles of the Baroque—the sacred and the profane, the spiritual and the physical, the artificial and the natural. And thus, an artist of paradoxes was suited to a paradoxical age.

NOTES

1. De Dominici, 1742, III, 1-24.

2. Coniglio, 1967.

3. Brown and Elliott, 1980.

4. Martínez, 1866.

5. Chenault, 1969.

6. Chenault, 1969; Bousquet, 1980. Both Chenault and Bousquet advise that this payment was for dues, in the sense of a tax levied on artists, and not necessarily for an entrance fee into the academy or the annual membership dues.

7. Viñes, 1929; Sarthou Carreres, 1947; Mateu y Llopis, 1953.

8. The history of the Ribera Family is complicated by the baptismal record of July 3, 1602, in the parish register of the church of San Marco dei Tessitori (di Palazzo), in Naples, for Anna Ribera, daughter of a Simone Ribera and Vitoria Bricchi. (Salazar, 1894.) Perhaps coincidentally, the family of Jusepe de Ribera's future wife lived in this parish for many years, and later Jusepe settled there. The name Ribera was common, however, and that this ''Simone'' was Jusepe's father is uncertain; no presently available documents confirm that Simón ever left Spain. Indeed, the church register of Santa Tecla records that on January 30, 1607, Simón Ribera, a shoemaker, and Margarita Anna Seleres were married (Viñes, 1929, p. 21.)

9. Palomino, 1715-1724, II, 63, 291.

10. Darby, 1938, p. 46.

11. Pacelli, 1977.

12. Causa, 1970.

13. Lurie and Mahon, 1977.

14. Prohaska, 1975, p. 3; Pacelli, 1977. Other works by Caravaggio probably painted in Naples include *The Penitent Magdalen,* known through numerous copies (see Bodart, 1970); *Christ Bound to the Column,* Rouen; *Salome with the Head of Saint John the Baptist,* London; *The Denial of Saint Peter* (see Marini, 1973); and a *Martyrdom of Saint Ursula.* See London, (Whitfield and Martineau), 1982, pp. 121-135.

15. Stoughton, 1980. See also: Stoughton, 1974; Stoughton, 1978; Prohaska, 1978; Pacelli, 1978; London (Whitfield and Martineau), 1982, no. 5, pp. 111-113.

16. Prohaska, 1975; Naples (Bologna and Causa), 1977; Stoughton, 1977, p. 366.

17. Mancini (1614-1621), ed. Salerno, 1956-1957, I, 149-150. Mancini's biography of Ribera provides us with fascinating information about the rather bohemian life of the artist and also furnishes some important clues for Ribera's precipitous departure from Rome and his life in Naples:

And coming then to Rome he worked by the day for those who make shop and trade of painting

through the labors of such youths as he. Siezing this opportunity, comporting himself well, he made himself known for a clever fellow and came into a great reputation and a very great profit. But as time went on, he became weary of working and, living in such a way that he spent much more than he earned, he was forced and compelled by debt to leave Rome and to go to Naples where, having been taken in by Giovanni ***, the Sicilian, a painter and a most singular man who makes little [things] of wax and clay and now is a more than ordinary painter, he married one of his daughters and, doing various works with those good results to which he was accustomed, he was introduced to the Viceroy, whence now with a salary and in splendor he lives in that city where, still spending as he always does, and that more than his wife and an honorable appearance in court require and demand, nonetheless, no longer a day laborer, with the rapidity of his work together with [good] coloring and good understanding he meets the expenses of his splendid [life].

[Ribera] is much admired by Signor Guido [Reni] who praises his resolution and coloring, which latter is for the most part by way of Caravaggio, but shaded more and bolder.

Here in Rome he was more than a little eccentric in his behavior, and although he was very shrewd, nonetheless he was sometimes caught up, as he was when one year at Easter, not being confessed, more through neglect than deliberately, or for some other reason, fearing that if he did not act something worse would happen, he asked his friend to obtain for him a *non gravetur,* not knowing that they [the Vicar and the Holy Office] did not have such a thing as a *non gravetur,* nor did the court of the governor handle such cases. Nonetheless with this simplicity was joined a rhetoric which served him in times of need, as was seen many times by the most illustrious governor Giulio Bunterenti, before whom he was often brought *pro suspicione fugae per dare* [for suspicion of fleeing his debts]; so well did he plead that the governor would have him released and, in fact, give him money, accepting the Spaniard's promise that in recompense he would paint him some pictures; he neither returned the money nor painted the pictures. Another time in the same way and for the same reason he was brought before the governor, to whom he once again made his usual pledge, and once again the governor paid his debts, adding however, the following words: ''I know that you are a crafty scoundrel and men like you and better I send to jail by the hundreds; notwithstanding all this, in view of your talent, I wish to spare you''. Thus freed from the hands of the gaolers and from the presence of the governor, without returning the money or giving its equivalent in painting as he had agreed and had promised, he departed for Naples. And in truth he acted in bad faith, because when he wanted to work he earned five or six scudi a day, so that with thrift he could quickly and easily have paid everyone. Nor could his many creditors be satisfied with less than such a wage, even supplemented as it was by his few household furnishings, which were these:

Mattresses, [rented] for six
persons . . . . 1 lot
Double blankets used for covers
and bedlinens . . . . .1 lot
Napkins and tablecloths of as-
sorted design . . . . —
Large plates of multiple use . . . . .1 lot of 100
Drinking glasses and saucers . . . . . . .1 lot 100
Seats on bricks . . . . .10 lots

Notwithstanding all his extravagant ways he had a very great reputation. And what is a greater marvel, men that have taste for painting, that were creditors of loans of money, with his chattering, words and tricks, giving them hope of doing that for which they hoped, he turned them aside with sweet words. But the innkeepers, bakers, delicatessen owners, fruit vendors and Jews, [seeing that] he was slow in the payment of his debts, beat on his door and sent bill collectors with documents called citations at all hours of the night, who finally, doubting that they would ever get their money, departed.

He made many things here in Rome, and in particular for ***, the Spaniard, [he made paintings] which have five half figures representing the five senses, very beautiful, a Christ Deposed and another, which in truth are things of most exquisite beauty.

18. Scannelli, 1657, pp. 85, 202.

19. Felton, 1976, pp. 32-33. Three of the early paintings presented here as autograph works of Ribera have not been fully received into the canon of Ribera's oeuvre by all scholars. (See Spinosa, 1978, especially nos. 214, 262, 273.) Works discussed or illustrated in this essay are accepted by the present writer.

20. Bissell, 1981.

21. Felton, 1976, p. 35, fn. 12; London (Pérez Sánchez), 1976, no. 27, pp. 48-52; Pérez Sánchez, 1978; Rodríquez-Buzón, 1982.

22. London (Maclaren and Braham), 1952, no. 235, pp. 92-94.

23. De Dominici, 1742, III, 23-24 and 122-134; Fiordelisi, 1898, pp. 181-187; Darby, 1962, p. 307; Prohaska, 1975, pp. 3-11. Ribera was a witness to three wills made by Azzolino (December 9, 1633; May 15, 1641, March 14, 1644). In these documents, Gian Bernardino corrects a mistake made many years earlier in a document taken in Palermo which records his father as Antonio Azzolino when actually his name was Andrea Ragano whose family was from Acquaviva (di Funte), and not from Sicily. Gian Bernardino Ragano, alias Azzolino, died on December 12, 1645 at the age of 73 and was buried at the Church of Santo Spirito di Palazzo.

24. Rodríguez Marín, 1920; Felton, 1976, p. 38; London (Pérez Sánchez), 1976, no. 25, pp. 47-48; Pérez Sánchez, 1978; Rodríquez-Buzón, 1982.

25. Trapier, 1952, p. 20; London (Pérez Sánchez), 1976, no. 25, p. 48.

26. Gnudi and Cavalli, 1955; Baccheschi, 1971. See also Baldinucci, 1681, fol. 129, who confirms Ribera's Roman sojourn and recognizes Ribera's debt to Guido Reni. His account reads: ''Jusepe de Ribera, called 'lo Spagnoletto,' of a wretched way for [developing his] talent for painting, ran away from his father and went straightway to Rome, where he gave himself to designing works of importance and particularly to copying things of Guido [Reni] from whom he learned the manner of coloring frescoes. He made some figures of his [own] hand which he sold in order to live a rather miserable life. Because he drew well, in a short time he was made a member of the Academy.

27. Causa, 1973.

28. Strazzullo, 1978.

29. Darby, 1953, p. 74.

30. Tormo, 1922.

31. Strazzullo, 1978; in London (Whitfield and Martineau), 1982, pp. 45-48: E. Schleier, ''The Bolognese Tradition and Seicento Neapolitan Painting.''

32. When G. B. Carracciolo worked in the Cappella del Tesoro, he was given a room in the Cathedral complex. See Stoughton, 1974, p. 48.

33. Faraglia, 1885, pp. 449-450; Prota-Giurleo, 1953, pp. 102-104

34. Coniglio, 1968, pp. 251-267.

35. Ruffo, 1916, pp. 44-47.

36. Faraglia, 1892, p. 673. Beginning in the middle of June, 1651, Jusepe de Ribera began a correspondence with the prior of the Monastery of San Martino which indicates the troubles the artist was experiencing and his need for financial assistance. These letters, all from 1651, also refer to Ribera's *Communion of the Apostles*.

• • •

To the most reverend Father and Master, most respectfully,
I had resolved to come in person to pay my respects to your most reverend sir and to satisfy this obligation. Afterwards, I changed my mind and have reserved [the visit] for a feastday in order not to lose time in attending to the painting. In the meantime, I am sending my son and my son-in-law to pay respects, and to take pleasure in your gentility. I request of your reverend sir, to give an order of payment to me of some money and to send it to me with [the aforementioned]. The burdens of the household are great, considering the requirements [of living]; and I for the life of me, do not do anything with the brush except for San Martino. I force myself to keep cheerful that the painting at the present moment proceeds with all diligence. With that end I pay my respects and kiss your hand. At my home, 20 June 1651, your most reverend sir's obedient servant, Jusepe de Ribera

● ● ●

To the most reverend Father and Master, most respectfully.
When I awaited some relief worthy of the hand of your most reverend sir, yesterday came the father who brought the payment from the father vicar of fifty ducats with which had I not had them, I could not have set straight the circumstances of the household, and Praises to God, they were not to become for me the burdens that even the greatest pleasures are not able to withstand. Work continues; nevertheless, I request of your reverend sir the favor of giving the order of payment for another sum of money that for such purposes my son comes to you, and I conclude by reaffirming my loyalties and kissing your hand. At my home, 23 June 1651, your most reverend sir's obedient servant, Jusepe de Ribera

● ● ●

Most Reverend Father
I inform your reverend sir that as of yesterday afternoon there has arrived the news of the death of my dear son-in-law Giovanni Leonardo Sersale, so truly your reverend sir's servant. I supplicate myself for your aid of 100 ducats because I must make many mourning arrangements, and I am lacking and there are matters that cannot wait; and I pray you to do this favor for me with all speed, and considering the circumstances which I am under, grant me the favor of excusing me for this burden; and may Our Lord concede many years to the Life of the House [monastery], today the 6th of September 1651. I serve your reverend sir and kiss your hand. Jusepe de Ribera

37. Prota-Giurleo, 1953, pp. 107-110.

38. Sarthou Carreres, 1952, p. 47; Prota-Giurleo, 1953, p. 101.

THE PRINTS AND DRAWINGS OF RIBERA
Jonathan Brown

Figure 50
Ribera. *Saint Sebastian*, Bibliothèque Nationale, Paris

Figure 51
Ribera. *Saint Bernardino of Siena*, Bibliothèque
Nationale, Paris

Jusepe de Ribera can rightly claim a place as one of the most inventive printmakers and draftsmen of his age.[1] Yet his interest in these two graphic media was markedly different. Printmaking was a passing fancy, employed by the artist during a brief time, primarily as an adjunct to his principal activity as painter. Drawing, on the other hand, remained a lifelong passion, and in this medium the artist expressed aspects of his personality hardly to be glimpsed in his pictures. Despite these fundamental differences in his approach to the graphic arts, Ribera's prints and drawings have a common element — they display a masterful and original use of line as an expressive artistic medium. As a painter, Ribera was a brilliant interpreter of an existing tradition; as a graphic artist, he sought and discovered new ways to use existing techniques.

RIBERA AS PRINTMAKER

Ribera's first activities as a printmaker date from around 1615-1620, the same time as his earliest-known paintings. In fact, it is difficult to attribute any of his prints to his pre-Neapolitan career (before 1616). While the assumption is reasonable that he made drawings from the start of his career, his interest in printmaking did not flourish until he had settled in Naples. Then in the 1620s, Ribera experienced an intense and short-lived fascination with etching.

Ribera probably was attracted to this medium, rather than to woodcuts or engravings, because etching was closely related to drawing and relatively simple to execute. Engraving and woodcutting demand greater technical control than etching does, and they are also more time-consuming. Ribera was interested in immediate results and immediate effects. Such interest accounts for the fact that his etching technique never became especially complicated. It also accounts for his relative indifference to the technical subtleties of the medium. Unlike Rembrandt, the greatest printmaker of the age, Ribera was not inclined to rework his copperplates or to try to achieve varied tonal effects through complicated acid-biting procedures. Neither was he a careful printer; several of the etchings, even in the earliest impressions, are marred by random surface scratches and flaws, which suggest that no great care was taken in handling the plates. Yet within these self-imposed limits, Ribera was able, for the first time in the history of printmaking, to realize the full potential of etching as a pictorial graphic art, capable of reproducing the rich effects of light, shadow, and texture inherent in painting.

The origins of Ribera as etcher are probably to be seen in two small prints, one depicting *Saint Sebastian* (fig. 50), the other *Saint Bernardino of Siena* (fig. 51).[2] These prints are little more than schematic line drawings made on a copperplate. A comparison of these works to a typical pen drawing of the 1620s (fig. 52) suffices to make the point. The prints, like the drawing, use vigorous lines of nearly uniform thickness with little or no crosshatching. Thus, the shadows are transparent, obviating not only the contrasts between light and dark but also the sense of relief.

Figure 53
Ribera. *Saint Jerome and the Trumpet,* Metropolitan
Museum of Art, New York

Figure 52
Ribera. *Saint Sebastian,* Ashmolean Museum, Oxford

These two prints cannot be dated precisely, although stylistic evidence suggests a date around 1616-1620. However, in 1621, Ribera signed and dated a larger, more ambitious work, *Saint Jerome and the Trumpet* (fig. 53).[3] This print combines passages of the utmost subtlety with others that can only be called clumsy. The finest accomplishment of the etching is clearly the figure of the saint, which shows Ribera thinking as an etcher, not as a draftsman. Without sacrificing the energy of his crisp linear manner, Ribera begins to discover the possibilities of crosshatched strokes to reproduce varying densities of shadow and also to model the structure of the body. He also introduces the use of drypoint and a few engraved lines in places where he wants to deepen the shadows. Finally, he employs a stippling effect by means of tiny, flecked strokes which create an intermediate tone on the saint's torso. These several techniques, combined with Ribera's mastery of form, allow him to recreate appearances of light and surface texture with convincing authority, as perhaps can best be seen in the marvelous still life of books and a skull in the lower left corner.

Contrary to this meticulous use of the needle is the scrawling, undisciplined treatment of the background. The looping strokes used to defined the surface of the rock lie purposelessly on the paper, defeating the illusion of volume. The sky is crudely defined by parallel strokes that collide with the outline of the rocky mass. In addition, every impression of the print so far discovered is marred by two pairs of parallel lines running from the top to the bottom of the plate, which must be the result of an accidental abrasion. The cause of these marks is a mystery, but they do impugn the artist's sense of craftsmanship.

Figure 54
Ribera. *Lamentation,* Gabinetto Nazionale delle Stampe, Rome

Figure 55
Ribera. *Penitence of Saint Peter,* British Museum, London

Figure 56
Ribera. *Penitence of Saint Peter,* (detail of Figure 55)

An unsigned, undated print associated with *Saint Jerome and the Trumpet* is the *Lamentation* (fig. 54), which is technically less advanced and may have preceded *Saint Jerome.*[4] Except for the limited stippling on Christ's body, the artist uses fairly wide, crosshatched strokes to create the darker areas, and his handling of the burin is sometimes careless, notably in the shadow between the Virgin Mary and Saint John, which is further confused by the lines running parallel to Christ's body. Once again, the sky is treated in a summary manner and is delineated by parallel lines that flatten the entire area. These infelicitous passages have distracted some writers, myself included, both from recognition of the points of contact between the *Lamentation* and Ribera's earlier prints, and from attention to the moving but restrained representation of emotion which is characteristic of the artist.

A second print, signed and dated 1621, is the superb *Penitence of Saint Peter* (fig. 55).[5] With this work, Ribera becomes a mature printmaker. The transformation from novice to master seems at first too rapid to be true. However, the differences are not as great as they initially seem. In essence, Ribera here exercises greater control over the same techniques he employs in *Saint Jerome and the Trumpet.* The results are a greater sense of refinement of detail and power of effect, which become clear when a detail is isolated for scrutiny (fig. 56). By carefully modulating the shadows and skillfully using the white of the paper for highlights, Ribera produces a powerful image of the saint. Once again, however, he is more attentive to the figure than to the background. The definition of the rocks, although more convincing in appearance than in the background of the *Saint Jerome,* is still cursory in comparison with the saint. However, the glimpse into the distance background is economically and effectively rendered.

Close in style to this print is a second version of *Saint Jerome and the Trumpet* (hereafter called *Saint Jerome and the Angel;* fig 57).[6] Recently, attempts have been made to date this sheet to 1626, primarily because the composition shows some kinship to two paintings of the same subject done in this year.[7] However, the style of *Saint Jerome and the Angel* is not compatible with Ribera's other prints from the later 1620s, whereas it fits nicely with his prints from around 1621. But if Ribera here improves the composition by the introduction of the angel, he does little to correct the haphazard treatment of the rocky background, which closely resembles this motif in the first version of the theme.

A final figure composition of this group is the *Poet* (fig. 58), one of Ribera's most successful prints and memorable inventions.[8] Much careful thought and research have been invested in determining the identification of the poet here represented, but it seems likely that Ribera was creating a type rather than a portrait of a specific individual.[9] Using only parallel and crosshatched lines, Ribera produced a powerful image of poetic inspiration. Small pockets of pitch-black shadow around the face and in the drapery help to create an imposing figure in deep thought. The inspired juxtaposition of a monumental figure and a large masonry block reinforces the ponderous, meditative mood of this brilliant image.

Figure 57
Ribera. *Saint Jerome and the Angel,* Hispanic Society of America, New York

Figure 58
Ribera. *Poet,* Metropolitan Museum of Art, New York

In 1622, Ribera turned his attention from figural compositions to physiognomy. Two groups of prints, one consisting of three, the other of two etchings, can be dated to this year. First is a collection of three sheets showing details of the head and face (figs. 59, 60, 61); each sheet is signed, and one is dated 1622. These prints belong to a tradition of artists' instructional manuals which developed during the sixteenth century.[10] The immediate prototype is found in two collections of engravings specifically designed for beginning artists, one of which appeared in 1608, the other in 1619.[11] The precise motive for Ribera's interest in the subject is unknown. He was, of course, a skilled draftsman who carefully trained himself in the practice of figure drawing, and if nothing else, these prints demonstrate his mastery of the art. But why he should have felt the need, even in passing, to help educate fledgling artists remains as a mystery, although such sheets may have served to train his apprentices. Whatever Ribera's motives, the *Studies of Ears* and the *Studies of Eyes* are routine examples of the patternbook tradition.[12]. The third sheet, however, moves from basic instruction in drawing to something more complicted, the representation of expression.[13] Ribera's choice of expressions offers a dramatic contrast between meditation and fear or pain, between hushed silence and raucous sound. (In fact, the ''shrieking mouth'' reappears in Ribera's own work, in the figure of Marsyas in the two paintings of *Apollo and Marsyas* of 1637).

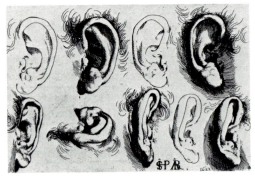

Figure 59
Ribera. *Studies of Ears,* British Museum, London

Figure 60
Ribera. *Studies of Eyes,* British Museum, London

Figure 61
Ribera. *Studies of Nose and Mouth,* British Museum,
London

Figure 62
Ribera. *Large Grotesque Head,* British Museum,
London

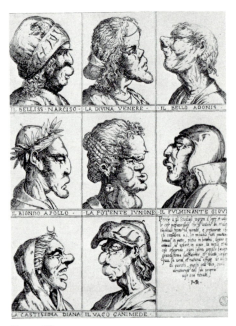

Figure 63
Martino Rota. *Pagan Deities,* Uffizi, Florence

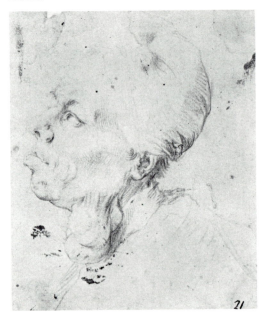

Figure 64
Ribera. *Study for Large Grotesque Head,* Whereabouts
unknown

Figure 65
Ribera. *Small Grotesque Head,* British Museum,
London

Figure 66
Ribera. *Study for Small Grotesque Head,* E. Schapiro,
London-Paris

The other prints in this group of physiognomic studies represent grotesque heads.[14] Ribera's interest in the grotesque is evinced mainly in his prints and drawings. Inspired by the examples of Leonardo da Vinci, artists of the sixteenth century became increasingly fascinated by the world of the grotesque, and obviously Ribera studied the subject with some care.[15] The *Large Grotesque Head* (fig. 62), in fact, appears to be derived from a large sixteenth-century print by Martino Rota (fig. 63),[16] a derivation that is even more apparent in Ribera's preparatory drawing for the etching (fig. 64).[17]

The *Small Grotesque Head* (fig. 65), signed and dated 1622, is somewhat less extravagant. In this instance, too, a preparatory drawing (fig. 66) has been discovered which is closer to the print and seems to have been made to guide the execution of the plate.[18]

By the end of 1622, Ribera had created the majority of his prints. Beyond this date, only four complete compositions are known. However, in these four works, the artist achieved new heights of technical subtlety and virtuosity. From 1624 are two masterpieces, the theatrical *Martyrdom of Saint Bartholomew* (fig. 67),[19] which is signed and dated, and the serene *Saint Jerome Reading* (fig. 68).[20] In these prints, Ribera worked with close attention to detail, making expanded use of his stipple-like technique to add tonal variety to the compositions. Another device, the use of very faint drypoint incisions, produces a gray middle-tone with a smudgy effect (fig. 69). And on some impressions of *Saint Jerome Reading,* a thin film of ink, left on the plate after wiping, modulates the stark dark-light contrasts of the earlier prints. The combination of consummate draftsmanship and a powerful artistic imagination establishes these compositions among the major creations of seventeenth-century printmaking.

In 1628, Ribera executed another great etching, the *Drunken Silenus* (fig. 70), which is based on his painting of two years earlier (cat. no. 6).[21] From a technical standpoint, this print is the artist's masterpiece, demonstrating the complete command of the etcher's needle. The evocation of texture is especially notable — the bristly hair of the satyrs, the rough-hewn wood of the vat, and the smooth expanse of Silenus' flesh are all vividly brought to life. One small detail is perhaps the most telling of Ribera's mastery — the rushing flow of liquid from the wineskin to the vessel held aloft by Silenus.

How extraordinary, then, that this great print should be Ribera's last but one, that his final print should be done a full twenty years later, and that this late print, executed after an incapacitating illness, should be as fine as the *Drunken Silenus*! The etching, the *Equestrian Portrait of Don Juan de Austria* (fig. 71), is signed and dated 1648.[22] A glance at the print convinces us that time had not diminished the skill of this great etcher.

Ribera's sudden decision virtually to stop making prints after 1630 comes as a surprise. While in some respects his half-hearted dedication to the medium is typical of many Italian Baroque painters, it is strange that Ribera should have

Figure 68
Ribera. *Saint Jerome Reading,* British Museum,
London

Figure 67
Ribera. *Martyrdom of Saint Bartholomew,* British
Museum, London

Figure 69
Ribera. *Saint Jerome Reading,* (detail of Figure 68)

Figure 70
Ribera. *Drunken Silenus,* British Museum, London

Figure 71
Ribera. *Equestrian Portrait of Don Juan de Austria*,
British Museum, London

Figure 72
Ribera. *Martyrdom of Saint Bartholomew*, British
Museum, London

given up printmaking just when he had mastered the art. We shall probably never have a certain explanation of his motives, but is impossible to evade the question because of its importance for understanding Ribera's work as an etcher.

Inevitably, any attempt to explain the vicissitudes of Ribera's interest in etching involves a discussion about the reasons why he cultivated the art in the first place. Although these motives are ultimately unknowable, one or two points seem to suggest themselves. First, it is obvious that Ribera lacked a true vocation as a printmaker. His relative indifference to the mechanical niceties of the medium indicates this fact. For him, etching was more of a pastime than a profession, and once he had attained his primary artistic goal as an etcher, he seems to have been satisfied with his achievement. In the broadest terms, Ribera sought to create the graphic equivalent of the ''tenebrist'' manner made popular in painting by Caravaggio (and practiced by Ribera himself in the years he was making the prints). Having achieved this ambition in a thoroughly convincing way, he evidently saw no further need to continue the experiment, and the fact that the *Equestrian Portrait of Don Juan de Austria* of 1648 is technically identical to the *Drunken Silenus* of 1628 seems to indicate that Ribera ceased to be challenged by the medium.

In addition to these purely artistic considerations, there was perhaps another, more practical reason for learning to etch. Possibly Ribera wanted to use the prints to broadcast knowledge of his artistic excellence to a public beyond his circle of clients in Naples.[23] Support for this hypothesis is evident in the relationship of the prints to the paintings. Of the eight figural prints executed in the 1620s, six can be related more or less directly to his earlier paintings (the *Don Juan de Austria* is also based on a picture).

The relationship of Ribera's prints to his paintings has been a topic of interest to students of the artist, especially in recent years.[24] When I first studied this topic in 1973, I proposed that generally the prints were created independently of the pictures. This idea is no longer tenable, having been put to rest by the cleaning and restoration of the paintings in the Colegiata de Osuna (see above, cat. no. 4 and figs. 118, 119, 120) and their return to the canon of Ribera's authentic works,[25] and by the discovery of what I believe to be a copy of the *Martyrdom of Saint Bartholomew*, mentioned as being among Ribera's earliest paintings in Naples (see above, fig. 12).[26] In the Osuna pictures, we see two of the compositions later reworked in prints — *Saint Jerome and the Angel* and the *Penitence of Saint Peter* — while the copy of the *Martyrdom of Saint Bartholomew* clearly provides the prototype for the print of the same subject. The *Drunken Silenus*, as has always been known, depends on Ribera's painting of the subject, dated 1626. While no exact model for the *Lamentation* has yet been discovered, the etching perhaps reproduces the picture described by Mancini as a *Christ Deposto*,[27] and also partly corresponds to the composition of the famous *Pietà* of San Martino of 1637. Thus only *Saint Jerome Reading* and the *Poet* are left as ''fatherless'' prints among the major figure compositions.

Figure 73
Guercino. *Saint Jerome and the Angel,* San Gerolamo, Rimini

Figure 74
Antonio de Pereda. *Penitence of Saint Peter,* Museo Lázaro Galdiano, Madrid

Figure 75
Jacques-Louis David. *Saint Jerome and the Trumpet,* Cathedral, Québec

The relationship between paintings and prints supports the idea that Ribera, perhaps for no other reason than vanity, took up etching because he wanted his art to become widely known, and he may also have expected that by the fame of his prints he would secure commissions from abroad. If such circumstantial argument is valid, then he probably stopped making prints either because the strategy failed to attract customers or succeeded well enough to justify a decision to stop. Ribera's high rate of pictorial production during the 1630s suggests that the latter hypothesis is the more likely.

Having noted these considerations about Ribera as printmaker, it is nonetheless a mistake to regard the figural compositions in his etchings as mechanical replicas of the pictures. In fact, in every instance the prints mark an improvement — and often a remarkable improvement — over the prototype in painting. A comparison of either of the Osuna paintings with the corresponding prints makes this fact evident. Even in prints after mature works like the *Drunken Silenus,* the alterations, if less important, add interest, variety, and harmony to the original version. These changes reflect Ribera's preferred mode of working, which was to vary the set composition of a given theme rather than to invent anew. In at least one instance, we can see how he restudied a composition as he converted it from painting to print. A drawing of the central motif of the *Martyrdom of Saint Bartholomew* (fig. 72) rearranges the poses of the two central figures.[28] In the painting (fig. 12), the saint's leg is bound by a crouching figure, while the knife-wielding executioner halts his grisly task of skinning the martyr and looks at his companion. In the drawing and subsequently in the print, the saint, his hands tied above his head, kneels on a rock as the executioner intently goes about his business. The fact that Ribera made a preparatory study for the print suggests that he regarded the etching as deserving of his full artistic attention, which was only logical if he intended them to attract customers.

Whether or not the prints succeeded in this purpose, they unquestionably made Ribera's art widely known, and among his audience were painters who adapted Ribera's compositions in their own works. Although he lived in the southernmost part of western Europe, Ribera, thanks to his prints, became one of the best-known, most imitated artists of the seventeenth century. The number of paintings by major and minor artists alike which were inspired by Ribera's prints is beyond counting.[29] Two examples by seventeenth-century Spanish and Italian painters, both of whom copied Ribera's *Saint Jerome and the Angel* (see above, fig. 57), must serve to represent all the other similar derivations. No less an artist than Guercino used the print as the starting point for his painting in San Gerolamo, Rimini (fig. 73), while the Spaniard, Antonio de Pereda, inventively retained the pose of the saint but changed his identity from Jerome to Peter (fig. 74). And even more than a century and a half after its creation, the print was still exerting a hold on artists who had to represent Saint Jerome. In 1780, Jacques-Louis David recast Ribera's bony hermit as an incongruously well-nourished version of the ascetic saint (fig. 75).[30] Thus, Ribera's brief encounter with the art of etching proves to have had lasting consequences for the history of painting.

Figure 76
Ribera. *Christ Beaten by a Tormentor,* British Museum, London

Figure 77
Ribera. *Susanna and the Elders,* Uffizi, Florence

Figure 78
Ribera. *Study for Adoration of Shepherds,* Uffizi, Florence

RIBERA AS DRAFTSMAN

If printmaking was an episode in Ribera's career, drawing was a constant concern. Somewhat over a hundred drawings have been plausibly attributed to Ribera, but there is reason to believe that this number represents only a small part of his production. According to the eighteenth-century Neapolitan writer, Bernardo De Dominici, the artist drew almost every day of his life.

> In the evening he also used to make drawings of what he would paint the following day, and, as soon as he had decided what he wanted to do, he made finished drawings either in pen or with wash and watercolor, and more often with red chalk, although sometimes he used black chalk. And then he painted that figure from a live model . . . His continuous study [of drawing] is witnessed by the large number of his drawings that can be found.[31]

Although written almost a century after Ribera's death, this account is fundamentally credible, at least by the evidence of the surviving works, which leave no doubt that Ribera was a facile, versatile draftsman. As De Dominici stated, most of the drawings are executed in one of two media: pen and brown ink, occasionally heightened with wash, and red or red and black chalk. The two media were differently used in accordance with their inherent qualities.

With chalk in hand, Ribera frequently made careful, patient, finished drawings in a manner now called "academic." These drawings, in the "grand" style of Italian draftsmanship, are devoted to presenting a sculptural interpretation of the human figure. The most highly finished chalk drawings appear to date from the years before 1630, as for example *Christ Beaten by a Tormentor* (fig. 76).[32] Within firmly drawn outlines, Ribera sensitively models the play of light over the forms by means of closely spaced, carefully modulated lines which shade into the filmy area created by the side of the crayon. Shadows cast by the figures are represented by thicker, heavier, diagonal strokes, as on the plinth which supports Christ. Much the same technique is evident in the drawing *Susanna and the Elders* (fig. 77),[33] in which the whiteness and smoothness of the skin are accentuated by enclosing the figure in a veil of exceedingly thin strokes that strike the contours of the body at an angle. These effects are virtually identical to the ones used in the etchings and show Ribera in his most refined graphic mode. Later in life, Ribera's chalk drawings became looser and more discursive, as seen in what is perhaps a preparatory study (fig. 78)[34] for the shepherds in the painting of the *Adoration of the Shepherds* (fig. 46) of 1650 (Paris, Musée du Louvre).

While Ribera could, and sometimes did, make rather careful pen drawings (see above, fig. 52), he also developed a wiry, shorthand manner of drawing which expresses a taut, nervous energy and forms a complete contrast to the massive, monumental style of his paintings. In a drawing of an unidentified subject, probably done in the 1620s (fig. 79),[35] the figures are reduced to schematic forms by jerky lines which pulsate as if electrically charged. Subsequent drawings become ever more cryptic, yet ever more affecting. A

Figure 79
Ribera. *Sleeping Nude with Cupids and Man,* Fitzwilliam
Museum, Cambridge

Figure 80
Ribera. *Study for Massacre of Innocents* (recto), A.
Battesti, Toulouse

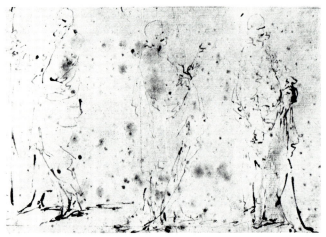

Figure 81
Ribera. *Study for Saints Peter and Paul,* Gabinetto
Nazionale delle Stampe, Rome

Figure 82
Ribera. *Saint Peter,* 1637, Museo Provincial de Alava,
Vitoria

Figure 83
Ribera. *Adoration of the Shepherds,* Metropolitan Museum of Art, New York

Figure 84
Ribera. *Crucifixion of Saint Peter,* Academia de Bellas Artes de San Fernando, Madrid

Figure 85
Ribera. *Hercules at Rest,* Dr. John A. Cauchi, Rabat, Malta

vibrant study for the *Massacre of the Innocents* (fig. 80),[36] for which no painting is known, leaves much to the imagination; only the head and arms of the woman and the limp body of the slain infant are delineated by the terse, crumpled lines which are Ribera's hallmark. By the mid-1630s, this graphic style is pushed to the brink of abstraction in drawings such as the sheet of studies (fig. 81)[37] for paintings of *Saint Peter* (fig. 82) and *Saint Paul,* both dated 1637, in which the contrast between drawing style and painting style is truly impressive. In the 1640s, the pen drawings, like the chalk drawings, lose some of their crispness (fig. 83),[38] although their quality remains high and the powers of imagination undiminished.

Of all of Ribera's drawings, his few with brush and wash are understandably the closest in their effects to his paintings. A beautiful study for the *Crucifixion of Saint Peter* (fig. 84)[39] and another for a lost picture of *Hercules at Rest* (fig. 85),[40] the pose of which Ribera borrowed from his print of *Saint Jerome and the Trumpet,* exemplify this aspect of his draftsmanship.

Endowed with superior gifts as a draftsman, Ribera constantly used the medium for a variety of purposes, among these the preparatory drawing. As previously noted, preliminary drawings for identifiable paintings are relatively few in number. But other drawings also show the method of trial-and-error typical of Ribera's practice in his preparatory studies, although for these drawings related paintings have yet to be found. A typical example is the study for the figure that has been identified as *Cain Slaying Abel* (fig. 86)[41] As De Dominici observed, Ribera made preparatory studies in pen and ink and in chalk, following the analytical procedure used by most Italian and Italianate draftsmen. (Indeed, the use of this procedure, the "classical" style of the finished chalk drawings, and the keen interest in figure studies suggest that Ribera was trained in the atelier of an Italian painter.) First, he would essay the poses for the main figures of the composition, sketching the possibilities on a single sheet. For instance, in 1632 he executed a large-scale *Tityus* (fig. 33), which depicts a figure from classical mythology who was punished for a crime against the gods and, like Prometheus, was visited daily by a vulture who feasted on his entrails. The preliminary study, executed in pen and ink with wash (fig. 87),[42] explores two compositional schemes. The upper composition shows the bird about to alight on the manacled figure, who regards the arrival with understandable apprehension. The lower version, which was adopted for the paintings, is more dramatic and visually effective. Here, the vulture menacingly spreads its wings wide while the bound Tityus throws back his head in anguish.

The preliminary study for another gruesome scene, *Apollo and Marsyas* (fig. 88),[43] a subject known in two paintings of 1637 (figs. 165, 166), concentrates on the protagonists; the study excludes the satyrs in the right background and the landscape at the left. In his staccato style of pen drawing, Ribera comes close to the final composition. Once again, the major change in the painting involves a heightening of emotion, achieved by showing Marsyas screaming wildly with the pain of his punishment.

Figure 86
Ribera. *Study for Cain Slaying Abel,* Uffizi, Florence

Figure 87
Ribera. *Study for Tityus,* Gabinetto Nazionale delle Stampe, Rome

Figure 88
Ribera. *Study for Apollo and Marsyas,* Gabinetto Nazionale delle Stampe, Rome

Figure 89
Ribera. *Study feor Pietà,* Gabinetto Nazionale delle Stampe, Rome

Figure 90
Ribera. *Group of Figures* (recto), Private Collection, Paris

After the composition was set, Ribera sometimes isolated individual figures or groups of figures for further study and sketched them in a summary way, although a figure or a part of a figure may be worked out with close attention. An example of the first practice is found in an energetic ink and wash drawing of the dead Christ and Saint John (fig. 89),[44] which was incorporated without change into the moving *Pietà* of San Martino (1637; fig. 25). Another drawing in the same vein is a study of figures in red chalk apparently intended for an unknown painting (fig. 90).[45] At times, Ribera concentrated on a small detail within a composition, as seen in a drawing of the head of a helmeted soldier (fig. 91),[46] who belongs in the supporting cast in a now-lost painting of *Samson and Delilah,* which is known through a finished chalk drawing of the entire composition (fig. 92).[47]

This finished drawing represents a final category of preparatory study, in which the artists carefully rendered the composition as it would be painted. While we cannot be certain that finished drawings were invariably made by Ribera for each of his paintings, there are other examples of the type, one of which is a splendid red and black chalk drawing of *David and Goliath* (fig. 93) related to a picture once in the Spanish royal collection and now destroyed.[48]

The study of Ribera's preparatory drawings reveals an important aspect of his artistic practice, for the drawings allow us to see how carefully he planned his compositions and sought the right effect for the subject at hand. But drawings were both an adjunct to Ribera's profession as a painter and also an outlet for

Figure 91
Ribera. *Study of Helmeted Soldier,* Museo del Prado, Madrid

Figure 92
Ribera. *Samson and Delilah,* Museo Provincial de Bellas Artes, Córdoba

Figure 93
Ribera. *David and Goliath,* Private Collection, New York

Figure 94
Ribera. *Men Hauling Carcass of a Deer,* Gabinetto Nazionale delle Stampe, Rome

Figure 95
Ribera. *Blind Friar Led by Man,* Mr. and Mrs. John Steiner

Figure 96
Ribera. *Blacksmith and Other Figures,* Uffizi, Florence

the expression of the most inventive artistic imaginations of the seventeenth century. The artist we know from Ribera's pictures is a forceful interpreter of religious and mythological themes. However, another aspect of the artist which is revealed only in the drawings shows him to have been enthralled by the humorous, the bizarre, the outlandish, the capricious, the grotesque, and the cruel. Speculation as to the reasons for Ribera's fascination with the unheroic aspects of life is pointless: that Ribera's drawings reveal such aspects with startling pungency is readily apparent.

Some of Ribera's capricious drawings appear to derive from his observations of the world around him, although these drawings can hardly be called documentary records of seventeenth-century Neapolitan life. Transformed by the artist's imagination and rendered in his terse, notational style, the subjects hover between the factual and the imaginary. (It is also possible that certain genre-like themes represent literary texts as yet unidentified.) Two drawings with relatively matter-of-fact subjects show how the commonplace is transformed by Ribera's pen. One depicts a man hauling a carcass of a deer (fig. 94),[49] the other a blind friar being led through the streets by a guide wearing a skullcap (fig. 95).[50] A third example is a fascinating drawing of a blacksmith at work, assisted by a woman fanning the fire with bellows. On one side, a man approaches the central group, gesturing with his right hand (fig. 96).[51] In all these drawings, the stylization of the figures, the absence of a background, and the spare use of accessory details impart an unreal quality to the humdrum activities.

Figure 97
Ribera. *Man and Page,* Kurt Meissner, Zurich

Figure 100
Ribera. *Fantastic Scene,* Whereabouts unknown

Figure 98
Ribera. *Hermit Saint Praying and Other Figures,*
Ecole des Beaux-Arts, Paris

Figure 101
Ribera. *Grotesque Head with Figures,* Pennsylvania
Academy of the Fine Arts, Philadelphia

Figure 99
Ribera. *Grotesque Figure Waving Stick,* California
Palace of the Legion of Honor, San Francisco

Figure 102
Ribera. *Standing Figure with Small Figure, Holding
Banner, on His Head,* Metropolitan Museum
of Art, Harry G. Sperling Fund, New York

Figure 103
Ribera. *Grotesque Scene,* Museo Bassano del Grappa

Almost imperceptibly, this type of subject approaches the realm of the grotesque, and here Ribera was master. A forceful drawing of the late 1620s represents a man and a page (fig. 97),[52] an unexceptional subject transformed by the humorous treatment of the faces. A comparable but even stronger drawing shows a bald hermit in a dance-like pose praying before a crucifix (fig. 98).[53] To the left, two other praying figures strike exaggerated devotional poses, while the right three figures, a mother and child with a man, half-hidden by the hillock, impassively gaze at the scene. The step from this strange world to the realm of pure imagination is short.

Ribera's imagination spawned a variety of bizarre and grotesque types. An introduction to this netherworld of the natural order is provided by a figure with a cape, holding a stick which he shakes menacingly (fig. 99).[54] Although from the feet to the neck the figure appears normal, the face suggests a weird, distorted mask with a large nose, mustache, high cheeks, and slanted eyes. In the right margin of the sheet, Ribera sketched both a frontal and profile view of the head, and thus intensified the exaggerated appearance.

Stranger still, a drawing in a similar vein (fig. 100) shows a gentleman in profile wearing a grotesque mask.[55] Over his body Lilliputian figures swarm; they swing from his nose, wrestle on his head, and balance on his sword. These agile, energetic little figures, stock characters of Ribera's imagination, scale the heights of a head as if it were a mountain (fig. 101)[56] and plant a flag atop the conquered summit (fig. 102).[57] Such figures also occur clambering over the remains of a dead tree in one of Ribera's more macabre and enigmatic drawings (fig. 103).[58]

Besides these capricious figures, a dark corner of Ribera's mind sometimes produced horrible images of cruel punishment and violent death. A few of these drawings record the barbaric practices of the day; for example, a representation of an inquisition scene in which the accused is raised on the hoist (fig. 104),[59] which causes the excruciating dislocation of the shoulders. A boldly signed sheet of the later years may also be factual in its subject matter (fig. 105).[60] But undoubtedly, two scenes of violent death and mutilation (figs. 106, 107) are purely imaginary. In one drawing, a figure is bound horizontally to stakes by the hands and feet, awaiting the impending blow from an executioner armed with a heavy ax.[61] The other drawing shows a landscape strewn with the remains of unspeakable violence — heads and limbs lie about like so much dead wood.[62]

Figure 104
Ribera. *Scene of Torture,* Rhode Island School of
Design, Providence

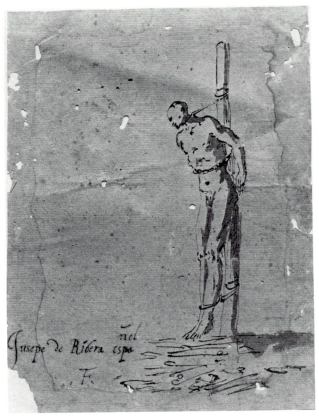

Figure 105
Ribera. *Man Tied to Stake,* California Palace of the
Legion of Honor, San Francisco

Related to these subjects, a large series of drawings shows men bound to trees and stakes, often in unusual and uncomfortable configurations (fig. 108).[63] And, on one occasion, Ribera produced a drawing which, despite its connection with an established iconographical tradition, can only be considered indelicate (fig. 109).[64]

Ribera's range as a draftsman thus runs the full gamut of themes from the sacred to the profane. And the variety of his techniques and uses of drawing is equally extensive. For this reason, Ribera's drawings offer us a glimpse into the recesses of his artistic imagination. In the preparatory studies, the artist carefully sought the right effect for the subject at hand, experimenting with gesture, pose, expression, and composition until he was satisfied with the result. This practice helped Ribera to realize the confident arrangement of pictorial elements which adds great authority to his paintings, and to achieve the often complicated, intricate poses of the figures. The fantastic drawings, on the other hand, show us another side of the public artist identified with those memorable, heroic versions of the major Christian themes. Together, the range of his thematic repertory and the pronounced individuality of his style place Ribera in a class with the great draftsmen of the Baroque.

Figure 106
Ribera. *Scene of Execution,* Teylers Museum, Haarlem

Figure 107
Ribera. *Scene with Tortured Men,* Biblioteca Reale, Turin

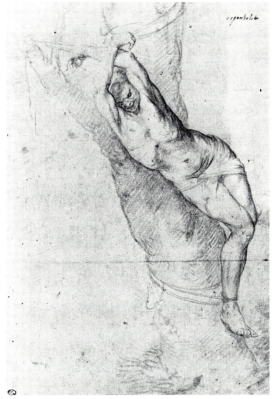

Figure 108
Ribera. *Man Tied to Tree,* Musée du Louvre, Paris

Figure 109
Ribera. *Man with Syringe,* Private Collection,
Munich-Vienna

NOTES

1. This essay is based on my earlier study, *Jusepe de Ribera: Prints and Drawings* (Princeton, 1973). However, I have endeavored to take account of the contributions to knowledge of the subject published since that date and to amend and revise my earlier opinions as necessary. Several of the prints have been recently catalogued, although without significant changes from my work of 1973, by Alba Costamagna in *Incisori Napoletani del '600* (Gabinetto Nazionale delle Stampe, Rome, 1981).

2. Brown, 1973, p. 66, nos. 1 and 2.

3. Brown, 1973, pp. 66-67, no. 4.

4. Brown, 1973, pp. 78-80, no. 17, where the attribution is rejected. The authenticity of the print is skillfully defended by Sopher, 1978, no. 158.

5. Brown, 1973, pp. 68-69, no 6.

6. Brown, 1973, pp. 67-68, no 5.

7. Felton, 1976, pp. 38-39 and Spinosa 1978, p. 96, no. 29. Both authors base their argument for the 1626 date on the assumption that the print is a variant of the painting in the Hermitage, dated 1626. This assumption supposes that Ribera never made variations on a composition after he etched it. But in at least one instance, the *Martyrdom of St. Bartholomew*, he continued to rework the composition after making the print. Given his habit of revising the compositions of certain themes, there is no inherent reason to believe that a print could not, in its turn, provide the starting point for another version of the subject in the painting. Also, it should be noted that an angel with a trumpet appears in a version of the scene now in the Colegiata de Osuna, which is datable to 1616-20. Therefore the motif was not new to Ribera's art when the print was made, as I believe it was, around 1621.

8. Brown, 1973, p. 66, no. 3.

9. Palm, 1973, identifies the poet as Virgil. Moffitt, 1978, convincingly refutes this hypothesis and proposes instead the name of Dante. Moffitt's learned discussion of the significance of the "withered-yet-blooming" tree is informative, but its application to the interpretation of the print is uncertain because this motif was frequently used by Ribera in a variety of contexts. Also, I fail to discern in the original the scholar's cap which Moffitt believes the poet to wear. To my eyes, the poet's head is uncovered. Therefore, I continue to accept the typological interpretation presented by Stechow in 1957.

10. Gombrich, 1969, pp. 156-172, discusses the origins and development of printed instructional manuals in the early seventeenth century.

11. Odoardo Fialetti (after Agostino Carracci), *Il vero modo ed ordine per disegnar* (1608); Olivieri Gatti (after Guercino, *Primi elementi per introdurre i giovani al disegno* (1619), to which Ribera's prints are very similar. Both books are discussed by Gombrich, 1969, pp. 161-162.

12. Brown, 1973, pp. 69-71, nos. 7-8.

13. Brown, 1973, pp. 71-72, no. 9.

14. Brown, 1973, pp. 72-73, nos. 10-11.

15. See Konečný, 1980, for a concise, illuminating discussion of this print and its relation to the tradition of the representation of grotesque subjects in the Renaissance.

16. Konečný, 1980, pp. 93-94, note 9. For another comparable grotesque head, see the anonymous drawing (late sixteenth-century Italian?) in the Pennsylvania Academy of the Fine arts, PAFA 283.

17. Whereabouts unknown; 161 x 127 mm, red chalk on white paper with watermark of encircled bird. Collections: Christie's, April 15, 1980, no. 30. The drawing in Naples, Capodimonte, mentioned by D'Amico, 1978, no. 94, as a preparatory study for the print is in my opinion a copy; see Brown, 1973 p. 73.

18. London-Paris, E. Schapiro; 147 x 107mm, red chalk on white paper. Collections: Rey de Villette (Lugt 2200a), in his sale, Berlin, 1931, no. 926, as Annibale Carracci.

19. Brown, 1973, pp. 73-74, no. 12.

20. Brown, 1973, pp. 74-75, no. 13.

21. Brown, 1973, pp. 75-76, no. 14. Chenault Porter, 1979, identifies the satyr as Pan and also suggests a bewildering variety of possible sources for the pose of Silenus, thus demonstrating that it was a commonplace in the art of antiquity and the Renaissance. Also, as Trapier, 1952, p. 241 noted, a comparable pose was used by Ribera in an earlier drawing of *Samson and Delilah* (Córdoba, Museo de Bellas Artes), which is a study for a lost painting in the Spanish royal collection; see below for further discussion of this drawing.

Bellini, 1975, pp. 19-20, proposes the attribution to Ribera of a print (Naples, San Martino), which is a composite of motifs from the *Drunken Silenus* and *Saint Jerome Reading*. As Spinosa, 1978, p. 95, no. 25, notes, this print is a *derivazione* and is related to the numerous collections of prints after Ribera described by Brown, 1973, pp. 83-86, nos. 30-37.

22. Brown, 1973, pp. 77-78, no. 16. Ribera collaborated with an anonymous engraver on a print of around 1629-33; see Brown, 1973, pp. 76-77, no. 15.

23. This hypothesis is advanced by Darby, 1953, p. 71, and partly supported by Felton, 1976, p. 34, who, however, recognizes the importance of the changes made by Ribera when adapting the composition of a painting to a print.

24. Felton, 1976.

25. See London (Pérez Sánchez), 1976, no. 27 and 1978; Felton, 1976, p. 35; and Spinosa, 1978, pp. 94-95, nos. 21-24, for views on the authenticity of these works, which are datable to ca. 1616-20.

26. Felton, 1976, pp. 31-34, accepts the painting as authentic. Like Spinosa, 1978, pp. 129-30, no. 262, I believe that the execution is too stiff and clumsy to be attributable to Ribera and that the painting and the related drawing also published by Felton are probably copies of the work described by De Dominici.

27. The identity of this picture has been much discussed, but without conclusive results. For a summary of the opinions and the relevant references, see Spinosa, 1978, p. 98, no. 38 and p. 140, no. 411. The proposal that the print reflects this lost composition, like the others advanced so far, is hypothetical and circumstantial. However, if we accept that most of the figure compositions in the prints are based on pictures, and that the print could have been executed around 1620, then the *Lamentation* is entitled to consideration as a possible reflection of the painting mentioned by Mancini.

28. Brown, 1973, p. 159, no. 8. To my mind, the drawing is more closely related to the print than to any painting of the subject, including the version in the Galleria Pallavicini, Rome, which in any case is a debatable attribution (see Spinosa, 1978, p. 93, no. 18, for a discussion of the problem).

29. For examples, see Brown, 1973, pp. 38-61.

30. For this painting, see Schnapper, 1974, p. 384.

31. De Dominici, 1742, III, 18.

32. Brown, 1974, p. 368, no. 3. Information on the technique, dimensions, and provenance of drawings mentioned in this essay is provided only in the case of previously unpublished works. Otherwise, reference is made to a place in which this information and further bibliography can be found. The references are not necessarily to the initial publication of a drawing.

33. Vitzthum, 1967, p. 32, no. 44.

34. Vitzthum, 1967, p. 31, no. 43.

35. Brown, 1973, p. 163, no. 15. Palm, 1975, p. 81, suggests that the female figure may be Ariadne. While the pose is undoubtedly related to the Ariadne type found in antique works of art, it is difficult to be definitive about the identification of the subject because of the imprecise representation of the male figure.

36. Collection A. Battesti, Toulouse; 116 x 197 mm, pen and brown ink on white paper; inscribed in ink upper right corner: 22. Verso, figure holding hand on breast, partially trimmed. Provenance unknown.

37. Vitzthum, 1967, p. 29, no. 39.

38. Brown, 1973, pp. 174-175, no. 33.

39. Brown, 1973, pp. 169-70, no. 24.

40. Brown, 1973, p. 168, no. 22.

41. Vitzthum, 1967, p. 35, no. 50.

42. Brown, 1973, pp. 166-67, no. 20.

43. Vitzthum, 1967, p. 30, no. 40.

44. Vitzthum, 1971, p. 83.

45. New York, private collection; 221 x 217 mm, red chalk on beige paper; inscribed in brown ink, lower left: "spagnoletto." Verso, figure kneeling on a cloud or rock, and detail of arm and hand holding staff; red chalk; inscribed in brown ink, upper left: "Spagnoletto." Collection: Sotheby's, July 11, 1979, no. 133.

46. Pérez Sánchez, 1972, p. 119. The connection of this drawing with the Córdoba *Samson and Delilah* was made by Muller, 1976, p. 609, where the subject is incorrectly identified as *Jael and Sisera*.

47. Trapier, 1952, p. 240.

48. New York, private collection; 260 x 432 mm, red and black chalk on white paper; inscribed in brown ink, lower right: "De Gusepe de Ribera el Españoleto, 1624"; upper right: "Solis"; lower left: "20 R.ˢ" Collections: Francisco de Solís (1629-84); Christie's, July 8, 1975, no. 125. The inscription with the artist's name and date does not seem to be autograph. The drawing is mentioned by Muller, 1976, p. 609.

49. Brown, 1974, p. 370, no. 14.

50. John and Alice Steiner Collection; 187 x 140 mm; black chalk and brown wash on white paper. Collections: Pietro Scarpa (1973).

51. Vitzthum, 1971, p. 80.

52. Foster-Hahn, 1969, p. 114, no. 88.

53. Paris, Ecole des Beaux-Arts, no. 302; 277 x 209 mm; red ink and red wash on white paper, laid down; inscribed in brown ink, lower left: "Rivera." Collections: J. Masson (Lugt Suppl. 1494a).

54. Hellman, 1915, no. 253.

55. Brown, 1973, p. 148.

56. Philadelphia, Pennsylvania Academy of the Fine Arts, PAFA 8; 170 x 104 mm; pen and brown ink with brown wash over some black chalk, on buff paper; inscribed on former mount: "Orig¹ de Spagnoletto, da Napoli." Provenance unknown.

57. New York, Metropolitan Museum of Art, Harry G. Sperling Fund, 1981.395; 212 x 102 mm; pen and brown ink with brown wash; inscribed in banner, probably in artist's own hand: Nicolò Simonelli''; on verso: "Simonelli." Collections: Nicolò Simonelli (fl. 1630-60); Sotheby's, April 9, 1981, no. 89. Nicolò Simonelli, who served in the households of Cardinals Brancacci and Chigi, was a noted Roman collector and connoisseur. He is documented as having been in contact with Pieter van Laer and Pier Francesco Mola. Passeri mentions his sponsorship of Salvator Rosa in 1638, which suggests that he had acquaintances in Naples, perhaps including Ribera among them. This raises the possibility that the

drawing may have been executed by Ribera as a
present to Simonelli.

58. Vitzthum, 1971, p. 81.

59. Brown, 1973, p. 174, no. 32.

60. Brown, 1973, pp. 176-77, no. 36.

61. Brown, 1973, pp. 173-74, no. 31.

62. Vitzthum, 1967, p. 33, no. 46.

63. Vitzthum and Monbeig-Goguel, 1967, pp. 12-13,
    no. 20. For a discussion of the ''bound man'' theme,
    see Brown, 1972.

64. Vienna-Munich, private collection; known to me
    only from a photograph. Dimensions and medium
    unavailable. For a discussion of the theme, see
    Donald Posner, *Watteau: A Lady at Her Toilet* (New
    York, 1973), pp. 43-46.

CATALOGUE

Since the submission of my Ph.D. dissertation, *Jusepe de Ribera, a Catalogue Raisonné,* to the University of Pittsburgh in 1971, a number of paintings by Ribera have come to light and many of his works have undergone conservation. Additionally, the discovery of signatures and dates on several works, the publication of scholarly studies on seicento art, and the exchange of information and ideas by interested colleagues have helped to clarify the artist's evolution. Some paintings for which participation of studio assistants was suggested in my dissertation are accepted here as fully autograph; others rejected as by Ribera are included in this study as accepted works. This catalogue supercedes the thesis in representing my views on the artist and his work.

I am grateful to Dr. William B. Jordan, who made many substantive contributions to this publication and assisted in the writing of the catalogue.

CF

Figure 110
Jacob de Backer. *The Sense of Taste,* ca. 1580, etching,
Rijksmuseum, Amsterdam

Figure 111
Vincenzo Campi. *Fish Market,* 1580, Kirchheim
[Mindelheim], Fugger Collection

The Five Senses
(Catalogue numbers 1-3)

Ribera's series of the Five Senses makes a special contribution to a theme that has immediate antecedents in the sixteenth century when a number of artists, mostly from northern Europe, began to explore it. One example of such treatment is the series painted and etched by Jacob de Backer (ca. 1560-ca. 1591) (fig. 110). These compositions, designed as allegorical confections with large nude or semi-nude figures in landscapes, and with varied symbols appropriate to the different senses, follow the general patterns of the Dutch Mannerists.[1] The Netherlandish tradition of market scenes, with moralizing overtones, painted by Pieter Aertsen (1508-1575) and his pupil Joachim Beuckelaer (ca. 1530-ca. 1574), who had been active in Parma, certainly influenced the Cremonese Vincenzo Campi (ca. 1530-1591) when in 1580 he executed a series of five paintings for the dining room of the Fugger Castle at Kirchheim. These latter works (fig. 111), while they are big showpieces, contain genre elements that would shortly be isolated as the subject matter of independent paintings—for example, the man eating beans at the left, a detail that has been compared to Annibale Carracci's famous *Bean Eater* (fig. 112) of 1583-1584.

Both Campi's and Carracci's figures are coarse peasants devouring the most ordinary of meals with unabashed gusto. Although allegorical or symbolic meaning has been suggested for Annibale's painting, as well as for his two paintings of *The Butcher Shop* (ca. 1580), (Christ Church, Oxford; Kimbell Art Museum), the most general interpretation is that they are basically genre scenes.[2] Such imagery probably came to Annibale by way of the Bolognese Bartolomeo Passarotti (1529-1592), whose *Butcher Shop* (Galleria Nazionale, Rome) is only one of several of his paintings revealing a spirited and refreshing new naturalism. During his travels from Naples to Parma and the year or more that he spent in Rome in 1615-1616, Ribera probably encountered this growing interest in genre subjects.

Definitely pertinent to Ribera's development of the theme of the Five Senses were Caravaggio's half-length figures of languid young men placed behind tables and engaged in activities designed to elicit a sensual response from the viewer. *The Lute Player,* now in the Hermitage, Leningrad, was famous almost from the moment of its creation; the painting can be interpreted as a *Sense of Hearing,* just as the Borghese *Boy with a Basket of Fruit* can also be the *Sense of Taste.* The Longhi Collection *Boy Bitten by a Lizard* (fig. 113) has, in fact, been associated with the *Sense of Touch.* Certainly, one of the effects, if not the objective, of such compositions was to call up associations with sensual pleasures.[3]

Ribera's series of the *Five Senses* may be the first treatment of the subject as a group of naturalistic, portrait-like images. Ribera presents the subjects in much the same way that painters were beginning to show the saints and their

Figure 112
Annibale Carracci. *The Bean Eater,* 1583-1584,
Galleria Colonna, Rome

Figure 113
Caravaggio. *Boy Bitten by a Lizard,* ca. 1593, Longhi
Collection, Florence   (Alinari)

attributes—in simple, direct compositions that focus the eye and the mind
according to the conceptual discipline engendered during the Counter
Reformation under the influence of Ignatius of Loyola's *Spiritual Exercises.* The
heightening of the senses advocated in Loyola's treatise had an undeniable
effect even on secular attitudes, and it is surely no coincidence than an artistic
preoccupation with the theme of the senses occurred at the same time that
many artists were sharpening the sensory focus of naturalism.

Judging from the several extant copies, Ribera's compositions enjoyed some
popularity, yet the older, more elaborate treatment of the subject lingered, as
in, for example, Jan Breughel's five canvases from 1617-1618 (Prado
1394-1398). Breughel painted two other canvases which also entered the
Spanish royal collection: one represents *Sight and Smell* (Prado 1403); the other
Taste, Hearing, and Touch (Prado 1404).

Shortly after its completion Ribera's series of the *Five Senses* is recorded in the
early literature of art. Giulio Mancini (1558-1630), physician to Pope Urban
VIII Barberini (1623-1644) and astute critic of the styles and trends in the art
of his time, wrote a brief biography of Ribera in *Considerazioni sulla Pittura* in
which he states:

> He made many things here in Rome, and in particular for ***, the
> Spaniard, those having five half-figures representing the five senses, very
> beautiful, a Christ Deposed and another, which in truth are things of most
> exquisite beauty.[4]

Documents from the Roman archives establish Ribera's presence in Rome for
the annual Easter census taken there in April of 1615 and again in March of
1616.[5] He is also recorded in May of 1616 as having paid dues in the
Accademia di San Luca, Rome. This information confirms Mancini's account
of Ribera in Rome and lends support to the dating of the *Senses* to those years.

The history of these paintings is complex. Mancini omitted the name of the
Spaniard for whom Ribera painted them in Rome. During the first two years
that Mancini was writing his text, the Spanish Ambassador to Rome was the
Duke of Osuna, who, as Viceroy of Naples from 1616 to 1620, is known to
have been one of Ribera's important patrons. Osuna may have been the
mystery patron, although many of Ribera's clients at the time were probably
Spaniards.[6]

The *Sense of Touch* (cat. no. 1) and the *Sense of Taste* (cat. no. 3) were in the
collection of Prince F. F. Youssoupoff in Moscow and St. Petersburg prior to
the Revolution of 1917 and then passed to Duveen in New York. They had
been attributed to Velázquez, to Antonio Puga, and then (by Martin Soria) to
Pietro Novelli, ''Il Monrealese,'' a Sicilian follower of Ribera. In 1963 a Paris
dealer showed Roberto Longhi a series of paintings representing the *Five Senses*
and inscribed: TACTVS, ORDORATVS, AUDITVS, VISSVS, and
GVSTVS. (These copies later passed through the Dorotheum in Vienna to

Figure 114
Bartolomeo Passarotti. *Man with a Lute,* 1576,
Museum of Fine Arts, Boston

Figure 115
after Ribera. *The Sense of Hearing,* (from an original
work ca. 1615), Europahaus, Vienna

Figure 116
after Ribera. *The Sense of Smell,* (from an original work
ca. 1615), Europahaus, Vienna

Europahaus, a corporation on the outskirts of Vienna.) Longhi, remembering the Mancini text, published the series in 1966 as copies of the Ribera paintings and reattributed the Hartford *Sense of Taste* to Ribera. In 1968 Schleier recognized the *Sense of Touch* in the Norton Simon Collection as another of the original canvases by Ribera. The Franz Mayer *Sense of Sight* was attributed to Gérard Douffet when it was published in 1964. Without knowing of its location in Mexico City, the present writer published a photograph of this painting as a Ribera, indicating that it was formerly on the New York art market (Felton, 1969 [actually issued in 1972]). Spear published its present location in 1972. The *Sense of Taste* and the *Sense of Touch* were shown together in the important *Caravaggio and His Followers* exhibition held at the Cleveland Museum of Art in 1971. The present exhibition marks the first recorded occasion of the showing together of the three known paintings from the series.

Although copies exist of the other two paintings in the series, the originals of the *Sense of Hearing* and the *Sense of Smell* have not been located. Passarotti's *Man with a Lute* (fig. 114), dated 1576, now in the Museum of Fine Arts, Boston, is a prototype of the former. Figures (115) and (116) illustrate the copies now at Europahaus in Vienna.

Ribera has made these symbolic paintings much more powerful than any previous representations of the Senses by having chosen as his models ordinary, unidealized human types and by focusing on their individual physical traits and respective attributes. Each of the figures engages us in a way that calls upon our own sensory experience, and therefore the meaning of each work impresses us directly rather than through allegory. In that respect, they are also a part of the genre tradition represented by Carracci's *Bean Eater.* The young Ribera demonstrates his understanding of the innovation and strengths of Caravaggio's art, but he interprets this heritage to satisfy his own demand for an even more rugged and dramatic semblance of reality.[7]

NOTES

1. Czobar, 1972, pp. 317-327. Similar thematic series including the seasons and the months have a much longer tradition in European art and their frequent association with Christian symbolism is only the more immediate development from classical antecedents.

2. Wind, 1976, pp. 93-96; Posner, 1971, I, 12-20; Martin, 1963, p. 263.

3. A parallel development in which groups of figures are gathered to enjoy the pleasures of food, wine, song, and spirited companions is continued well into the seventeenth century.

4. Mancini (1614-1621), ed. Salerno, 1956-1957, I, 149-150.

   > Fece molte cose qui in Roma et in particulare per ***, spagnolo, quale ha cinque mezze figure per i cinque sensi molto belle, un Christo Deposto et altro che invero son cose di esquisitissima bellezza.

   This treatise was mainly written between 1614 and 1621, but Mancini continued to edit it until he died in 1630.

5. Chenault, 1969, pp. 561-562; Bousquet, 1980, pp. 105-106.

6. Konečný suggested in 1973 that this dating is necessarily uncertain since Ribera returned to Rome and Mancini continued to edit his text; however, the style of the paintings does not support a later dating. See also Felton, 1969.

   Numerous copies of Ribera's paintings of the *Five Senses* are known. One complete set, plus a duplicate of the *Sense of Taste,* is in the Collection d'Estoup in Murcia. The catalogue of the d'Estoup collection (Martínez Ripoll, 1981) was brought to my attention by Dr. Lois Drewer. Another complete set of the *Five Senses,* with Latin inscriptions, is in Vienna. Also, in the estate inventory begun on April 6, 1655, following the death of Don Diego Phelipez de Guzmán, Marquis of Leganés, on February 12, separate paintings representing each of the *Five Senses* are recorded. These paintings are all attributed in the inventory to Jacob Jordaens: no. 576, the *Sense of Touch;* no. 577, the *Sense of Sight;* no. 578, the *Sense of Smell;* no. 579, the *Sense of Hearing;* no. 581, the *Sense of Taste.* (See López Navio, 1962, pp. 34-35) Dr. John Spike recognized these descriptions as matching the paintings by Ribera; however, the inventory lists them as being three-quarters *varas* square.

7. A painting dated 1632 of a blind man holding an antique head has been misidentified as the *Blind Sculptor from Gambassi* (Prado 1112). It may belong to a second series of the *Five Senses* representing the *Sense of Touch. A Man Holding a Mirror,* known in several versions, may be a companion *Sense of Sight.* Ribera painted a third series of the *Five Senses* in 1637, of which three subjects are known (see cat. no. 20).

1 *see color plate*

Figure 117
Ribera. *The Sense of Touch,* 1632, Museo del Prado,
Madrid

1

Sense of Touch

Canvas, 116 x 88.3 cm (45¾ x 34¾ in)
Painted ca. 1615-1616
The Norton Simon Foundation, Pasadena
Pasadena, California

In the *Sense of Touch,* Ribera has dramatically heightened the impact of his subject by presenting a blind man, his eyes tightly shut, who is unable to see the painting of a man's head lying, foreshortened, on the table in the foreground. The blind man holds in his coarse hands a finely chiselled antique sculptured head. The intense concentration expressed by his face focuses our imaginations on the contact between his fingertips and the surface of the marble he holds. The painting explores a marvelously Baroque idea which the artist could not resist treating again in a signed and dated work of 1632 (Prado 1112) (fig. 117).

This very early work shows at its most primitive stage Ribera's preoccupation with the pictorial representation of texture. The face and hands are thickly painted and somewhat labored when compared to his virtuoso brushwork of a decade later. His painting technique contrasts with that of Caravaggio, who carefully modulated values, producing a smoother and more continuous surface. With Ribera, values and textures are established by permitting deeper layers of darker hue to be exposed in the crevices formed by the coarse-bristled brush dragged through wet paint. Using the brush somewhat as a sculptor uses a chisel, Ribera deliberately exploits the effects of natural light raking across the highs and lows of textured paint.

PROVENANCE: Prince F. F. Youssoupoff, Moscow and St. Petersburg; with Duveen Bros., Inc., New York; The Norton Simon Foundation, Los Angeles, 1965, no. F. 65.1.52 P.

EXHIBITIONS: Palm Beach, 1964, no. 2; Hartford, 1967; San Francisco, 1968-70; Cleveland (Spear), 1971, no. 56, illus.

BIBLIOGRAPHY: Mancini (1614-1621), ed. Salerno, 1956-1957, I, 149-150; Milicua, 1952, pp. 309-322; Longhi, 1966, pp. 74-78; Schleier, 1968, pp. 79-80, illus.; Paoletti, 1968, pp. 425-426; Felton, 1969, pp. 2-11, illus.; Spear, 1972, pp. 149-150; Volpe, 1972, pp. 72-73; Pepper, 1972, p. 178; Konečný, 1973, pp. 85-92; Felton, 1976, pp. 31-43, illus.; Spinosa, 1978, no. 3, illus.; Pasadena, California (Hermann), 1980, p. 43.

VERSIONS: Murcia, Collection d'Estoup; Vienna, Europahaus (from Collection J. Braz).

2

2
Sense of Sight
Canvas, 114 x 89 cm (45 x 35 in)
Painted ca. 1615-1616
Collection Franz Mayer
Mexico City

In contrast to the brutish model personifying the *Sense of Touch,* the model Ribera chose for the *Sense of Sight* has a face of acute intelligence even though his unpretentious dress assures us he is not a man of wealth. The face is modeled with a more highly developed chiaroscuro, perhaps to emphasize the visual metaphor. The man, who holds a telescope in his hands, looks out at us across a table on which are a mirror, a pair of spectacles, and a cap with colored feathers. The right side of the face is worked with heavy impasto, brushed to give relief to the furrows in his brow and a structure to his eye, cheek, and nose. The left eye and cheek are more thinly painted and concealed in shadow. The rough and swollen hands are those of a laborer, with large knuckles and darkened nails.

PROVENANCE: Sale, Hôtel Drouot, Paris (ca. 1941, as Velázquez); with Bensimon, Inc., New York, 1952 and Paris 1971; Collection Franz Mayer, Mexico City, on loan to the Museo de San Carlos, Mexico City, until 1982.

BIBLIOGRAPHY: Mancini (1614-1621), ed. Salerno, 1956-1957, I, 149-150; Milicua, 1952, pp. 309-322; Mexico City, 1963, pl. 38; Longhi, 1966, pp. 74-78; Felton, 1969, pp. 2-11, illus.; Cleveland (Spear), 1971, pp. 149-153; Spear, 1972, pp. 149-150, illus.; Konečný, 1973, pp. 85-92, illus.; Felton, 1976, pp. 31-43, illus.; Spinosa, 1978, no. 4, illus.

VERSIONS: Murcia, Collection d'Estoup; Vienna, Europahaus, (from Collection J. Braz).

3 *see color plate*

3
Sense of Taste
Canvas, 116.8 x 88.3 cm (46 x 34¾ in)
Painted ca. 1615-1616
Wadsworth Atheneum, Hartford
The Ella Gallup Sumner and Mary Catlin Sumner Collection

To represent the *Sense of Taste,* Ribera depicts a corpulent gypsy wearing tiny gold earrings. His frayed and soiled gray shirt strains and puckers to close around his fleshy girth. Clearly focused deep-brown eyes impart his serious purpose toward the meal he is about to enjoy. The pasta, or squid, sprinkled liberally with cheese, overflows a decorated pottery bowl; olives, spilling from a paper-cone, and a hard-crust roll complement the meal. He raises his glass of wine in anticipation of the gustatory pleasures awaiting him.

The *Sense of Taste* is aesthetically the most successful of the three paintings. The modeling of the figure's ruddy face and hands is extremely skilled, and its overall naturalistic presence is more subtle in the transitions from light to dark. In comparison with the half-length youths of Caravaggio, Ribera's figure is astoundingly naturalistic, and Giulio Mancini's praise for this series of paintings by the young artist is hardly surprising.

PROVENANCE: Prince F. F. Youssoupoff, Moscow and St. Petersburg; with Duveen Bros., Inc., New York; Wadsworth Atheneum, 1963. 194.

EXHIBITIONS: Hartford, 1963; Cleveland (Spear), 1971, no. 55, illus.; London (Whitfield and Martineau), 1982, pp. 226-227, no. 119, illus.

BIBLIOGRAPHY: Mancini (1614-1621), ed. Salerno, 1956-1957, I, 149-150; Milicua, 1952, pp. 309-322; Longhi, 1966, pp. 74-78; review of Longhi, A.E.A., 1966, p. 232; Schleier, 1968, pp. 79-80; Paoletti, 1968, pp. 425-426; Felton, 1969, pp. 2-11, illus.; Spear, 1972, pp. 149-153; "High Flavors," *Apollo,* 1972, p. 247; Spear, 1972, pp. 149-150; Volpe, 1972, pp. 72-73; Pepper, 1972, p. 178; Konečný, 1973, pp. 85-92; Felton, 1976, pp. 31-43, illus.; Spinosa, 1978, p. 92, no. 2, illus.

VERSIONS: Florence, Collection Rampini (from Collection Rossi, Forlì); Leningrad, Hermitage; Murcia, Collection d'Estoup; New York, Collection Adela Holzer; Vienna, Europahaus (from Collection J. Braz).

4

Figure 118
Ribera. *Saint Jerome and the Angel*, ca. 1616-1620,
Parish Museum, Collegiate Church, Osuna

4

The Martyrdom of Saint Sebastian
Canvas, 179 x 139 cm (70½ x 54¾ in)
Painted ca. 1616-1618
Museo Parroquial de Osuna
Colegiata de Osuna

This *Martyrdom of Saint Sebastian* and three other paintings by Ribera—a *Saint Jerome and the Angel of Judgment* (fig. 118), a *Martyrdom of Saint Bartholomew* (fig. 119), and a *Penitent Saint Peter* (fig. 120)—were incorporated into the elaborate Baroque altar of the Collegiate Church of Osuna in 1770. Mounted on panels, probably at this time, the canvases eventually split along the joint lines. They have also suffered considerable other damage from the effects of time and climate.

With the exceptions of Justi (1889) and Tormo (1916), most historians (Ponz 1764, Mayer 1923, and Trapier 1952) considered the works to be replicas or studio versions of original paintings by Ribera. The paintings have only recently been scientifically examined in the laboratory of the Prado Museum. The *Saint Sebastian,* the first to be restored, was exhibited in London and Paris in 1976, where it was convincingly defended by Pérez Sánchez as an authentic work by Ribera and a hallmark of his early painting style. Since then, the entire series has been returned from the laboratory to the Parish Museum at Osuna. In recent publications, the four paintings have been accepted into the canon of Ribera's authentic works.[1]

In 1982 Rodríquez-Buzón published records from Osuna which he believes indicate that these paintings may have been commissioned from Ribera by the Duke and Duchess of Osuna about 1616-1617. He documents the journey of Abbot Don Diego de Salvatierra from Osuna to Naples in 1617 to discuss church business with the Duke, who was then Viceroy of Naples. In another document referring to the council meeting of the Collegiate Church held on April 13, 1627, it is noted that Doña Catalina Enríquez de Ribera, by then Dowager Duchess of Osuna, sent ten "excellent paintings" from Italy, including a *Crucifixion.* Rodríquez-Buzón assumes with good reason that this work is Ribera's *Calvary* (fig. 21). The conclusions which he draws are that the four paintings of saints by Ribera were commissioned during the discussions between the Abbot and the Duke beginning in 1617. The documents certainly do not prove that. As elsewhere noted, the *Calvary* was surely a later commission awarded to Ribera by the Duchess or a member of her family and may have been meant for a funerary chapel for the late Duke.[2]

The patron of these works, Don Pedro Téllez Girón, Grand Duke of Osuna, was an illustrious general, successful in his military career in Flanders and in campaigns against the Turks. Following his appointment as Spanish Ambassador to the Holy See, he was awarded the coveted post of Viceroy of Naples. Fomenters of court intrigues and rivalries in Madrid seized upon his

Figure 119
Ribera. *Martyrdom of Saint Bartholomew,* ca. 1616-1620,
Parish Museum, Collegiate Church, Osuna

Figure 120
Ribera. *Penitent Saint Peter,* ca. 1616-1620, Parish
Museum, Collegiate Church, Osuna

lavish life in Naples as an excuse to bring charges of embezzlement against him. On June 4, 1620, he left from Naples under arrest to stand trial in Madrid, where he was found guilty of treason, imprisoned, and died in 1624 at the age of forty-five. Lope de Vega and Quevedo, loyal friends and servants of the Duke's, wrote tributary verses to his memory. The Duchess of Osuna, daughter of the 4th Marquis of Tarifa and immensely wealthy in her own right, strongly pleaded her husband's innocence.[3] Until her own death in 1635, she made the Osuna ancestral lands in Andalusia, and the Collegiate Church in particular, her personal projects, and she founded two convents and a seminary.

The *Martyrdom of Saint Sebastian* and the other three paintings of saints by Ribera at Osuna share basic stylistic features with the paintings of the *Senses.* The figure of Saint Sebastian has been tightly drawn with the outlines of the form sharply defined. The position of the legs and lower torso is strikingly similar to that of the classical sculpture known as the *Niobid* (Museo

Nazionale, Rome),[4] and a sculptural compactness gives weight as well as volume to the figure. Ribera's brushwork is careful and deliberate, lacking the vigor and virtuosity of his later method. Shadows are dense and seem to encroach upon the limbs and body rather like the dramatic darkness found in such paintings by Caravaggio as the Kansas City *Saint John the Baptist* (fig. 178) or the Borghese *Madonna of the Serpent.* The flesh tones are ruddy as in the *Sense of Touch* and the *Sense of Sight.* Ribera has taken pains to paint clearly the lines in Sebastian's palms, fingers, and wrists and to model the bulging veins on his forearms, pressed by the ropes tied above his elbows.

For all its assertive naturalism, Ribera's painting also relates very much to the more classicizing Bolognese tradition, as Pérez Sánchez has shown (1976). Particularly, the posing of the figure before such a low horizon line and against an expansive landscape with blues recalls the works of Guido Reni. Yet the protagonist seems to be thrust into the foreground and into the spotlight in a manner that sets the work quite apart from the milder ways of Bologna. The single arrow that pierces the saint's abdomen graphically details his particular form of torture, but the clear brown eyes, idealized face, and open gesture express his transported preparation to die for his faith.

Radiographic examination has shown that the artist reworked the head of Saint Sebastian from a frontal position to the final three-quarter, raised profile. On close inspection the left eye of the original head can be seen to the right of the present left eye. The earlier position of the head is similar, only in reverse, to that of Christ in Ribera's *Derision of Christ* in the Brera Gallery (fig. 13) or the Cogolludo *Preparation of Christ for the Cross* (fig. 19). The final pose is similar to that of the principal figure in the *Martyrdom of Saint Lawrence* now in London (fig. 17).

NOTES

1. Felton, 1976, pp. 31-43, illus. 4; Pérez Sánchez, 1976, no. 27, illus. p. 50; Pérez Sánchez, 1978, [20-23], illus.; Spinosa, 1978, p. 94, no. 21, illus.; Rodríquez-Buzón, 1982, pp. 62-63, 72-78, illus.

2. Mayer, 1923, p. 30; Felton, 1976, pp. 31-43, illus.

3. Rodríquez Marín, 1920, p. 22.

4. The poses are so alike that Ribera must have known some antique version of the figure. He could not, however, have known the Museo Nazionale version, which was not unearthed until 1906.

PROVENANCE: Collegiate Church of Osuna until 1978; Museo Parroquial de Osuna.

EXHIBITIONS: London (Pérez Sánchez) 1976, no. 27, illus. p. 50; Paris (Pérez Sánchez) 1976, no. 45, illus.

BIBLIOGRAPHY: Ponz, 1776, IV, 163; Justi, 1889, p. 343; Tormo, 1919-1920, pls. 887-880; Mayer, 1923, p. 30; Trapier, 1952, p. 23; Felton, 1976, pp. 31-43, illus. 4; Pérez Sánchez, 1978, [20-23], illus.; Spinosa, 1978, p. 94, no. 21, illus.; Rodríquez-Buzón, 1982, pp. 62-63, 72-78, pl. XIII.

5 *see color plate*

5

Saint Peter and Saint Paul

Canvas, 126 x 112 cm (49⅝ x 44⅛ in)

Signed, lower center: *Josephus Ribera Hispanus Valen / tinus Civitatis Setabis Aca / demicus Romanus*

Painted ca. 1618-1620

Museé des Beaux-Arts, Château des Rohan, Strasbourg

Although this painting bears an evident and genuine Latin inscription in which Ribera signs his name and states that he is a Spaniard from the city of Valencia, a native of Játiva, and Roman Academician, the work was catalogued by Haug in 1938 as a painting by Gérard Douffet, a Flemish follower of Ribera. It was subsequently attributed by Mayer (1945) to Pietro Novelli ''Il Monrealese,'' who had worked in Ribera's studio and to whom Soria had also ascribed the paintings of the *Five Senses* (see cat. nos. 1, 2, 3). Recent scholarship has returned this and several other early paintings to Ribera, helping to give a more clearly defined idea of the formative phase of his career.

Ribera dramatically uses symbols in this painting. Saint Paul holds his great sword upright just to the left of the center of the composition; in the foreground, Saint Peter's keys are placed on the stone ledge between the saints. The open volume, symbolizing Paul's epistles, and the great parchment scroll held by both men are treated as a pictorial *tour de force* of light and shadow. The colors assigned to the robes of each saint follow traditional iconography. Saint Paul's dark red mantle and green robe emerge from the shadows and are rather generalized in their structure, not unlike the garment in the *Sense of Touch;* Saint Peter's deep ochre mantle is brightly highlighted along the edges of the folds as the light falls upon it from the left.

The dynamics of Ribera's habitual x-shaped composition are enhanced by Saint Peter's glance across to Saint Paul and, in turn, by Saint Paul's direct gaze toward the viewer. The ledge supporting the still-life elements also serves to penetrate the viewer's space, counter-balancing Saint Paul's receding right arm holding the sword. The scroll is meant to articulate the space in between these extremes. All considered, there is a certain youthful over-zealousness about this composition; nevertheless, the work is powerful and effective. A date slightly before 1620 seems appropriate.

PROVENANCE: Sale, G. Rothan, Paris, Gallerie Georges Petit, 29-31 May 1890, lot 233; Musée des Beaux-Arts, Strasbourg, 1890, no. 103.

BIBLIOGRAPHY: Loeser, 1896, p. 286, as Ribera; Strasbourg, 1912, p. 78 as Ribera; Strasbourg (Haug), 1938, p. 76, no. 103 as Douffet; Mayer, 1945, pp. 83-92, illus. as Novelli; Trapier, 1952, p. 262, fig. 170, as Douffet; Spinosa, 1978, p. 93, no. 13, illus.

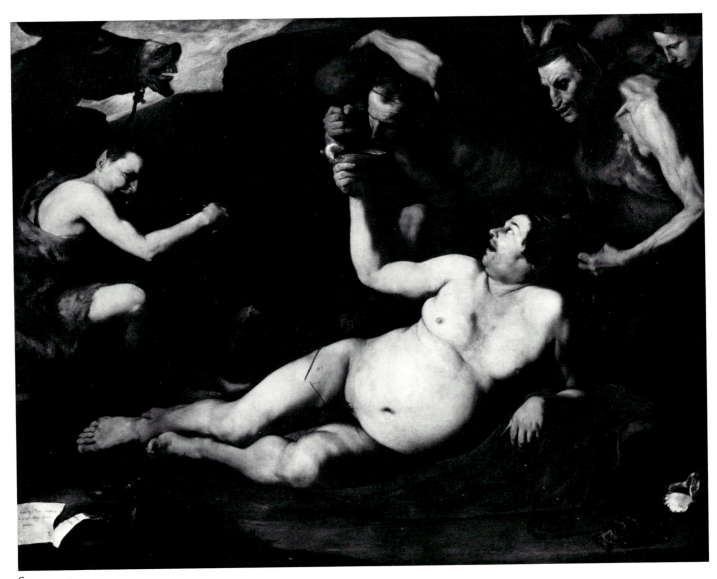

6 *see color plate*

6

The Drunken Silenus
Canvas, 185 x 229 cm (72⅞ x 90⅜ in)
Signed, lower left, on a cartello:[1] *Josephus de Ribera, Hispanus, Valentin / et adccademicus Romanus faciebat / partenope / .6..*
Museo e Gallerie Nazionali di Capodimonte, Naples

During his travels in Italy, the painter and author Joachim von Sandrart saw a painting of *Silenus* in the collection of Gaspar Roomer, the immensely wealthy Flemish merchant, whose villa he visited at Monteoliveto in Naples. Sandrart's account was published in 1675. About fifty years later, Antonio Palomino referred to the *Silenus* formerly in Roomer's collection as one of Ribera's notable works. De Dominici, in 1742, also comments on the painting and on an etching of the subject (fig. 70) which Ribera made two years later, in 1628.

Prior to Roberto Longhi's discovery and attribution to Ribera in 1966 of the *Sense of Taste* (cat. no. 3), the *Drunken Silenus* was considered the earliest reliable example of the painter's youthful, naturalistic style. Today, it seems like an example of a second phase, or of his early maturity. Ribera signed and dated three paintings in 1626, the *Drunken Silenus* and two versions of *Saint Jerome and the Angel of Judgment,* Leningrad (fig. 124) and Naples (cat. no. 7). All three signatures use the Latin form of his name and nationality, and the first two call attention to the artist's membership in the Roman Academy.

The classical subject of this painting was unusual in Ribera's oeuvre at this time. Indeed, the patron may have been responsible for its choice and for specific details of iconography. Gaspar Roomer's taste and erudition suggest such a possibility. His collection, housed at several locations in Naples, included works by Rubens and Jordaens with which this painting might have been compatible.[2]

According to some ancient authorities, Silenus was the son of Pan, Greek pastoral god of fertility. In contrast to the half-beast, half-man anatomy of Pan and other satyrs, Silenus had a completely human body. His unbridled appetites, however, led to his obesity and to his reputation as the drunken progenitor of satyrs. He adopted Dionysus (Bacchus) as his son; hence, he is shown in Ribera's painting with a wreath of grape leaves on his head, sampling the product of the winery or huge vat behind him. In addition to his base, self-indulgent character, Silenus is often credited with dispensing homely philosophies and wisdom.

In Ribera's painting, the goatish old satyr, Pan, supports the head of his son, Silenus. Ribera identifies Pan by several attributes. In the right foreground of the painting, he has placed a conch shell: Pan's death was announced by the sailor, Thamus, by means of a conch shell, and the conch was also the origin of the lyre. Beside the conch is the tortoise, sacred to Pan and symbol of sloth.

Figure 121
after Giulio Romano. *Silenus and Winemakers,* Crocker
Art Museum, Sacramento, California

The shepherd's crook is a symbol of Pan as a shepherd. Especially related to the events of Pan's life are the wreath of coniferous needles on his head and the spotted animal skin wrapped around his body. The former is a reference to Pan's love for the nymph Pitys, who was metamorphosed into a fir tree to escape his lust; the latter refers to his occupation as a shepherd as well as to his animal nature.[3]

The boy below the donkey at the left is omitted in the etching. Perhaps he could be identified as the young Dionysus whom Silenus raised from early childhood. Later the two traveled together, with Silenus mounted on a donkey and supported by young satyrs because he was too obese to walk. In the etching Ribera also has changed the attributes of Pan: the conch shell and the tortoise are replaced by reed pipes, making his identification more obvious. The etching also shows two children lying at Silenus's feet next to a wooden tub, one sleeping and one drinking wine from a shell. These figures come from Mantegna's *Bacchanal.* Trapier suggests that the serpent which tears apart the *cartello* on which Ribera placed his signature in the painting may have been derived from El Greco's *Martyrdom of Saint Maurice;*[4] however, he probably never saw El Greco's painting. Silenus's dual characteristics of wisdom and vulgarity are compared with those of Socrates; therefore, the serpent could represent wisdom. In the etching, the signature, without the serpent, is on the stone block at the lower right.

In 1979, J. Chenault Porter published a detailed analysis of the composition, concentrating on its iconographic content. Chenault drew attention to a resemblance between the lower half of the figure of Silenus and a similar detail in a print by G. B. Cavalieri made after a fountain sculpture in the gardens of the Palazzo Margarita (formerly the Palazzo Boncompagni-Ludovisi) in Rome. She also suggests that the image of a reclining Silenus derives from the famous classical sculpture of Silenus placed along the Via del Babuino in Rome late in the sixteenth century. Further, Chenault postulates that a more revealing source for Ribera's composition is to be found in a drawing (fig. 121) in the E. B. Crocker Art Museum, Sacramento, California, made after Giulio Romano's now lost fresco in the Loggia della Grotta of the Palazzo del Tè in Mantua. In addition to the physical resemblance of the Silenus type used by Ribera, the drawing incorporates a donkey, a wine vat, and a small satyr to support Silenus's head. Trapier suggested that another parallel to Ribera's composition is to be found in an etched design by Annibale Carracci for the Farnese silver salver.[6] All of these parallels suggest the more likely conclusion, drawn by Spinosa, that Ribera, as other artists of his time, was familiar with Hellenistic relief sculpture, which may have served as a source of inspiration to all of them in approaching such classical themes.

Whatever the sources of Ribera's composition may be, they are of relatively minor interest when we confront a work as staggeringly brilliant as his *Drunken Silenus.* In all its repellent explicitness, it is one of the greatest examples of Baroque naturalism thoroughly imbued with the classical spirit. In the introduction to this catalogue, Ellis Waterhouse relates the painting to the art of Guido Reni—an insight that is on the mark, though no artist of his time could equal Ribera in the cogency of his pictorialization. Although the surface and some of the colors of the painting have changed over the years (the blue drapery on which Silenus reclines has totally oxidized), the robust figures demonstrate Ribera's breathtaking ability to capture the reality of flesh and the characteristics of surface textures.

Upon the death of Gaspar Roomer in 1674, his vast estate was divided among his family, friends, and charities. A share was left to Ferdinand van den Einden, the son of Roomer's partner, who also collected paintings. In turn, van den Einden's estate was inherited by his three daughters, one of whom, Giovanna, married Giuliano Colonna.[7] In 1688, Luca Giordano catalogued the Colonna paintings, which included several works by Ribera.[8] The *Silenus* is not specifically mentioned, although a larger painting of *Bacchus* is catalogued. It is not likely that Ribera's pupil, Giordano, would have failed to identify his master's famous *Drunken Silenus.* Its whereabouts is not known until the end of the eighteenth century.

NOTES

1. Following a recent restoration, three digits of the date came off with old repaint; however, the date of 1626 has been on the painting for many years and it is likely that it was placed there with good reason during a previous restoration. Because Ribera's etchings that correspond with his paintings always were made later, the painting of the *Drunken Silenus* must come before the etching which is dated 1628. This sequence is borne out by the structural changes in the etching, which improve the composition.

2. Ceci, 1920, pp. 160-165.

3. Graves, 1955, pp. 101-102.

4. Trapier, 1952, p. 39

5. Chenault Porter, 1979, pp. 41-54.

6. Trapier, 1952, pp. 37, 43.

7. London (Whitfield and Martineau), 1982, pp. 227-228.

8. Colonna, 1895, pp. 29-30.

PROVENANCE: Perhaps painted for Gaspar Roomer, Naples; Galleria of the Prince of Francavilla (not in the inventory of 1802), Naples, which went to Palermo, 1802; returned to Naples, 1806; Museo Nazionale, Naples; Museo di Capodimonte, No. 298.

EXHIBITIONS: Florence, 1922, no. 817; London (Whitfield and Martineau), 1982, pp. 227-228, no. 120, illus.

BIBLIOGRAPHY: Sandrart, 1675, p. 278; García Hidalgo, 1691; Palomino, 1724, III, 877; De Dominici, 1742-1744, III, 16-17; Colonna, 1895, pp. 29-30; Ceci, 1920, pp. 160-164; Gigliolo, 1922, pp. 201-231; Mayer, 1923, p. 197; De Rinaldis, 1928, p. 261, illus.; Trapier, 1952, pp. 36-39, illus.; Parks, 1954, pp. 4-5; Causa, 1957, pl. 18; Gaya Nuño, 1958, no. 2271; Waterhouse, 1962, p. 175, illus.; Spinosa, 1978, p. 95, no. 28, illus.; Chenault Porter, 1979, pp. 41-45, illus.; Ruotolo, 1982, p. 15.

7 *see cover*

7

Saint Jerome and the Angel of Judgment
Canvas, 262 x 164 cm (103½ x 64⅝ in)
Signed, bottom right: *Josephus de Ribera / Hispanus Valentin / Setaben. . .*
Partenope, F. 1626
Museo e Gallerie Nazionali di Capodimonte, Naples

Saint Jerome is the most frequently painted subject in Ribera's oeuvre.
Paintings of the saint are among the artist's earliest known works (fig. 118),
and during the last months of his life, Ribera treated the subject twice again
with new understanding (figs. 47, 48). Jerome surely held an enormous
fascination for the artist and his clients; indeed, Ribera realized in these works
some of his most moving images.

Jerome (Eusebius Hieronymus Sophronius) was born about 342 A.D. into a
wealthy family in Dalmatia. First educated by his father, he completed his
studies in Rome under the famous pagan grammarian Donatus. To his native
Illyrian tongue he added a mastery of Latin and Greek. After pursuing a life
of ease and luxury in Rome, Jerome was converted to Christianity and was
baptized about the year 366. Desiring to use his considerable education and
skills for his newly acquired faith, he traveled to Gaul where he became a
monk. Then recognizing his need to journey to the lands where Jesus had
lived, Jerome departed for Palestine, arriving in Antioch in 374. Two of his
companions died there of a virulent illness, and in a delirium of his own,
Jerome saw himself called before the Judgment of Christ and asked to identify
himself. When he answered that he was a Christian, the reply came: "Thou
liest, thou art a Ciceronian: for where thy treasure is, there is thy heart also."
Profoundly disturbed by this dream, Jerome withdrew from the life he had
known and spent four years as a hermit in the Syrian desert. In his pursuit of
the abstemious life, he gave up the classics. Yet, try as he did, he was greatly
plagued by his imagination and his fixations on physical desire. To distract
himself from these torments, he took up a new study that was to change his
life: "When my soul was on fire with bad thoughts, as a last resource I became
a scholar to a monk who had been a Jew, to learn of him the Hebrew alphabet;
and, from the judicious rules of Quintilian, the copious flowing eloquence of
Cicero, the grave style of Fronto, and the smoothness of Pliny, I turned to this
language of hissing and broken-winded words. What labor it cost me, what
difficulties I went through, how often I despaired and left off, and how I began
again to learn, both I myself who felt the burden can witness, and they also
who lived with me. And I thank the Lord, that I now gather such sweet fruit
from the bitter sowing of those studies."[1] After years as a hermit, Jerome
returned to Rome where he preached against the laxity of the Church. Three
years later, he returned to a monastery in Bethlehem and remained there until
his death in 420 A.D., at nearly eighty years of age. The fruit of Jerome's
career as a linguistic and Biblical scholar was his monumental standard Latin
text of the Bible, produced during his long residence at Bethlehem. This
Bible, known as the Vulgate, was the text upon which virtually all Christian

exegesis was based for over a thousand years, and the Council of Trent in the sixteenth century reaffirmed Jerome's text as the authorized Latin Bible for the Catholic Church.

Beyond his work as a Biblical scholar, Saint Jerome was a prolific writer. A substantial corpus of his works survives, including many letters, which give a vivid portrayal of his strong, often abrasive character, his fiery temperament, and the strong positions he took on major issues of his day. Living as he did in the waning years of the Roman Empire, a time of great upheaval and diverse theological opinions, it is significant that Jerome spoke out strongly for the authority of the Papacy. In a letter to Pope Saint Damasus, he wrote: "I am joined in communion with Your Holiness, that is, with the chair of Peter; upon that rock I know the Church is built. . . . Order me, if you please, what I should do." In the wave of church reform still sweeping over Italy and Spain in Ribera's time, this noble father of the Church, at once so palpably human and so rigorously austere in his denial of the flesh, became even more of a hero than he had previously been. As a paradigm of the spirit trapped in the flesh, he became the very personification of one of the ironies of human existence that most fascinated the baroque imagination. As an outspoken reformer and one of the early defenders of the legitimacy of the Papacy, he became a welcome player in the Counter Reformation's growing cast of characters and was especially suitable for the anti-Lutheran campaign of the period.

In Ribera's monumental composition of 1626, Saint Jerome is represented as a man of advanced years startled by the angel at the upper right blowing the trumpet of the Last Judgment. The books, inkwell, quill pen, and Hebrew scroll in the right foreground suggest his scholarly pursuits, but the trumpeting call to Judgment was an event from earlier in Jerome's life. The lion in the shadows at the far left alludes to the story of Saint Jerome's removing a thorn from the paw of a lion, which then became his loyal companion. Though the artist combines these events and symbols from several periods of the saint's life, the dramatic coherence of the painting justifies the violations of Jerome's personal chronology.

This *Saint Jerome and the Angel of Judgment,* painted for the church of the Trinità delle Monache in Naples, was placed in a chapel on the Epistle side of the main altar.[2] This church, which was destroyed by an earthquake in 1897, was considered one of the most beautiful examples of the Neapolitan Baroque style ever constructed. Designed by the architect Francesco Grimaldi in the Greek Cross plan, it was begun in 1621 with work progressing rapidly during the next few years. Documents of payment show extraordinarily high sums paid for various work. Ribera's father-in-law, Gian Bernardino Azzolino, painted altarpieces and many frescoes in the church, and the intarsia, the finest in the city, was designed and executed by Cosimo Fanzago with marble sent from Genoa by Marcantonio Doria. Ribera also painted another great altarpiece for this church (see cat. no. 14). When the monastery was suppressed in 1813, the paintings were removed to the newly established Museo Napoleonico.[3]

Figure 122
Caravaggio. *Saint Matthew and the Angel,* 1601-1602,
Contarelli Chapel, San Luigi dei Francesi, Rome
(Alinari)

Ribera never surpassed the grandeur and clarity he achieved in this *Saint Jerome.* Scarcely ten years before, he had painted exactly the same subject for the Duke of Osuna (fig. 118), and by 1626 he had transformed himself from a still-groping tenebrist painter into a mature master not only steeped in the light and drama of Caravaggio, but also tempered by the classicism of the Carracci and Domenichino. Caravaggio's influential style clearly caught the young Ribera's imagination, and the Lombard's *Saint Matthew and the Angel* (fig. 122), painted in 1601 for the Contarelli Chapel in San Luigi dei Francesi, Rome, must have been on his mind when he was designing the composition of this *Saint Jerome.* The scale and proportions of the two paintings and the relationships of the principal figures to the angels are very close. The classical nobility distinguishing Ribera's paintings from the raw naturalism of many works by Caravaggio is also found in a late *Saint Jerome* by Guido Reni (fig. 123), who seems to have benefited from a knowledge of Ribera's compositions.

Figure 123
Guido Reni. *Saint Jerome and the Angel of Judgment*,
1635-1642, Kunsthistorisches Museum, Vienna

Ribera's progress as a highly refined and elegant draftsman is demonstrated by the etchings he produced during the early 1620s, among which are two versions of *Saint Jerome and the Angel of Judgment* (figs. 53, 57). These are splendid works, but the composition in this painting of 1626 has been simplified and the space greatly clarified over what was possible through the mere use of line and shading.

The main lines of force in Ribera's painting run diagonally across the canvas from corner to corner, interacting like a great "X." The strongly lighted forms cast dark shadows, but Ribera shows his mastery of the half-shadow in the subtle definition of form. Certain forms, such as the saint's left forearm, seem to emerge gently from shadow, while the hand, backlighted by a grayish radiance, stands out solidly in space. On the side from which the light emanates, the contours of Saint Jerome's right forearm and back are razor-sharp and give the figure its sense of weighty volume and taut energy. The voluminous red drapery across his knees provides the principal color accent (the blue of the angel's robe has long since oxidized from its original brilliance). The drapery is rather thinly painted in comparison to the white loin cloth, which is defined with richly brushed impasto. The hair and beard have been modeled with individual strokes of a coarse, narrow brush, building to a surface of bristling texture. A few dabs of white accent the eyes, the nose, and the cheeks, giving them the appearance of real flesh. The sculptural hands attest to Ribera's skill both in drawing and in handling the brush. They have been worked with strong, rapid strokes of heavy paint, highlighted here and there with touches of red, black, and white. The nails are carefully outlined in pink and black, with flecks of white to indicate their curvature. The overall impression of the painting is one of palpable physicality and presence — heightened indeed by the play of light on the brilliantly arranged still-life elements of the Hebrew scroll, the books, and the skull.

Figure 124
Ribera. *Saint Jerome and the Angel of Judgment*, 1626,
Hermitage, Leningrad

At this moment in his career, one year after his interview with Jusepe
Martínez, in which he acknowledged his success in Naples and confided
his reasons for not returning to Spain, Ribera had achieved the full promise
of his talents. He was an artist whose debt to Caravaggio was undeniable,
but whose independence and singular greatness were even more striking.
By 1626 Ribera had established himself as one of the great masters of Europe,
the equal if not the better of those contemporaries and predecessors to whose
work his paintings are often compared.

A rather less heroic composition of this subject, also signed and dated 1626, is
today preserved in the Hermitage in Leningrad (fig. 124).

NOTES

1. Butler, III, 686-693.

2. Fiordelisi, 1898, pp. 181-187.

3. Spinosa, 1978, p. 96.

PROVENANCE: Church of the Trinità delle Monache, Naples; Museo Napoleonico,
Naples, 1813; Museo Borbonico, Naples; Museo e Gallerie Nazionali di
Capodimonte, 1959, no. 312.

EXHIBITIONS: Naples (Ortolani), 1938, p. 34; Bordeaux (Martín-Méry), 1955, no.
47; London (Whitfield and Martineau), 1982, p. 228, no. 121, illus.

BIBLIOGRAPHY: Sarnelli, 1697, p. 312; Celano (1692), ed. Chianni, 1859, IV,
662-678; De Dominici, 1744, III, 11; D'Afflitto, 1834, II, p. 92; Sigismondo, ed.
1824, p. 63; Spinazzola, 1898, p. 48; Fiordelisi, 1898, p. 185; Rolfs, 1910, p. 298, fig.
107; Mayer, 1922, pl. 200; Mayer, 1923, p. 40, pl. III; Naples (De Rinaldis), 1929, p.
262, no. 312; Pillement, 1929, p. 75, illus.; Trapier, 1952, pp. 57-59, figs. 33-34; Gaya
Nuño, 1958, no. 2276; Naples (Molajoli), 1960, p. 52, no. 312; Spinosa, 1978, p. 96,
no. 30, illus.

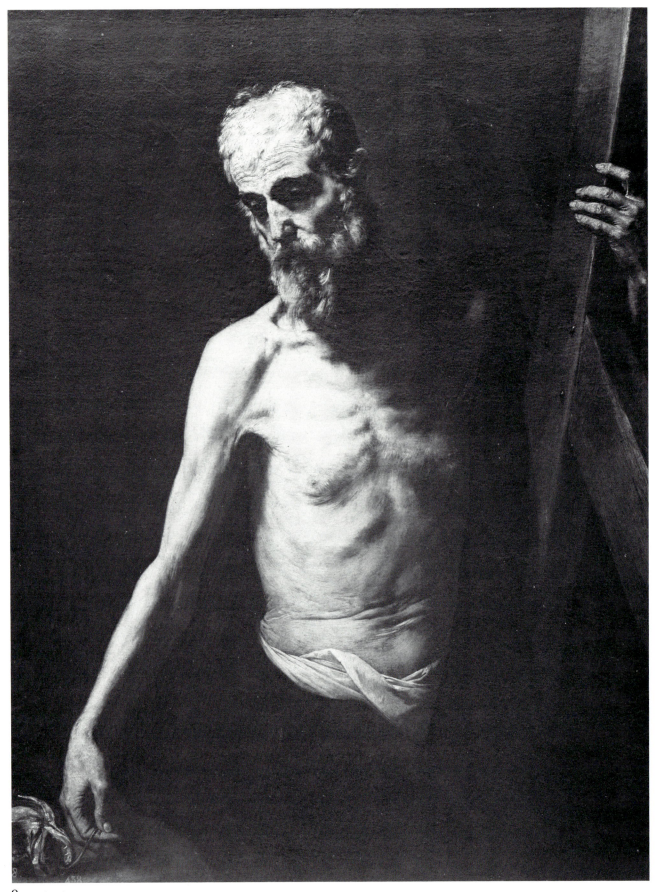

8 *see color plate*

8

Saint Andrew with His Cross
Canvas, 123 x 95 cm (48⅜ x 36½ in)
Painted ca. 1630-1632
Museo del Prado, Madrid

Saint Andrew was born in Galilee and became a fisherman with his brother Simon Peter at Capernaum on the Lake of Tiberias. Jesus, having left Nazareth when John the Baptist was imprisoned, went to live in Capernaum and there began his active ministry. The first Apostles whom he called were these brothers.

As far as we know, Ribera's earliest depiction of Saint Andrew is the half-length composition of about 1620 now in the Picture Gallery of the Church of the Gerolomini in Naples (fig. 125). One of Ribera's early masterpieces is a large, multi-figured composition representing the *Martyrdom of Saint Andrew*, dated 1628 and now in the National Museum in Budapest (fig. 126), a dynamic work that shows the saint about to be crucified on an x-shaped cross.

Saint Andrew, the quiet, reflective defender of the mysteries of the Cross, is known to us from *The Golden Legend.* Founding churches and baptizing as he traveled to fulfill his mission, Andrew settled finally at Patras in Greece. The area's proconsul, Aegeus, angered that his own wife had converted to this new religion, confronted Andrew and challenged his teachings. When Andrew refused to worship false idols, Aegeus had him bound by the wrists and the feet to a cross, at the sight of which the old man is said to have exclaimed: "O good Cross, ennobled and beautified by the limbs of the Lord, long desired, constantly loved, ceaselessly sought, take me away from men and return me to my Master, in order that He, having redeemed me by thee, may receive me from thee!" For two days Andrew remained on the Cross, preaching to the multitudes that gathered. When Aegeus' soldiers sought to remove him from this torture, they were miraculously repelled. Praying for deliverance in death, Andrew was engulfed in a glorious light and his soul soon departed from his body.[1] In the earliest images of Saint Andrew, he is shown with a Latin cross. At Autun in the tenth century, he was first shown with an x-shaped cross. From the fourteenth century onward, the x-shaped, or saltire, cross was always used, and it became known as the cross of Saint Andrew, eventually finding its way even into the British flag (legend holds that the saint visited Scotland, where he is revered as the patron saint).[2]

Set against a deep-brown background, the figure of Saint Andrew embraces the cross of his martyrdom with his left arm and holds in his right hand a fish caught by a great hook. This latter allusion refers to his being a fisherman and to Christ's words to Andrew and Peter: "Follow Me, and I will make you fishers of men." The bare-chested old saint with furrowed brow, shaggy head,

Figure 125
Ribera. *Saint Andrew,* ca. 1620, Picture Gallery, Church of the Gerolomini, Naples

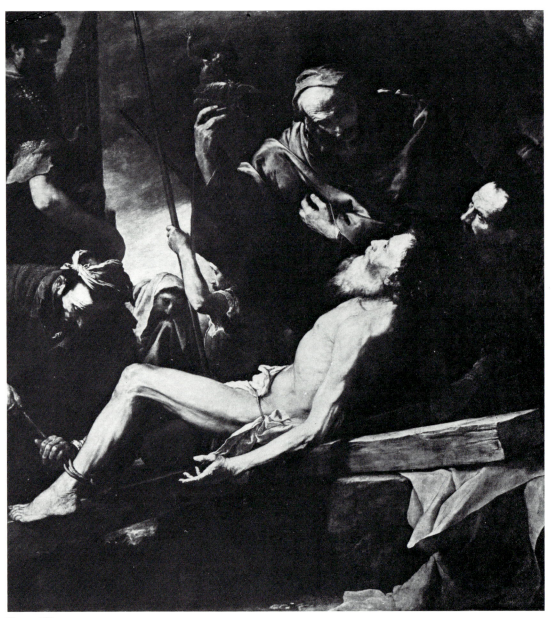

Figure 126
Ribera. *Martyrdom of Saint Andrew*, 1628, Hungarian
National Museum, Budapest

Figure 127
Ribera. *Saint Simon,* ca. 1630, Museo del Prado, Madrid

and bearded face appears melancholy. He emerges from the deep shadows engulfing him and stands before us with the simple grace of a man who has worked with his body. A bright light from the left defines his noble countenance and his strong but aged torso. The gnarled hands with swollen knuckles bear witness to a life of manual labor.

Ribera's representation of this simple, isolated figure is profoundly moving. So powerful is the visual presence of the image that the painting affords the viewer a spiritual encounter. The artist has focused his virtuosity on the amazing lifelikeness of the figure, and in doing so, he achieves one of the most memorable images in Christian iconography.

The *Saint Andrew* is similar in conception and execution to the *Saint Simon* in the Prado (fig. 127), which obviously has been cut down from its original size. Both paintings have a royal provenance and were inventoried at the Escorial in December 1700, when they were described as being the same size (1 ½ x 1 ¼ *varas*).[3] Both paintings likely date from about 1630 to 1632.

NOTES

1. Voragine, 1948, pp. 7-16.

2. Farmer, 1978, p. 17.

3. Archivo de Palacio, Madrid, Registro 242, fols. 128r-128v, 129r.

PROVENANCE: El Escorial, 1700, 1837; Museo del Prado, no. 1078.

EXHIBITIONS: Geneva, 1939.

BIBLIOGRAPHY: Mayer, 1923, p. 75; Tormo, [1912]; Trapier, 1952, p. 96, fig. 60; Sarthou Carreres, 1953, illus. p. 23; Madrid (Museo del Prado), 1972, pp. 547-548; Spinosa, 1978, pp. 98-99, no. 42, illus.

Figure 128
after Ribera. *Fable of Bacchus,* Collection of Princess
Caroline Schönburg-Laserna, New York

Figure 129
Teoxenia, Hellenistic Relief, British Museum, London

The Fable of Bacchus
(Catalogue numbers 9 and 10)

August L. Mayer claimed in 1915 that the two heads catalogued here were among the fragments of a lost *Fábula de Baco* recorded in the 1686 inventory of the Real Alcázar of Madrid, where they were in the ''Room where his Majesty used to dine.'' It can be added here that the large work was also listed as No. 99 in the 1666 inventory of paintings in the same room. During the fire that ravaged the palace in 1734, the large canvas was badly damaged. Fragments of it were taken to the Buen Retiro Palace, and one such fragment was mentioned in 1800 by Ceán Bermúdez. In 1888 when these two heads had already been moved to the Prado, Danvila published the inventory descriptions of four fragments which had been at the Buen Retiro and which were presumed to have been from the same painting. The subject and the original composition remained a mystery. In 1927, Mayer published a photograph of a previously unknown copy (fig. 128), which he attributed to Luca Giordano, that confirmed that three of the heads he had published in 1915 were indeed part of the lost original and, somewhat startlingly, that the entire composition closely followed a Hellenistic marble relief known in several versions (fig. 129).[1] In 1943, Delphine Fitz Darby published a thorough study of the problems associated with the lost painting and its fragments. Among her contributions was the observation that an engraving of the antique composition published by Antoine Lafréry in the *Speculum Romanae Magnificentiae* (fig. 130) in 1549 was an even closer source of Ribera's work. The unusual fact of the artist's having copied so closely an antique source seems to suggest a direct commission.

Most authorities who have treated the subject tend to agree that the Duke of Alcalá was the most likely patron of this work. Both Darby and Trapier date the painting to the period after the *Drunken Silenus* (cat. no. 6) of 1626 and probably to the years 1629-1631, when Alcalá was Viceroy of Naples.[2] Darby presumes that the commission was given by Alcalá on behalf of King Philip IV and suggests that Ribera's painting was part of a program of classical subjects in the royal dining room that included Massimo Stanzione's *Bacchanal* (Prado 259) (fig. 131), a painting of analogous composition and dimensions (237 x 358 cm).[3] Whether Stanzione's painting was originally conceived as a pendant to Ribera's is impossible to establish with present knowledge, but it seems probable that the two were installed in proximity to one another shortly after their creation, perhaps as a consequence of their complementary subjects and compositions.

Darby points to an intriguing iconographic parallel between Ribera's composition and a Bacchic myth related in Rodrigo Caro's *Antigüedades y Principado de la Illustrissima Ciudad de Sevilla . . .* (Seville, 1634). According to the myth, Dionysus (Bacchus) journeyed in his old age to Bética, the ancient name for the area around Cádiz, where he easily converted the monotheistic inhabitants to his rites. His rites established there, Bacchus withdrew, leaving as his regent the god Pan, who renamed the region Pania (Hispania). In

Figure 130
Antoine Lafréry. "Ikarios Relief," from *Speculum Romanae Magnificentiae,* 1549, Avery Library, Columbia University, New York

Figure 131
Massimo Stanzione. *Bacchanal,* ca. 1630, Museo del Prado, Madrid

Figure 132
Ribera. *Head of Pan,* Collection of Princess Caroline Schönburg-Laserna, New York

building his case for these ancient ties between Spanish history and the pagan gods, Caro cited the authority of several ancient authors and said that he had also studied relics of antiquity in the possession of the Duke of Alcalá. As noted, one of the versions of the marble relief upon which Ribera's composition is based was in Alcalá's ancestral home. In Ribera's painting, the robed figure being divested of his sandals is Dionysus; the obese, near-naked figure behind him, with grape leaves in his hair and holding pipes, is Pan. The *Bacchanal* by Stanzione appears to depict the revelry of the Béticans in their newly acquired and spirited rites.[4]

Of the four fragments which Mayer in 1915 associated with Ribera's lost work, one fragment, a young, wreathed diety (Spinosa no. 90.3), appears to have no relation after all with either this painting or Ribera's hand, an opinion implicit in its omission from the discussion of the fragments in the Prado catalogue (1122). A fragment of the head of Pan (fig. 132), formerly in the collection of Henry J. Miller of Pittsburgh, and now in the collection of Princess Caroline Schönburg-Laserna of New York, is probably that part of the lost original described in the Buen Retiro inventory as "figura de Dios Baco."[5] A fourth fragment, representing the group of human heads ("tres cabezas sobre una mesa"), was associated with the lost work in the Buen Retiro inventory but is unknown today.[6] To judge from the copy of Ribera's painting, the group of heads at the left was painted in a naturalistic way that lent a gruesome note to the composition, when, in fact, in the antique reliefs, the heads were actually theatrical masks.

NOTES
1. 1) In the library of the Palazzo Farnese, Rome, during Ribera's lifetime and then in the late eighteenth century in the National Archaeological Museum, Naples; 2) in the Villa Montalto, Rome, and now in the British Museum; 3) in the Villa Albani, Rome, and now in the Louvre; 4) in the antique sculpture collection of the Duke of Alcalá, Casa de Pilatos, Seville, which originated with his great-grandfather Don Perafán de Ribera, who was Ambassador to Rome (Pope Pius V gave him the collection) and Viceroy of Naples, 1566-1572.

2. Spinosa suggests a possible alternate date of 1634-1636, which is difficult to reconcile with the style of the known fragments, but we cannot completely rule out this later date, because dating of a lost work on the basis of such fragmentary clues is risky.

3. Pérez Sánchez (1970, p. 538) suggests that the Stanzione was part of a cycle of paintings of Roman subjects executed by various artists about 1634 for the new Buen Retiro Palace, even though the picture seems never to have been hung with them: the inventories of both 1666 and 1686 place the picture in the same room of the Alcázar as Ribera's painting.

4. Identification of the subject of these reliefs as *Dionysus and Icarius* was proposed by E. Q. Visconti (*Il Museo Pio-Clementino*, IV, Milan, 1870, pp. 172 ff.) and by T. H. Dyer (*On Imitative Art*, London, 1882, pp. 172 ff.). (see Darby, 1943, p. 145, fn. 13.) The term "teoxenia," a visitation of a god to a mortal, is the general category for such a subject. In this Attic legend, Dionysus brought his gift of wine to Icarius, who shares it with the country people. Fearing that they had been poisoned, the people killed Dionysus. Icarius' daughter Erigone searched for Dionysus, and when she found his body, she hanged herself in despair. Although the woman leaning on her hand in the relief composition does not figure in Caro's story, his version of the wanderings of Dionysus has the most significance for a Spanish patron, because of its inclusions about Pan and other Bacchic followers.

5. The dimensions of the painting in the collection of Princess Schönburg-Laserna (ex-Miller collection) are 48 x 37 cm, and not 55 x 40 cm as given in Spinosa, 1978, pp. 106-107, no. 90⁴.

6. Darby, 1943, p. 141, fn 4.

163,

9

10

9

A Sibyl
(a fragment from *The Fable of Bacchus* [*Teoxenia*])
Canvas, 67 x 53 cm (26⅜ x 20⅞ in)
Painted ca. 1629-1631
Museo del Prado, Madrid

PROVENANCE: Alcázar, Madrid (from at least 1666); fragment saved from the fire in the Alcázar of 1734; Buen Retiro Palace, Madrid; Museo del Prado, no. 1122.

BIBLIOGRAPHY: De Dominici, 1742, III, 17; Ceán Bermúdez, 1800, IV, 191; Danvila, 1888, pp. 173-174; Madrazo, 1913, pp. 221-222; Mayer, 1915, pp. 309 ff.; Mayer, 1923, pp. 79-80; Mayer, 1927, pp. 159-160; Pillement, 1929, illus.; Darby, 1943, pp. 140-150, fig. 3; Trapier, 1952, pp. 53-54, fig. 28; Sarthou Carrares, 1953, pp. 14-65, illus. p. 51; Gilbert, 1953, pp. 70-81; Madrid (Museo del Prado), 1972, p. 557; Causa, 1972, p. 284, illus.; Spinosa, 1978, pp. 105-106, no. 90.1, illus.

10

Dionysus
(a fragment from *The Fable of Bacchus* [*Teoxenia*])
Canvas, 55 x 46 cm (21⅝ x 18⅛ in)
Painted ca. 1629-1631
Museo del Prado, Madrid

PROVENANCE Alcázar, Madrid (from at least 1666); fragment saved from the fire in the Alcázar of 1734; Buen Retiro Palace, Madrid; Museo del Prado, no. 1123.

EXHIBITIONS: Geneva, 1939, no. 75.

BIBLIOGRAPHY: De Dominici, 1742, III, 17; Danvila, 1888, pp. 173-174; Mayer, 1915, pp. 309 ff.; Mayer, 1923, pp. 79-80; Mayer, 1927, pp. 159-160; Darby, 1943, pp. 140-150, fig. 4; Trapier, 1952, pp. 53-54, fig. 29; Sarthou Carrares, 1953, pp. 14-65, illus. p. 51; Gilbert, 1953, pp. 70-81; Madrid (Museo del Prado), 1972, p. 557, no. 90.2 illus.

11 *see color plate*

11

Magdalena Ventura with Her Husband and Son
Canvas, 196 x 127 cm (77 ¼ x 50 in)
Signed and dated in the Latin inscription below
Painted in 1631
Museo Fundación Duque de Lerma, Hospital de Tavera, Toledo

Towards the end of the winter of 1631, Ribera put the finishing touches on a painting which because of its subject matter was destined to carry his fame through the ages. He signed it with a factual Latin inscription, unique by its length in all his career, from which we learn of the scientific purposes of painting and something about the sitter, the artist, and the patron:

EN MAGNV[M] NATURAE
MIRACVLVM

MAGDALENA VENTVRA EX / OPPIDO ACVMVLI APVD / SAMNITES VVLGO EL A / BRVZZO REGNI NEAPOLI / TANI ANNORVN 52 ET / QVOD INSOLENS EST CV[M] / ANNVM 37 AGERET COE / PIT PVBESCERE, EOQVE / BARBA DEMISSA AC PRO- / LIXA EXT VT POTIVS / ALICVIVS MAGISTRI BARBATI / ESSE VIDEATVR / QVAM MV / LIERIS QVAE TRES FILIOS / ANTE AMISERIT QVOS EX / VIRO SVO FELICI DE AMICI / QVEM ADESSE VIDES HA / BVERAT. / IOSEPHVS DE RIBERA HIS / PANVS CHRISTI CRVCE / INSIGNITVS SVI TEM- / PORIS ALTER APELLES / IVSSV FERDINANDI II / DVCIS III DE ALCALA / NEAPOLI PROREGIS AD / VIVVM MIRE DEPINXIT / XIIIJ KALEND. MART. / ANNO MDCXXXI.

The inscription is superimposed on a stone plinth at the right. It begins with four words written in large capital letters, easily legible from a distance, which announce: GREAT WONDER OF NATURE. Standing next to the plinth in absolute frontality is the rather stout figure of a middle-aged woman dressed in an elaborate country costume, holding a swaddled infant in her arms. The baby's lips are poised on the verge of nursing from a large, exposed breast, which is modeled with rich chiaroscuro and given a highly physical presence, unlike the breast of any Madonna of Charity in Italian or Spanish seicento painting. Perhaps the instant before one has seen this detail, perhaps the instant after, the viewer notices too that the rugged face of the figure is heavily bearded. An audible gasp may be heard when the viewer realizes that he is confronting, face to face, a bearded lady. Over her right shoulder in the background stands the shadowy figure of a perplexed old man. Having seen this much, most people would want to read more of the inscription. It tells us that the woman's name is Magdalena Ventura and that she is from the town of Accumoli, or in the vernacular, from the Abruzzi, in the Kingdom of Naples. Fifty-two years old at the time of this portrayal, she was thirty-seven when "she began to become hairy and grew a beard so long and thick that it seems more

Figure 133
Ribera. *The Duke of Alcalá,* 1629, from Parrino, *Teatro eroico de' Vicere di Napoli,* 1692

like that of any bearded gentlemen than of a woman who had borne three sons by her husband, Felici de Amici, whom you see here.''

Ribera continues the inscription with a Latinized form of his name, describing himself as a Spaniard and as a member of the Order of the Cross of Christ, a great honor for a painter, which Pope Urban VIII had bestowed upon him at Saint Peter's on January 29, 1626.[1] Ribera continues by calling himself ''another Apelles in his time,'' a comparison with the fabled painter to Alexander the Great and since the Renaissance a common epithet for painters; rarely, however, do painters thus refer to themselves in their signatures. Finally, Ribera states that he painted the picture from life on orders from Ferdinand II, Third Duke of Alcalá, Viceroy of Naples, on February 16, 1631.

Fernando Afán de Ribera y Enríquez (1570-1637), Third Duke of Alcalá (fig. 133), was from a renowned and cultured noble family of Seville. Possessor of several other aristocratic titles, he was a Knight of the Order of Alcántara and, throughout his life, served the Crown in numerous diplomatic posts. From August 1629 to May of 1631, he was Viceroy of Naples. An intellectual of considerable accomplishment and an avid collector of books and works of art, Alcalá became one of Ribera's most notable patrons, and probably took this portrait with him to Spain in 1631. The painting passed by descent from his family first to the Dukes of Medinaceli and later to the Dukes of Lerma. Except for a brief period during the Napoleonic wars, when it was taken to Paris for the Musée Napoléon, the portrait has never changed hands except through descent, and consequently it is extremely well-preserved.

Alcalá probably was already familiar with the portrait of another bearded lady named Brígida del Río (La Barbuda de Peñaranda), who had come to the court of Madrid in 1590. In 1603, her portrait by Juan Sánchez Cotán (fig. 134) was recorded as having been delivered to Juan Gómez de Mora, the Aparejador de Palacio, and it became part of the royal collection.[2] Timid in its naturalism by comparison to Ribera's work, the painting nonetheless reveals a hardly surprising interest on the part of the educated elite in such anatomical anomalies. Interest in dwarfs and pictures of them was strong in Spain, as it had been in other European courts since the Renaissance.

Ribera's own interest in bizarre subjects is amply revealed in his two etchings of *Grotesque Heads* (figs. 62, 65) and related drawings (figs. 64, 66), which are not unlike those of Leonardo da Vinci. This had its parallel in an interest in unusual events: the large canvas entitled *The Battle of the Women* (fig. 135) (Prado 1124), signed and dated 1636, is thought to document the story of two women who, in 1552, fought a duel over a contested lover. The artist, however, has succeeded in giving the scene of combat the timelessness of an antique bas relief. Ribera's painting of a *Clubfooted Boy* (cat. no. 33) is not just a vivid depiction of a freak of nature, but contains a moral lesson as well. The *Dwarf with a Dog* (fig. 182), painted in 1643, is perhaps closer in its essence to the *Magdalena Ventura.*

Figure 134
Juan Sánchez Cotán. *The Bearded Woman of Peñaranda*, 1590s, Museo del Prado, Madrid

Figure 135
Ribera. *Battle of the Women*, 1636, Museo del Prado, Madrid

Ribera's *Magdalena Ventura* is one of the most stunning examples of the artist's unrelenting naturalism. He knew it would shock; he strove to make it the more shocking in its lifelikeness by depicting the afflicted mother in the act of nursing her child. Such explicit truthfulness to nature supports the bravura of Ribera's inscription. By equating himself with Apelles, the most famous ancient exponent of a naturalistic style, Ribera means to set himself apart from all his contemporaries; he has even surpassed Caravaggio as the ultimate practitioner of naturalism. He intends also to flatter the Duke with his implicit parallel with Alexander of Macedon. The inscription, of course, is not required for the viewer to feel the brimming sense of modernity in Ribera's work. The self-confidence expressed in his signature is palpably evoked by the self-assurance of the picture.

On top of the plinth at the right is a small still-life with a spindle, a symbol of female domesticity, and a snail. As Rof Carvallo (1975) has pointed out, the latter, a symbol of the hermaphrodite, underscores the bizarre and darkly erotic side of the subject.

NOTES

1. Chenault, 1976, pp. 304-307.
   The document of Ribera's investiture is found in the Vatican's archivio Segreto, Segreteria dei *Brevi* (Urbanus VIII), v, 709, fol. 488, 488r, 490.

2. Cavestany, p. 138; Pérez Sánchez, 1982, p. 191, no. 169.

PROVENANCE: Duke of Alcalá, Naples and Seville; Dukes of Medinaceli; sent to Paris during the Napoleonic invasion; restored to Spain on the order of Louis XVIII; Academia de Bellas Artes de San Fernando, Madrid, in the catalogues of 1818, 1829; later restored to the Medinaceli family; Dukes of Lerma; Duke of Lerma Foundation, Toledo.

EXHIBITIONS: Bordeaux (Martín-Méry), 1955, no. 49; Brussels, 1970, no. 21; London (Pérez Sánchez), 1976, no. 28, illus. p. 51; Paris (Pérez Sánchez), 1976, no. 47, illus.; Munich-Vienna, 1982, no. 70, illus.

BIBLIOGRAPHY: Ponz, 1776, IV, 163; Madrazo, 1884, pp. 87, 301, 302; Tormo, 1916, pp. 11-16, illus.; Mayer, 1923, p. 197; Pillement, 1929, pp. 38-39; Beroqui, 1933, p. 155; Mayer, 1947, p. 293; Pantorba, 1949, p. 33; Toledo (Cardona), 1951, p. 18; Trapier, 1952, pp. 70-71, fig. 45; Gaya Nuño, 1955, p. 707; Ainaud, 1955-1956, p. 116; Hodge, 1969, pp. 1693-1696, illus.; Rof Carvallo, 1975; Spinosa, 1978, p. 100, no. 99, illus.

VERSIONS: Collection Ruiz de Alda, Madrid (copy). Ceán Bermúdez (1800, IV, 193) mentions a small-scale copy as having hung in La Granja Palace; the copy is unknown today.

12

Figure 136
Ribera. *Saint Joseph and the Young Jesus,* ca. 1632,
Museo del Prado, Madrid

12
Blind Beggar and His Boy
Canvas, 124.5 x 101.7 cm (49 x 40¹/₁₆ in)
Signed, lower left: *Jusepe de Ribera / español , F, 163.* [last digit illegible]
Painted ca. 1632
Allen Memorial Art Museum, Oberlin College, Oberlin, Ohio,
R. T. Miller, Jr. Fund

Few literate people looking at this painting in the seventeenth century, especially those in Spain or Spanish Naples, could have failed to recognize in it the subjects of one of the most famous of picaresque novels, *Lazarillo de Tormes,* first published anonymously in 1554. The tale of the harsh and cruel blind man and his wily beggar boy, forced to outwit his master to obtain his share of the food and alms, had become famous throughout Europe, and in fact, the name "Lazarillo" had become synonymous in Spanish-speaking lands with "beggar boy." Thus, in painting this picture of a blind man raising his alms cup while he rests his left hand on the shoulder of a youth, the artist created an image rich in literary associations, but, more importantly, one familiar to him from the streets of Naples. As Spinosa has noted, Ribera does not really illustrate the picaresque tale; he concentrates on the profound humanity and the moral import of the subject. The piece of paper attached to the blind man's cup bears the inscription "Dies Illa / Dies Illa," a repetition of the second phrase of that segment of the Requiem mass announcing the Last Judgment: "Dies Irae, Dies Illa" (Day of Wrath, That Day). The note is a reminder of the importance of charity for us all in the final accounting of "That Day."

It has been noted often that Ribera used the same model in this painting as in the *Sense of Touch* (Prado 1112), dated in 1632 (fig. 117).[1] The last digit of the date on the Oberlin picture is illegible; nevertheless, the painting is sufficiently close in execution to the Prado work to suggest that the two were probably painted around the same time. Another painting depicting *Saint Joseph and the Young Jesus* (Prado 1102), also from about 1632, makes use of a similar composition in which a man and a boy are shown in a three-quarter length format (fig. 136).

NOTE

1. Darby (1962) proposes that the subject is the Philosopher Carneades rather than the traditional but mistaken identification as Giovanni Gonnelli, the blind sculptor of Gambassi.

PROVENANCE: Dr. Carvalho, Château de Villandry; Allen Memorial Art Museum, 1955, 55.9.

EXHIBITIONS: Oberlin, 1957, no. 2; Richmond, 1961; Indianapolis (Carter and Peat), 1963, no. 66; Minneapolis, 1966.

BIBLIOGRAPHY: Mayer, 1923, p. 20; Milicua, 1952, pp. 296-298; Angulo Iñiguez, 1957, pp. 59-62; Buck, 1957, pp. 62-69; Rogers, 1957, pp. 49-58; Stechow, 1957, pp. 12-13; "Bibliografía," 1957, p. 344, pl. 3; "Noticias de arte," 1957, pp. 339-340, illus.; Gaya Nuño, 1958, no. 2329; Gaya Nuño, 1961, pp. 53-61; Wethey, 1963, pp. 206-208; Konečný, 1973, p. 89, n. 8; Spinosa, 1978, p. 102, no. 64, illus.

13 *see frontispiece*

13
Saint Matthew
Canvas, 126 x 95 cm (49⅝ x 37⅜ in)
Signed, on rock, lower right: *Jusepe de Ribera español / ,F, 1632*
Kimbell Art Museum, Fort Worth, Texas

One of Ribera's great gifts was his ability to endow with the conviction of
portraits from life his many images of Christian saints and martyrs and of the
philosophers of antiquity. He adopted the *Apostolado* format developed in Spain
and Flanders at the turn of the seventeenth century, but with his highly
developed naturalism he made this format far more compelling than had
earlier painters.

Ribera's individual figures seem to possess unique personalities which establish
a bond of visual truth with the viewer. In this painting of *Saint Matthew,* the
convincing illusion of surface textures and the gentle and sensitive portrayal
of character typify the artist's depictions of the Apostles.

Saint Matthew is represented as a man just past middle years. His warm,
brown eyes have been averted from us in his quiet contemplation. Ribera
characterizes Matthew as the sensitive writer of the Gospel, a sharp contrast to
the rather illiterate peasant depicted by Caravaggio in his Contarelli Chapel
Saint Matthew and the Angel (fig. 22). The focal point of the composition is the
noble head of the figure. From the visual tour de force of the hands holding the
large book, Ribera builds his composition through the contours and curves of
the robe to the brightly-lit face. The virtuoso passages of hair, flesh, and worn
pages project dramatically from the dark, monochromatic background.

The surface of Saint Matthew's brown robe has no doubt suffered from past
cleanings, and the modeling of the folds has lost much of its plasticity;
nevertheless, the strength of the characterization remains because of the thick
paint used to model the face and hands (frontispiece). These passages
demonstrate vividly Ribera's method of working from the dark underpainting
to the lightest areas in a wet-on-wet technique of paint application. Especially
characteristic is the use of a stiff-bristled brush pulled across the wet paint on
the forehead to produce deep gouges approximating wrinkles.

Two other paintings of Apostles of almost the same dimensions are possible
companions to the *Saint Matthew.* In them, also, the modeling of the figures is
bold and vigorous, capturing a physical as well as a psychological presence of
the subjects. The *Saint Paul* (fig. 137), also signed and dated 1632 and now in
the Hispanic Society of America, is a close structural analogue to the Kimbell
painting, although the shadows in the *Saint Paul* are somewhat more dramatic.
The Prado's *Saint Peter* (1071) (fig. 138) is a well-preserved painting with a
somewhat brighter chromatic range of browns and ochres, and the figure has a
greater sense of volume, in part due to the lighter neutral background.

Figure 137
Ribera. *Saint Paul,* 1632, Hispanic Society of
America, New York

Figure 138
Ribera. *Saint Peter,* ca. 1632, Museo del Prado,
Madrid

The *Saint Matthew* is unusual among Ribera's works as his only surviving representation of one of the Evangelists. A painting of Saint John the Evangelist is recorded in old inventories of the Alcázar, but no mention is made of Saint Luke or Saint Mark. Whether or not any of these paintings belonged to a series is impossible to ascertain with present evidence; no known documentation confirms any *Apostolado* or Evangelist cycle of this size.

PROVENANCE: With M. Sano, Paris; Lord Wimborne, Cranford Manor, Dorset, England, November, 1867; Sale, Lord Wimborne, Christie's, London, March 9, 1923, no. 50; with Sedelmeyer, Paris, 1925; Jean Deschamps, Paris; with Newhouse Galleries, Inc., New York; Kimbell Art Foundation, 1966, AP 66.10.

EXHIBITIONS: Paris, 1925, no. 83

BIBLIOGRAPHY: Cranford Manor, 1888, p. 68, no. 163 (as a *Male Portrait*); Mayer, 1923, p. 197 (as lost); Fort Worth, 1972, pp. 59-61, illus. pp. 59, 61 and 1981, p. 152, illus.; Spinosa p. 103, no. 70, illus.

14 *see color plate*

14

God the Father, from the altarpiece of
The Holy Family Appearing to Saint Bruno and Other Saints
Canvas, 109 x 109 cm (43 ¼ x 43 ¼ in)
Painted ca. 1632-1635
Palazzo Reale, Naples

The history of this painting is not clear. The church from which it originated, the Trinità delle Monache, was destroyed by an earthquake in 1897; therefore, it is necessary to rely on written accounts in order to know something of its original commission and installation. Trapier was the first to assume that this *God the Father* is a fragment of the large *Holy Family Appearing to Saint Bruno and Other Saints* (fig. 139).[1] This assumption was based on a passage from De Dominici, who, writing in 1742, believed the large painting had been begun on commission for the Carthusian Monastery of San Martino but, rejected by the monks, was adapted and sold by Ribera to the nuns of the Trinità:

> Ribera had painted first the picture which was to be placed in the back of the choir corresponding to the High Altar, and in this picture he had represented in a glory of little angels God the Father, and below the Blessed Virgin who holds the young Jesus by the hand and in their company Saint Joseph. They appear, almost as in a vision, to Saint Bruno, who is kneeling, and to Saint Benedict, who adore the God Incarnate. This picture is similarly well painted and well conceived besides being very well designed, although in depicting the face of the Virgin he made use of a naturalness neither very beautiful nor tender; but there arose then so many altercations and disputes between him and the monks, perhaps because of the exorbitant price that he claimed for the picture, or even because of his very bad manners toward the painters selected and favored by the monks, that the monks finally concluded [the dispute] with the admirable choice of placing in that location a picture by Guido Reni, as in fact happened. But before Guido's painting (representing the Birth of the Lord) arrived in Naples, "lo Spagnoletto" sold his painting mentioned above to the nuns of SS. Trinità, adding the figure of Saint Bernardino of Siena with Saint Bonaventura as Cardinal, as one sees in the church already mentioned, in the large chapel on the Gospel side, where to our days it has received praise as a very good work by Ribera.[2]

De Dominici, given to embroidery of detail, is not always a reliable source, but there is usually an element of truth in what he says. It was common practice in such commissions for painter and client to agree on the price of a painting before work began; the cost was usually determined by the overall size of the composition, the nature of the background, the number and size of the figures represented, and the colors to be used. The archives of the Certosa di San Martino are unusually complete; moreover, because of a lawsuit brought by Ribera's heirs against the monastery, his work there (especially from 1638 on) is documented with great care. No mention is made of such a commission or

Figure 139
Ribera. *Holy Family Appearing to Saint Bruno and Other Saints,* 1632-1635, Palazzo Reale, Naples   (Alinari)

of a dispute during the artist's lifetime. It is difficult to believe that Ribera and the monks could have had an unfriendly dispute and then, just a few years later, have agreed upon a commission for some of the most important works in the church — a *Pietà* (fig. 25), the twelve Old Testament *Prophets* (figs. 29, 30), *Moses* (fig. 27), *Elijah* (fig. 28), the *Communion of the Apostles (Institution of the Holy Eucharist)* (fig. 49), a *Saint Jerome* (fig. 50), and a *Saint Sebastian* (cat. no. 38). One is inclined, then, to ask whether there might be some other explanation for this sequence of events than the rather simplistic one given by De Dominici.

Figure 140
Guido Reni. *Adoration of the Shepherds*, 1635-1642,
Church of the Certosa di San Martino, Naples

Figure 141
View towards the Choir, Church of the Certosa di San
Martino, Naples

Figure 142
Simon Vouet. *The Virgin Adored by Saint Bruno,* 1626,
Church of the Certosa di San Martino, Naples
(Alinari)

Guido Reni's *Adoration of the Shepherds* (fig. 140), *in loco* in the Certosa, is part of an elaborate installation with marble intarsia surrounding the painting itself.[3] That the installation was designed with no other painting in mind is beyond argument: Reni's picture and Ribera's differ in height and width (whether or not the *God the Father* was once attached to the latter). It is probable that Reni's painting was part of a larger plan for the iconography of the choir of the Certosa, which evolved during the 1630s and in which Ribera himself later played a major role.

As Causa discusses, the design of the choir area of the church of the Certosa was changed from the first plan of about 1590, to a second stage in the early 1620s, and again to its present configuration before 1638 (fig. 141).[4] Not all of the paintings commissioned for the choir during these years are still there. For example, Belisario Corenzio signed a quit-claim in 1624 stating that he had completed two paintings in oil for the choir of the church.[5] The subjects were *The Taking of Christ in the Garden* and a *Christ on the Cross;* unfortunately, their whereabouts today is unknown. Ribera's *Holy Family Appearing to Saint Bruno and Other Saints* is a fitting subject for a Carthusian church, because Saint Bruno was the founder of the Order. In fact, Simon Vouet painted *The Appearance of the Virgin to Saint Bruno* for the monastery in 1626 (fig. 142). With the architectural expansion of the structure and the evolution of a new iconographic scheme for the choir, however, the subject of Ribera's picture may no longer have been appropriate. Indeed, there is a consistent program established by the paintings that remain there today in which the *Holy Family* could play no part.

Key to the existing iconographic program is Guido's altarpiece of the *Adoration of the Shepherds,* painted during the years 1635-1642. It establishes the Eucharistic focus of the whole, to which all the paintings conform.[6] Facing each other to the right and left of the Reni are a *Last Supper* from the studio of Veronese and Ribera's *Communion of the Apostles,* commissioned from the artist in 1638 but not delivered until 1651. Next to these are Stanzione's *Christ at the Marriage of Cana,* signed in 1639, and Caracciolo's *Christ Washing the Feet of the Apostles,* which had been painted in 1622. Ribera's twelve Old Testament *Prophets* in the nave, his *Moses* and *Elijah,* and Stanzione's *Pietà* (fig. 26) on the entrance wall of the nave continue these symbolic references. The individual frescoes contribute additional themes and stories relating to the Holy Eucharist; others make typological references. Thus it is that Ribera's paintings, working in accord with the one by Guido Reni, play a major role in the Eucharistic program of the Certosa. This speaks of harmony, not of discord, as De Dominici had said. Writing a century later, De Dominici must have heard about "so many altercations and disputes between him [Ribera] and the monks" over the high price of a painting in the choir of the church; perhaps, not knowing that these disputes referred to a lawsuit brought by Ribera's heirs over the *Communion of the Apostles,* he confused the story.

The next part of De Dominici's account that must be examined is his statement that before the painting by Guido Reni arrived in Naples, Ribera sold the *Holy Family* to the nuns of the Trinità, adding the two figures at the left—Saint Bernardino of Siena and Saint Bonaventura. Such an addition, if indeed the figures were not there originally (and it is impossible to know without technical examination) would have expanded the scope of monastic life embraced by the painting considerably beyond the Carthusian Order. The more intriguing question, however, is how the *God the Father* was related to this picture.

It is easy to believe, as Trapier suggested, that the *God the Father* was once attached to the top of the *Holy Family.* The design, brushwork, and color are logical extensions of those in the larger painting. Two seraphic heads, one just to the left of center and one almost lost in the clouds in the left corner, look down, corresponding to those at the top of the large painting, some of which are looking up in the direction of something that is not now there. The attention of these little seraphim alone should alert us that something is missing, but there are also iconographical reasons for finding something missing. At the upper left of the Holy Family is the Dove of the Holy Spirit. Together with the image of the Christ below, we have two-thirds of the Trinity, an implausible construction. Furthermore, Mary, Joseph, and Jesus make up the so-called Earthly Trinity, and, except for the absence of God the Father, we have a Double Trinity, a common subject in the seventeenth century and an appropriate subject of an altarpiece for a convent of nuns dedicated to the worship of the Trinity.

As tempting as it is to believe that the picture was as described above, we must at least consider a possibility raised by an eyewitness description of the *God the*

Figure 143
Ribera. *Coat of Arms of the Marquis of Tarifa,* 1634
Bibliothèque Nationale, Paris

Father when it was still in the Trinità. Writing in 1873 a guidebook of Naples, G. A. Galante, who mentioned that the *Holy Family* altarpiece had long since been removed from the church, described a chapel on the Gospel side of the main altar, and referred to the *God the Father* still *in situ:* "il quadretto superiore de Dio Padre e dello Spagnoletto" ("the little picture, high up, of God the Father, is by "lo Spagnoletto").[7] Obviously, in Galante's time, the painting was installed high up over a large altarpiece that had been substituted for the *Holy Family.* In this regard, *God the Father* matched other small square paintings in the same church also placed above larger altarpieces — among them one over the altar on the Epistle side representing the *Sacrifice of Abraham* by Gian Bernardino Azzolino, Ribera's father-in-law. Therefore, it is possible either that Ribera's large painting with God the Father at the top was cut in order to conform to a pattern of small square paintings over large ones already established at the Trinità, or that the artist painted the *God the Father* in its square format and modified the larger painting especially for the Trinità site in order to convert what had been a *Holy Family Adored by Saints* into a *Double Trinity* suitable for its new home.

Trapier dated the *Holy Family* before or about 1635 because of a similarity between the painting and an etching commissioned by the Duke of Alcalá and published in that year as the frontispiece of a book of collected decrees of the realm of Sicily, over which he then ruled as Viceroy (fig. 143).[8] The rare etching shows three hovering putti holding a coronet above the coat of arms of the Marquis of Tarifa, one of the titles of the Alcalá family.[9] Although there are significant differences between the design of this detail in the etching and the painting, the two works are obviously connected, and the painting no doubt preceded the etching, as Trapier supposes. The vivid sky behind the figure of God the Father and behind the central group in the larger portion of the picture is similar to the sky in the *Holy Trinity* (Prado 1069) (fig. 144). Although usually dated 1635-1636, a version of this composition signed and dated in 1632 hangs in the Chapter Room of El Escorial; this version has been largely ignored in the literature.[10] Despite the dirty state and excessive restoration of the latter, it is a painting of the highest quality, which ought to serve as a basis for the redating of the unsigned version in the Prado. The highlighting of drapery, by delicately fluttering a loaded brush across the basic color of the fabric, accents the gown and robe of the Virgin in the *Holy Family,* much as it does the cloak of God the Father in the Holy Trinity of the Prado and El Escorial. The *Holy Family* may, therefore, date as early as 1632 or as late as 1635.

The fate of the *Holy Family Appearing to Saint Bruno and Other Saints* from the Trinità delle Monache is touched upon by Fiordelisi (1898), who writes that among the paintings removed from the convent at the time of the suppression of the monasteries in 1813 were the two large paintings by Ribera.[11] When the agent from the official ministry went to the Trinità delle Monache to make an inventory, he found that these paintings and several others were missing. The director of the Royal Museum confirmed that these works had already been removed to the museum, which later records them in the inventory of

Figure 144
Ribera. *The Holy Trinity,* ca. 1632, Museo del Prado,
Madrid

1820. In 1852, when the Prince of San Giorgio made a new inventory of the
museum, the *Holy Family* altarpiece was missing. Fiordelisi could not locate it
in 1898; perhaps it had by then been removed to the Palazzo Reale, where it
has been for many years.[12] As indicated above, the *God the Father* remained in
the church until the earthquake of 1897.

NOTES

1. Trapier, 1952, pp. 102-107; Spinosa, 1978, p. 105, nos. 88, 89

2. De Dominici, 1742-1744, III, 11-12

3. Garboli and Baccheschi, 1971, p. 114, no. 201. The commission to Guido Reni
   has not been satisfactorily explained. Malvasia cities two versions of the
   composition, one at the Certosa and one formerly in the Liechtenstein Collection

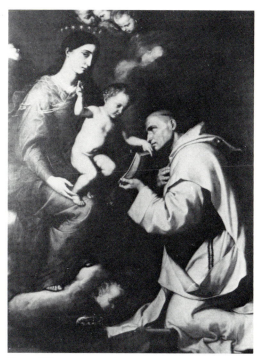

Figure 145
Ribera. *Madonna and Child Adored by Saint Bruno,* 1634,
Schloss Museum, Weimar

and now in London, as being in Guido's late style and "bozzate e imperfette."
Indeed, the paintings exhibit the characteristics of Guido's late works. Close
examination of the Naples composition permits one to see the vigorous, loose
brushwork, and the light, sketch-like touch of the master. These qualities are
especially apparent in the Christ Child and the figure bowing in adoration — most
notably in his drape, arm, and hand. Guido was in Naples only briefly from
December of 1620 to May of 1621 to take charge of the fresco decoration of the
Chapel of San Gennaro in the Cathedral. He left Naples when his life was
threatened and his servant was injured, supposedly by an attack from jealous local
artists. The negotiations for this commission for San Martino must then have been
conducted through intermediaries.

4. Causa, 1973, pp. 54-55.

5. Prohaska, 1978, p. 236, fn. 291. The entire unpublished document has been read
by Professor Michael Stoughton, who generously provided the translation.

6. For the Certosa di San Martino, see Tufari, 1854, and Galante, 1873, pp. 411-419.
To my knowledge, the iconographic program of the Church of the Certosa di San
Martino has never before been proposed.

7. Galante, 1873, pp. 363-365.

8. Trapier, 1952, pp. 101-102, fig. 61; Darby, 1953, pp. 68-69; Brown, 1972, p. 109,
fig. 21.
On June 17, 1635, the Duke of Alcalá wrote to Sancho de Céspedes:
A book of all the decrees of the realm is being printed here, and I should like the
frontispiece to be well etched; a drawing has been made which I send to you in
this letter so that you may have Joseph de Ribera etch it, giving him instructions
from me that it be done as if by his own hand and very quickly. Pay him
whatever may be right and send me the etched plate so that it may be printed
here and inserted in the book.
From Palermo, on July 12, he wrote again:
Joseph de Ribera etches plates excellently with *aqua ardiente* and in my time in
Rome, he had begun to etch. So see to it that he etches what I sent you, because
if he is willing to do it no one knows better how.

9. Darby, 1953, pp. 68-69.

10. Spinosa, 1978, p. 108, no. 98; El Escorial, 1967, illus. in color, p. 193.

11. Fiordelisi, 1898, pp. 185-187.

12. Trapier mentions another version of this subject, formerly in the Pappenhagen
Collection, Castel Hohenschwangau (Bavaria), which she had not seen, as a
possibility for the Trinità delle Monache altarpiece. That painting, signed and
dated 1634, is now in the Weimar Kunstsammlungen (fig. 145). Trapier, 1952, p.
102. Spinosa indicates that it may have been a "first thought" that Ribera
expanded into the large altarpiece and that the date of 1634 is appropriate to both.
Spinosa, 1978, pp. 104-105, no. 87, illus., 388 x 270 cm (152¾ x 106¼ in). It
seems to have no compositional bearing on the *Holy Family Appearing to Saint Bruno
and Other Saints.*

A painting of a similar subject, sold from the Oscar Falkman Collection in
Stockholm, represents the *Holy Family Adored by Two Carmelite Monks;* it is on loan to
the Kunsthaus, Zurich. Although attributed to Ribera in the sale catalogue, it
surely is by another hand. Christie's, London, Sale December 8, 1972, lot 48,
illus., 224 x 192 cm (88½ x 75½ in); Spinosa, 1978, p. 143, no. 463, illus.

PROVENANCE: Church of the Trinità delle Monache, Naples: Pinacoteca del Museo
Nazionale, Naples; Museo Civico Gaetano Filangieri, Naples; Palazzo Reale, Naples.

BIBLIOGRAPHY: De Dominici, 1742-1744, III, 11-12; Galante, 1873, pp. 363-365;
Fiordelisi, 1898, pp. 181-187; Trapier, 1952, p. 107; Gaya Nuño, 1958, no. 2300;
Naples (Acton), 1961, p. 31; Spinosa, 1978, pp. 105-106, no. 89, illus.

15

Figure 146
Rembrandt. *Belshazzar Sees the Writing on the Wall,* ca. 1636, National Gallery, London

15
Vision of Belshazzar
Canvas, 52 x 64 cm (20½ x 25¼ in)
Signed, lower right: *Jusepe de Ribera español / ,F, 1635*
Archbishop's Palace, Milan

This unusual painting derives from the story of Belshazzar's Feast as told in the Book of Daniel, Chapter V.

Belshazzar, the son of Nebuchadnezzar and King of the Chaldeans held a great feast in his palace, using as wine goblets the sacred golden vessels from the Temple in Jerusalem, which had been taken by his father. Suddenly, the fingers of a man's hand appeared and wrote cryptically on the wall: MENE, MENE, TEKEL, UPHARSIN. Puzzled and terrified, the king promised rich gifts and a third of his kingdom to any of the astrologers and wise men of Babylon who could interpret the meaning of the words. None could. Then the queen remembered a wise man named Daniel, who had prophesied during the reign of Nebuchadnezzar. Summoned, Daniel reminded the king that when Nebuchadnezzar had turned away from God, he was cast down to live among the animals. And now Belshazzar too had ignored God and had profaned the vessels of the Temple, whereupon God had moved his hand to write these words, which mean:

MENE: "God hath numbered thy kingdom, and finished it"
TEKEL: "Thou art weighed in the balances and art found wanting"
UPHARSIN: "Thy kingdom is divided, and given to the Medes and Persians"
That night, Belshazzar was slain; Darius, King of the Medes, took the kingdom.

In Ribera's time, perhaps the greatest treatment of this familiar theme, was Pedro Calderón de la Barca's magisterial *auto sacramental* entitled *La Cena del Rey Baltasar,* which was given a splendid first performance at the new Buen Retiro Palace in Madrid in 1634, the year before Ribera's painting was dated. In Calderón's play, the Old Testament subject received a eucharistic interpretation, with Belshazzar's profanation of the Temple vessels seen as the ultimate sacrilegious communion.

Unlike Rembrandt's masterful treatment of the subject in a multi-figure composition now in the London National Gallery (fig. 146), Ribera avoids a narrative approach to the events of Belshazzar's banquet. He created an hallucinatory image of a hand materializing out of a cloudy mist. The brilliant light and dark shadows suggest a palpable form casting a sharp shadow on the wall and creating the illusion of an actual hand suspended in space.

PROVENANCE: Cardinal Cesare Monti, Archbishop of Milan (d. 1650); Archbishop's Palace, Milan.

BIBLIOGRAPHY: De Dominici, 1742, III, 16; Nicodemi, 1914, pp. 279-287; Spinosa, 1978, pp. 107-108, no. 97, illus.

16 *see color plate*

16
Democritus
Canvas, 154.8 x 119.4 cm (61 x 47 in)
Painted ca. 1635-1637
From the Collection of the Earl of Pembroke at Wilton House,
Salisbury, Wiltshire

This painting, *Democritus,* is unique in Ribera's oeuvre in that it represents an ancient philosopher in a seated, full-length pose. Overlooked in the published literature of the artist, it is a magnificent work which the present occasion allows us to evaluate in relation to similar paintings from the 1630s.

Democritus is dressed in ragged clothing, indicating the poverty that resulted from his having spent an inherited fortune on travels throughout the ancient world. During his travels, he acquired a knowledge said by some to surpass that of any Greek before Aristotle. Cheerful in nature, he became known to posterity for laughing at the follies of men, hence his epithet "the Laughing Philosopher." The atomistic theory of matter which he developed also extended to the soul of man. According to his ethical system, man could obtain happiness by doing good for its own sake, rather than through fear of punishment or hope of reward. This ethic perhaps endeared him to Counter Reformation Catholics, who took a similar position in opposition to Lutheran reformists.

One of Ribera's earliest depictions of an ancient philosopher shows a grinning man wearing tattered clothes and holding a compass. This painting, dated 1630 (Prado 1121) (fig. 147), has since the eighteenth century been identified traditionally as of Archimedes; the figure was re-identified by Darby (1962) as Democritus (see cat. nos. 17-19). If her identification is correct, then the artist's conception of the physiognomic characteristics of this subject evolved considerably by the time the Wilton *Democritus* was painted. The three-quarter-length, standing figure in the Prado is an older, coarser type. His face is more weathered and his brow loftier in contrast to this handsome, younger man. Both philosophers peer sardonically toward the viewer; the Wilton *Democritus'* slight smile seems to comment on the thick folio he is perusing, while the Prado figure grins over the instruments of his philosophic pursuits. Such a change in depiction is not particularly troubling, especially since technical aspects of both paintings indicate that a span of a few years separated their execution.

Democritus is often paired with Heraclitus, known as "the Weeping Philosopher," who is seen in an example attributed to Ribera in the Kress Collection, Tucson. Another pair in half-length format, generally considered as by an imitator of Ribera, is in Genoa.[1] No work which could perhaps have been the pendant to the Wilton painting is known.

Ribera composes this figure with a rhythmic outline accenting the graceful

Figure 147
Ribera. *Archimedes (? Democritus),* 1630, Museo del
Prado, Madrid

geometry of the internal structures and emphasizing the sculptural weight of
the forms. The virtuosity of his brushwork and the muted color range of basic
earth tones, together with the gentle chiaroscuro in the modeling of the face,
hands, and legs of Democritus, are similar to those same qualities found in the
ex-Liechtenstein *Philosophers* (cat. nos. 17, 18, 19). Both the atmospheric
warmth suffusing the compositions and the descriptive detail of the tattered
garments further enhance the naturalistic strength of these paintings. Such
features were also employed for the *Philosopher* at Kingston-upon-Hull, which
Spinosa dates 1630-1632 but which could also be from somewhat later.

The monumental scale of this full-length figure calls to mind the *Saint Roch,*
dated 1631 (Prado 1109) (fig. 148), and the *Saint James Major,* dated 1631,
sometimes read as 1651 (Prado, 1083) (fig. 149). With its stylistic differences
from these works, the Wilton *Democritus* seems to date later in this decade.

NOTE:

1. Torriti, 1967, reproduces both paintings (figs. 45, 46), and although they are signed
   and dated 1635, he considers them to be replicas. They are excluded from Ribera's
   authentic works by Spinosa (1978, nos. 399, 400). This writer has not seen them.

PROVENANCE: Collection of the ''Cardinal de' Medici''; purchased either by Philip,
the 4th Earl, or Thomas, the 8th Earl of Pembroke; Earls of Pembroke, no. 238.

BIBLIOGRAPHY: Wilton House (Gambarini), 1731; Wilton House (Pembroke), 1968,
pp. 87-88, illus.

Figure 148
Ribera. *Saint Roch,* 1631, Museo del Prado, Madrid

Figure 149
Ribera. *Saint James Major,* (?) 1631, Museo del Prado, Madrid

The Ancient Philosophers
(Catalogue Numbers 17, 18, 19)

Ribera's imaginary portraits of the famous philosophers of antiquity represented an important contribution to the iconography of his time. The ancient Romans' fascination with the lives and effigies of the Greek philosophers, which is exemplified by such literary works as Diogenes Laertius's *Lives of Eminent Philosophers* and Lucian's satirical *Philosophers for Sale,* enjoyed a revival in humanistic circles of the seventeenth century. Certainly, Raphael's *School of Athens* revealed a similar interest on the part of High Renaissance intellectuals, as did Federigo da Montefeltro's Studiolo.[1]

Ribera seems to have set out to portray the ancient philosophers in a series of easel paintings, much like the format of an *Apostolado,* which he adapted from Spanish usage and perfected in his own manner. These figures are similarly original in artistic conception: Ribera avoids the idealized depiction characteristic of the Renaissance and shows his philosophers as flawed individuals. Yet for all of their individuality, they are endowed with a timeless dignity and monumentality. Though many of these philosophers are now unidentifiable, the literati of Ribera's time who commissioned these works must have taken delight in discoursing on the ways in which the portrayals revealed the subtleties of the philosopher's respective teachings. In a long and speculative article on the subject, Darby (1962) attempts to illuminate the study of these works and to facilitate identification of the respective philosophers. Despite her valiant effort, the subject remains obscure and difficult scholarly territory: as yet, few of Ribera's philosophers can be identified with certainty. The characterizations nonetheless are compelling.

Among Ribera's earliest depictions of ancient philosophers is the so-called *Archimedes* in the Prado, signed and dated 1630 (fig. 147), which Tormo[2] and Darby re-identified as Democritus and which Darby proposes may have been inspired by an antique bust belonging in Ribera's time to Cardinal Pamphilj (later Pope Innocent X) and now in the Capitoline Museum. Many individual works and groups followed (some of them obviously by imitators of Ribera). In the eighteenth century, De Dominici reported that many important contemporary collectors possessed paintings of philosophers by Ribera, among them the Prince of Avellino who had several.

In the catalogue of the Prince of Liechtenstein Collection, published in Vienna in 1767, six *Philosophers* from a series by Ribera are listed and identified as: *Aristotle, Plato, Crates, Anaxagoras, Diogenes,* and *Protagoras.* The 1780 catalogue similarly identified them, but assigned the works different inventory numbers. The 1931 catalogue by Kronfeld, based on the 1873 one by Miethke, assigned still other numbers to the paintings and named only three — *Diogenes, Archimedes,* and *Anaxagoras* — beyond the mere designation "A Philosopher." Because of the several changes of numbers and names, one cannot determine the original identities; only the names of Diogenes and Anaxagoras have

Figure 150
Ribera. *Diogenes,* 1637, ex-Collection Princes of Liechtenstein, Vaduz

remained constant. Both of the latter paintings are inscribed, and *Diogenes* (fig. 150) contains the attribute of a lantern, which the philosopher used in his search for an honest man. Obviously, in the nineteenth century the name of Archimedes was substituted for one of the names on the original list. All of the paintings have since been sold, and the locations of only those catalogued here are known to the author; two of the others have not been photographed. The facts relating to the series as a whole were first compiled in a study by Evan Turner, beyond which little has been added.[3]

The attempt to match the three figures here catalogued with the identifications of the 1767 Liechtenstein catalogue is facilitated by the fact that two of the original six — Diogenes and Anaxagoras — are inscribed, and the third, the Cynic philosopher Crates, famed for being grotesquely ugly and misshapen, cannot be one of these. There remain only Plato, Aristotle, and Protagoras to be matched with the right images.

In each of the three paintings, Ribera's style can be seen to have broadened, or loosened, considerably in comparison to the naturalism of the beginning of the decade. Although the authenticity of the series has been questioned in recent years, both by myself and by Spinosa who related the group to a painter in the circle of Fracanzano, a better understanding of the range of Ribera's style now requires that they be accepted and, indeed, recognized as typical examples of Ribera's work from the late 1630s.[4] The three have not been exhibited together since the series was originally dispersed.

NOTES

1. Darby, 1962, pp. 279-307. Montefeltro's collection of ''portraits'' of classical and contemporary writers and thinkers was with the Barberini family in Rome in 1631.

2. Tormo, [n.d.], pp 15f.

3. Turner, 1958, pp. 5-14.

4. Spinosa has reconsidered these paintings since the publication of his book (1978) and now accepts them as authentic works by Ribera.

17 *see color plate*

17

A Philosopher (? Protagoras)
Canvas, 126 x 100 cm (49⅝ x 39⅜ in)
Signed, lower right: *Jusepe de Ribera español / ,F, 1637*
Wadsworth Atheneum, Hartford,
The Ella Gallup Sumner and Mary Catlin Sumner Collection

Partly by the process of elimination, we can deduce that, of those philosophers
inventoried in the Liechtenstein Collection in 1767, this portrait may represent
Protagoras of Abdera (ca. 485- ca. 411 B.C.), the first of the Sophists.

A robust man whose once-black hair and beard are turning to silver and
white, he clutches a well-worn book in both hands and gazes with
determination. Like Aristotle, he is not portrayed as a ragged philosopher
but wears a voluminous cloak which is in keeping with the fact that Protagoras
became wealthy from payments he accepted for his teachings. He is best known
for his famous dictum on the relativity of all knowledge. "Man is the measure
of all things, of those which are, that they are; of those which are not, that
they are not."

PROVENANCE: Princes of Liechtenstein, Vienna and Vaduz before 1767; with
Newhouse Galleries, Inc., New York, 1957; Wadsworth Atheneum, 1957.44.

EXHIBITIONS: New York; Sarasota (Gilbert), 1961, no. 10 (as *A Greek Philosopher*).

BIBLIOGRAPHY: Vienna (Fanti), 1767, p. 105; Vienna, 1780, pp. 160, 169; Viardot,
1844, p. 257; Mayer, 1923, p. 201; Vienna (Kronfeld), 1927 and 1931, A 376;
Pantorba, 1946, p. 25; Gaya Nuño, 1958, no. 2328; Turner, 1958, pp. 5-14, fig. 1;
Darby, 1962, pp. 279-307, no. 73; Faison, 1968, pp. 466-477; Spinosa, pp. 138-139,
no. 401, illus.

18 *see color plate*

18

A Philosopher (? Aristotle)
Canvas, 124.5 x 99.1 cm (49 x 39 in)
Signed, bottom left: *Jusepe de Ribera español / ,F, 1637*
Indianapolis Museum of Art, Clowes Fund Collection

Since the 1950s when it entered the Clowes collection, this painting has been frequently exhibited, usually with the identification of Archimedes, which it acquired in the nineteenth century as a result of the geometric drawings on the papers in the foreground. Darby has argued strongly for the identification of the figure as Aristotle, shown as a doctor of learning wearing a scholar's skull cap (perhaps also to hide his baldness), a luxurious doctor's robe instead of the usual philosopher's tattered rags, and a carefully groomed goatee instead of a full philosopher's beard. She also points to the torn sleeve of the robe, or the *brachium exsertum,* found on ancient statues of the philospher and symbolizing his union with philosophy.

Whatever the identification, the figure, seen in profile supporting a large tome with his right hand and deeply meditating, conveys a tremendous sense of dignity. This scholar and teacher, looking down toward his books, papers, pens, and square, is obviously concerned with science, mathematics, and the order of things. His lean face and hollow cheeks are modeled with strong shadow. His left hand resting on the papers is a painterly *tour de force,* executed with an easy virtuosity that characterizes the works of the late 1630s.

PROVENANCE: Princes of Liechtenstein, Vienna and Vaduz before 1767; with Newhouse Galleries, Inc., New York, 1957; Dr. G. H. A. Clowes, Indianapolis, 1957.

EXHIBITIONS: Oberlin, 1957, no. 4; Indianapolis, 1959, no. 49; South Bend (Carter), 1962, no. 42; Bloomington (Hope), 1962, no. 31; Indianapolis and Providence (Carter and Peat), 1963, no. 70.

BIBLIOGRAPHY: Vienna (Fanti), 1767, p. 105; Vienna, 1780, pp. 160, 169; Viardot, 1844, p. 257; Mayer, 1923, p. 201; Vienna (Kronfeld), 1927 and 1931, A57; Pantorba, 1946, p. 25; Gaya Nuño, 1958, no. 2324; Turner, 1958, pp. 5-14, fig. 2; Darby, 1962, pp. 298f., fig. 9; Indianapolis (Fraser), 1973, p. 60, illus. p. 61; Spinosa, 1978, p. 139, no. 403, illus.; Indianapolis (Janson), 1980, pp. 71-74, illus.

19 *see color plate*

19

A Philosopher (? Plato)
Canvas, 124.3 x 99.1 cm (49 x 39 in)
Signed, left center: *Jusepe de Ribera español / ,F, 1637*
Mr. and Mrs. R. Stanton Avery

Among the most inspired of Ribera's portrayals of ancient philosophers is this one, which probably represents Plato. According to Darby, none of the ancient portraits of Plato bore sufficient identifying marks to have been recognized as such before the nineteenth century, when an inscribed herm came to light and served as the basis for placing the correct name on the type. Thus, Ribera necessarily relied primarily upon his imagination in creating a convincing likeness. He would, however, have had recourse to written descriptions of the philosopher, such as that of Diogenes Laertius' *Lives* (cited in Darby, 1962, p. 301), in which the sage is described with eyes and mouth that were never known to laugh and as ''frowning with eyebrows lifted high like a snail.'' Prominent among the features of Ribera's philosopher are the knitted brow and raised eyebrows. This painting from the Liechtenstein Collection must be the one identified in 1767 as *Plato*.

PROVENANCE: Princes of Liechtenstein, Vienna and Vaduz before 1767; with Newhouse Galleries, Inc. New York, 1957; private collection, New York, 1957-1973; with Newhouse Galleries, Inc., New York, 1973; Mr. and Mrs. R. Stanton Avery.

EXHIBITIONS: On loan to the Los Angeles County Museum of Art, 1973-1982.

BIBLIOGRAPHY: Vienna (Fanti), 1767, p. 105; Vienna, 1780, pp. 160, 169; Mayer, 1923, p. 197; Vienna (Kronfeld), 1927 and 1931, A372; Gaya Nuño, 1958, no. 2327; Turner, 1958, pp. 5-14, fig. 3; Darby, 1962, pp. 300-301; Los Angeles, 1975, pp. 184-185, no. 69, illus.; Spinosa, pp. 140, no. 412, illus.

20 *see color plate*

Figure 151
Ribera. *The Drunkard,* 1637, Private Collection, Geneva

Figure 152
Ribera. *Boy with a Pot of Tulips,* ca. 1637, National Gallery, Oslo

20
Girl with a Tambourine
Canvas, 59 x 45 cm (23¼ x 17¾ in)
Signed, right center: *Jusepe de Ribera / español ,F, 1637*
Mr. and Mrs. R. E. A. Drey, London

Martin Soria called this *Girl with a Tambourine* one of Ribera's greatest achievements in the art of characterization: "rude, robust, and rugged, [it is] intensely High Baroque, vehemently proclaiming enjoyment of life."[1] It was also Soria who first related the painting to the remarkable *Drunkard* (fig. 151), also signed and dated 1637, now in a Swiss private collection, and speculated that both paintings were part of a series of the Five Senses, with the Girl representing Hearing and the Drunkard, Taste. The *Boy with a Pot of Tulips* (fig. 152), an unsigned work of the same dimensions in the National Gallery of Oslo, is probably related to this same series (as the Sense of Smell). Spinosa reviews the published opinions in favor of and against its autograph status.[2] A fourth composition from this series might be the *Old Woman with a Spindle* (Sense of Touch), although an autograph version has not been identified.[3]

The paint surface of *Girl with a Tambourine* is richly textured, and strong shadows accentuate the coarse features of the model's animated face. Long wisps of her black hair are broadly brushed, framing the sides of her round cheeks, and an edge of a black-and-white braided ribbon is evident above her right ear. A white feather, which she has slipped into her hair from the left side, curls upward, accenting the diagonal thrust that is suggested by her fingers at the bottom left.

NOTES

1. Kubler and Soria, 1959, p. 241, illus.

2. Spinosa, 1978, p. 111, nos. 113, 114, 115.

3. The location of this painting is not known. See Spinosa, p. 136, nos. 371, 372. One such painting passed through Sotheby's London, June 25, 1969, lot 67, illus. See also, *Archivo Esp. Arte,* 44, April 1971, 216, illus.

PROVENANCE: Private Collection, Paris; Spanish Art Gallery, London; Mr. and Mrs. F. A. Drey, London; Mr. and Mrs. R. E. A. Drey, London.

EXHIBITIONS: London, 1938, no. 9; Southampton, 1946, no. 16; London (Maclaren), 1947,no. 24; Edinburgh (Waterhouse), 1951, no. 33; Stockholm (Nordenfalk), 1959-1960, no. 82; Barnard Castle (Ellis), 1962, no. 7; Barnard Castle (Young), 1967, no. 35; London (Kitson), 1973, no. 113; London (Braham), 1981, no. 19

BIBLIOGRAPHY: Gaya Nuño, 1958, no. 2318; Kubler and Soria, 1959, p. 241; Gaya Nuño, 1961, pp. 53-61; Crombie, 1962, p. 396, fig. 2; Harris, 1963, pp. 131-133, illus.; Causa, 1972, p. 279, illus.; Spinosa, 1978, p. 111, no. 114.

21 *see color plate*

21

Saint Christopher with the Christ Child
Canvas, 127 x 100 cm (49⅞ x 39⅜ in)
Signed, center right: *Jusepe de Ribera / español, F, 1637*
Museo del Prado, Madrid

Saint Christopher, one of Ribera's most remarkable paintings, stands out not
only among the many excellent works produced in his most prolific year, but
also as one of the most original and moving depictions of the subject in the
history of art. On a canvas of the size that he customarily used for half- or
three-quarter-length figures, Ribera here paints the head and shoulders of the
giant figure, whose robust masculinity contrasts with the tender Child Jesus
sitting on his shoulder.

According to his legend, Christopher, "the bearer of Christ" (from the Greek
ophorus and *Christos),* was a Canaanite of great stature and strength. Desiring
to use his prowess in service of the most powerful of rulers, Christopher
attached himself to a great king. On learning that the monarch feared Satan,
Christopher left the service of the king and sought this still stronger ruler.
Finding Satan, Christopher traveled with his new lord until he discovered
Satan's fear of Christ, and from a hermit Christopher learned of this greatest
of all rulers. He rejected the contemplative life of the hermit, preferring instead
a life of active service. The hermit told him of a wide stream, with a current so
swift that travelers had difficulty in crossing. Christopher built his hut on one
bank and worked tirelessly carrying across anyone who asked his aid. One
night he heard a child's voice calling him. He got up twice from his bed but
found no one. On the third call, he took a lantern and discovered a small child,
who asked to be carried across the stream that night. Taking his staff and lifting
the child onto his shoulder, Christopher began to ford the stream, but as he
was crossing, the winds rose, the waters became violent and he feared for his
charge, who was growing increasingly heavier. When with great difficulty
Christopher reached the other shore, he asked, "Who art thou, child, that
hath placed me in such extreme peril? Had I borne the whole world upon my
shoulders, the burden had not been heavier!" The child replied,
"Christopher, do not be surprised, for thou has not only borne all the world
upon thee, but thou hast borne Him that created the world. I am Jesus Christ,
the King."[1] Thus Christopher found his master and was converted to
Christianity.

Traditionally Saint Christopher is represented as a full-length figure, large in
relation to the surrounding landscape. Typical of this depiction is the work
executed about 1608 by the Roman painter Orazio Borgianni (1576/7-1616)
(fig. 153), who had been in Spain. Ribera's principal innovation was to focus
closely on the figure which turns in wonder at the weight of Christ. This
close-up view is similar to Ribera's approach in the large paintings of the
giants *Tityus* (fig. 33) and *Ixion* (fig. 34), painted in 1632, but the *Saint
Christopher* further develops this device. It more closely resembles the way

Figure 154
Gianlorenzo Bernini. *David with the Head of Goliath,* mid-1620s, Private Collection

Figure 153
Orazio Borgianni. *Saint Christopher and the Christ Child,* ca. 1608, formerly Art Market, London

Gianlorenzo Bernini aggrandized the prowess of the youthful *David* in a bust-length picture which includes the head of Goliath (fig. 154), a work usually dated in the mid-1620s. Both artists use the relatively small scale of the canvas to dramatize the enormity of something they depict: in Bernini's case, the huge head of Goliath, which does not fit within the picture space; in Ribera's, the hulking body of Christopher.

The paint surface of Ribera's painting is thick and sensuous. The brush has been deftly manipulated to give vivid texture to the flesh, whether in the bulging vein of Christopher's biceps, or the furrows of his questioning brow, or in the pale, dimply baby flesh of the infant Christ sitting on the giant's sinewy shoulder and resting His small hand on the saint's thick black hair. As was consistent with his style, Ribera sweeps the brush along the natural contours of the anatomy, creating definition of muscles and bone, softness and hardness, and allowing the brush patterns to interact with the wet paint of the flesh tones. He worked from a darker underpainting to the lighter tones on the surface while the paint layers were still wet. His method resulted in the brush's leaving natural, dark depths that took on representational function not only by defining shape and volume but also by evoking the tactile qualities of form.

The *Saint Christopher* seems always to have been in Spain; the circumstances of its commission, however, are not known. The terrestrial sphere on Christopher's shoulder is situated so that the Straits of Gibraltar and the Iberian peninsula are clearly visible. This reference to the gateway of Spain's expanding empire across the Atlantic and the implicit analogy with Atlas bearing the weight of the world on his shoulder are likely not to have been fortuitous.

NOTE

1. Quoted from Ferguson, 1971, pp. 199-200.

PROVENANCE: In the Alcázar, Madrid; saved from the fire of 1734; in 1772 in the Sacristy of the New Palace, Madrid; Museo del Prado, no. 1111.

BIBLIOGRAPHY: Trapier, 1952, pp. 136-139, fig. 87; Obuena, 1953, pp. 95-97, illus. p. 96; Francis, 1966, p. 341, fig. 4; Madrid (Museo del Prado), 1972, p. 554; Spinosa, 1978, p. 111, no. 116, illus.

22 *see color plate*

22
Virgin of the Immaculate Conception
Canvas, 255 x 177 cm (100 x 69¼ in)
Signed, lower right: *Jusepe de Ribera español / ,F, 1637*
Columbia Museums of Art and Science
Samuel H. Kress Collection, Columbia, South Carolina

The Virgin of the Immaculate Conception is one of the familiar religious
images of seventeenth-century art. In the hands of any but the greatest artists,
the image frequently becomes monotonous and pedantic. Ribera's
monumental canvases of the subject are among the most beautiful ever
painted.

The Doctrine of the Immaculate Conception, which affirms that Mary was
free from the stain of original sin from the moment she was conceived, was
rigorously debated in Rome during the 1610s and 1620s, with eminent
theologians traveling across Europe to attend Papal conferences on the subject.
The Order of the Immaculate Conception was founded in 1511, following a
vision experienced by Beatriz Silva of Portugal; however, the Church did not
then accept the belief as dogma. The controversial topic had great popularity
and support in Spain, but disputes were particularly acute even there.
Although Pope Gregory XV Ludovisi, in a directive issued in 1622, seemed to
favor the belief, no Papal decision was pronounced until 1854 when the
doctrine was officially decreed. As Hibbard points out, Urban VIII Barberini
showed some favorable disposition toward the proponents of the idea by
subsidizing the new Capuchin church in Rome dedicated to Santa Maria della
Concezione and laying its cornerstone in late 1626.[1]

Francisco Pacheco's *Arte de la Pintura,* in which the iconography of the subject is
treated in great detail, was not published in Seville until 1649 (manuscript
dated 1638); nevertheless, the compositional formulae had undergone major
changes during the Counter Reformation since Vasari's panel of the subject
was painted in 1540 for the Church of SS. Apostoli in Florence.[2] The
primary scriptural source used for the depiction is the vision of the
Apocalyptic Woman (Revelation 12:1): "And there appeared a great wonder in
heaven; a woman clothed with the sun, and the moon under her feet, and upon
her head a crown of twelve stars."

One of Ribera's masterpieces is the *Virgin of the Immaculate Conception* (fig. 155),
painted in 1635 for the high altar of the Convent Church of Las Agustinas
Descalzas in Salamanca. The huge painting, over five meters in height, is
among the most grand and theatrical depictions of the subject ever painted.
The graceful, classical figure of the Virgin, wearing a billowing blue mantle
over her iridescent white tunic, stands upon a crescent moon elevated in the
clouds amid full-sized angels and swarms of putti carrying Marian symbols.
All elements of the composition blend harmoniously in a convincing celestial
space and are subordinated to the radiant figure of the Virgin. God the Father

Figure 155
Ribera. *Virgin of the Immaculate Conception,* 1635,
Convent Church of Las Agustinas Descalzas,
Salamanca

Figure 156
View toward Altar, Convent Church of Las Agustinas
Descalzas, Salamanca

and the Dove of the Holy Spirit appear near the top of the composition, and below the Virgin, a landscape incorporates other references pertinent to her iconography.

As noted in the comprehensive study by Colin Eisler, the history of the Kress painting is also associated with the Salamanca convent.[3] When catalogued in the 1867 sale in Paris of the collection of the Marquis of Salamanca, this painting is described as having come from this convent. In 1916, referring to the entry in the Salamanca Sale catalogue but not knowing the whereabouts of the painting, Tormo wrote that, according to nuns still living in the convent, it had been in the cloistered section of the edifice until it was removed by a ''Duque patrono.''

The original patron of this convent, who was responsible for its decoration, was Ribera's most important patron of the 1630s, Don Manuel de Acevedo (de Fonseca) y Zúñiga, 6th Count of Monterrey.[4] The family of Monterrey, whose hereditary lands were in Salamanca, was closely allied with that of Don Gaspar de Guzmán, who became the Count-Duke of Olivares and Prime Minister to King Philip IV. The two men, who were cousins, married each other's sisters in 1607. Olivares, born in Rome in 1587, was personally familiar with the lucrative nature and the political importance of diplomatic appointments in Rome and Naples because his father had held them, and he promoted his brother-in-law's career with such favors. The closeness of the two men made it possible for Monterrey to be of great assistance to Olivares in obtaining works of art for the decoration of Philip IV's new Buen Retiro Palace.[5]

The Count of Monterrey began his diplomatic career on the Italian peninsula as Spanish Ambassador to Rome in 1628, succeeding the Duke of Alcalá, who then became the Viceroy of Naples. The Count served in that post until 1631, when he was appointed Alcalá's successor in Naples. His official entry into Naples was celebrated with a grand procession on May 19; his tenure as Viceroy lasted until November 2, 1637. During these years, he lived on a lavish scale, as documented by the many surviving accounts of building programs, festivals, and pageants.[6]

In addition to his family estates in Salamanca, the Count of Monterrey had a great house in the Prado de San Jerónimo, to which he added a picture gallery in the garden, and he also had another house nearer the center of the old city in the Plaza de Santo Domingo.[7] His patronage of artists and writers was used as an example to stimulate similar interests on the part of the King and Queen who, for example, were invited by Olivares on June 23, 1631, to attend new plays by Lope de Vega and Quevedo being performed at Monterrey's house in the Prado de San Jerónimo. In 1638 Sir Arthur Hopton, English Ambassador to the court of Philip IV, wrote home to Lord Cottington that when Monterrey returned to Madrid he ''brought with him the best [paintings] of Italy.''

Monterrey had intimate knowledge of the major artistic endeavors of the period in Italy. During his two years as Ambassador in Rome, important decorative cycles in the churches and palaces of the city were in various stages of completion. For example, Domenichino had finished his frescoes in San Andrea della Valle in 1622, and Giovanni Lanfranco was occupied with the dome frescoes in the same church from 1626 to 1628. Both artists, among the most widely sought painters in Rome, soon were awarded commissions for the most significant projects in Naples. Domenichino arrived in Naples in 1630-1631 to take charge of the decoration of the Cappella del Tesoro, and Lanfranco came in 1634 for a variety of private commissions and others for prominent churches. In a 1637 letter to Carlo Ferrante Gianfattori in Parma, Lanfranco wrote that he was one of the few painters favored by Monterrey, who had already commissioned two paintings from him for Philip IV.[8]

During his six-and-a-half years as Viceroy, the Count of Monterrey began his most ambitious artistic project—what was to become the Church and Convent of Las Agustinas Descalzas in Salamanca. Originally, Monterrey was going to build his chapel in Salamanca in the old church of the Ursuline nuns in which the patriarch of his family, Don Alonso de Fonseca, was buried in a tomb designed by Diego de Siloe and considered one of the most beautiful Renaissance works in Spain. As early as the autumn of 1633, plans for a great retable at Santa Ursula were complete.[9] The designs were under the direction of the Neapolitan architect Bartolomeo Picchiatti; a work schedule was stipulated, with completion of the project due by May 1634. Probably before the end of that year, Monterrey changed his mind about placing the altar there and decided to build the new Church and Convent of Las Agustinas;[10] his daughter was appointed Mother Superior with the name of Doña Inéz Francisca de la Visitación. Although construction was begun on the new building by 1636, it was not completed until 1687 (fig. 156). Brown and Elliott review a letter sent by Monterrey to Castel Rodrigo on February 26, 1636, in which the Count relates his founding of the convent and seeks advice on the transport of the statues, works of art, and other structures to Salamanca. He remarks on the shipment of fountains from Naples to Lisbon by the Duke of Alba and wonders if he could follow that route for the first part of his journey.[11]

The altarpiece as it exists today follows the intial plan of 1633 (fig. 157). The sculptures, executed by Giuliano Finelli, are the subjects ordered in that document: a *Crucifixion* at the crown of the retable and the *Virgin, Saint Mary Magdalen, Saint John the Evangelist,* and *Saint James Major* along the top of the marble altar frame. Cosimo Fanzago executed the marble columns and intarsia. Ribera's two paintings in the altarpiece, although not mentioned in the contract with Fanzago of 1633, were surely also commissioned that early, since one of them, the *Pietà* (fig. 158), is signed and dated 1634. The great *Virgin of the Immaculate Conception* at the center of the ensemble was completed in the following year. Life-size statues of the Count (fig. 159) and Countess (fig. 160) kneeling in prayer were also sculpted by Finelli.

Figure 157
High Altar, Convent Church of Las Agustinas
Descalzas, Salamanca

Figure 158
Ribera. *Pietà,* 1634, High Altar, Convent Church of
Las Agustinas Descalzas, Salamanca

A contract of April 1, 1636, mentions, in addition to more marble and other work by Fanzago, a painting of *San Gennaro* by Ribera, which is undoubtedly the work still in the convent and entitled today the *Apotheosis of Saint Januarius* (fig. 161).[12] The landscape observed from nature is rare in Ribera's oeuvre. The atmosphere has been infused with a pervasive golden tone, a quality which it shares with the Kress *Virgin of the Immaculate Conception.* The two paintings were probably painted about the same time.

The figure of the Virgin in the Kress *Immaculate Conception* is extremely close to that in the Salamanca canvas. The sway of the body, the positioning of the feet on the crescent moon, the tilt of the head, and the arrangement of the billowing drapery are all similar. Clearly visible pentimenti in the Kress picture show that originally the artist had painted the Virgin's arms crossed over her breast, just as in the Salamanca version. For whatever reason, he decided to change the hands to a gesture of prayer. Apart from these similarities of the two figures, Ribera created an entirely new composition in the Kress painting. He employed few of the Marian symbols that he used in the large picture, achieving a sense of celestial space and atmosphere wholly in keeping with the more intimate scale of the composition. Mayer (1934) pointed out the excellent qualities of design and execution of the Kress painting (then in a private collection in Paris). It is the finest of the smaller versions of the subject attributed to Ribera, although its state of preservation has no doubt dulled somewhat its original qualities.[13]

Figure 159
Giovanni Finelli. *The Count of Monterrey*, 1633-1636,
Convent Church of Las Agustinas Descalzas,
Salamanca

Figure 160
Giovanni Finelli. *The Countess of Monterrey*, 1633-1636,
Convent Church of Las Agustinas Descalzas,
Salamanca

Among Italian artists of the early Baroque years, Guido Reni's works of this
theme were particularly influential and gained for him a reputation with his
biographers for being especially devoted to the Virgin. Guido's radiant *Virgin of
the Immaculate Conception* (fig. 162), now in the Metropolitan Museum of Art,
was painted for the Infanta María, sister of King Philip IV. It was
commissioned in 1627 by the Duke of Alcalá, the Spanish Ambassador in
Rome during Reni's brief return from Bologna. The beautiful and elegant
young Virgin in this composition stands on a crescent moon over three
seraphic heads and is accompanied by a lovely angel on either side. Piously
holding her hands together in prayer, she gazes heavenward in an attitude of
devotion. A few years earlier, about 1623, Guido painted an *Immaculate
Conception* for the church of San Biagio in Forlì. Although it somewhat
resembles the painting from 1627, this Virgin crosses her arms upon her
chest; one little angel follows her example while its counterpart on the opposite
side holds his hands in prayer. Such a depiction was used by Denis Calvaert,
Reni's first master, in his *Assumption of the Virgin* painted about 1571. The
images of the Virgin of the Assumption and of the Immaculate Conception
were frequently merged in Guido's compositions. His *Assumption of the Virgin*
from 1616-1617, now in the church of Sant' Ambrogio in Genoa,
demonstrates such a confluence of themes.

Ribera certainly knew Reni's approach to the subject of the Immaculate
Conception, and the significance of Ribera's own such works can be judged in
comparison to those of his more famous colleague. In adapting his own image

Figure 161
Ribera. *Apotheosis of Saint Januarius,* ca. 1635,
Convent Church of Las Agustinas Descalzas,
Salamanca

Figure 162
Guido Reni. *Virgin of the Immaculate Conception,* 1627,
Metropolitan Museum of Art, New York

Figure 163
Ribera. *Virgin of the Immaculate Conception,* 1646,
[destroyed] Santa Isabel, Madrid

of the *Virgin Immaculate* to a smaller scale in 1637, Ribera arrived at a
composition that more closely resembles the intimacy of Reni's paintings.

Ribera painted another large *Virgin of the Immaculate Conception* (fig. 163),
signed and dated 1646, which was in Madrid in the Convent Church of Santa
Isabel until its destruction in the Spanish Civil War.[14] Prota-Giurleo (1953)
pointed out that this *Immaculate Conception* was the painting placed over the high
altar of the Royal Chapel of the Palazzo Vecchio in Naples and later was
transferred to the Royal Chapel of the Palazzo Nuovo in 1668 by the Viceroy
Don Pedro Antonio de Aragón, who took it back to Spain when he departed
in 1672. Celano, who considered this the most beautiful of all Ribera's
compositions, says that the painting was taken to Spain in the seventeenth
century. After 1672, it was replaced in the Palace of the Viceroys by an earlier
marble altarpiece designed by Cosimo Fanzago in 1639.[15]

NOTES

1. Hibbard, 1969, pp. 19-32.

2. Hibbard, 1969, p. 25, fig. 8.

3. Eisler, 1977, p. 207.

4. In most of the literature, Don Manuel is mistakenly referred to as 7th Count of Monterrey. He inherited the title from his father, Gaspar, the 5th Count of Monterrey; his heir, Inéz Francisca de Zúñiga, became the 7th Countess of Monterrey.

5. Brown and Elliott, 1980, pp. 13-14. Bernardo Monanni, secretary in Madrid of the Embassy of the Grand Duke of Tuscany, remarked in a dispatch dated November 26, 1633, that twelve cartloads of pictures had arrived from Monterrey for the Buen Retiro Palace. (Brown and Elliott, 1980, pp. 115, 123, and fn. 60.)

6. Coniglio, 1967, pp. 232-239.

7. Brown and Elliott, 1980, p. 116.

8. Trapier, 1952, p. 73.

9. Prota-Giurleo, 1957, p. 147. Documents concerning the history of the project and its decoration were discovered by U. Prota-Giurleo and published in 1957 in *Il Fuidoro,* a little-known Neapolitan journal. The November 28, 1633 document reads:

> En la Ciudad de Napoles en veynte y octo dias del mes de Noviembre de Mill y Seyscientos y treynta y tres años, ante mi Andres Fasano de Nap. eser°. p°. Juez de autos publicos y Testigos, pareciò presente el Cavallero Cosme Fanzago escultor y se obligò por servicio de Su Ex.ª el Sr. Conde de Monte Rey, Virrey deste Reyno de Napoles, de haçer un ornamento de marmol para el Altar Mayor de le Capilla que Su Ex.ª haçe en la Ciudad de Salamanca en el Convento de las Monjas de S.ᵗᵃ Ursola, con sus colunas, con las cinco figuras aussi mismo de marmol, che son un Cruçifisso con N.ʳᵃ S.ʳᵃ y S.ᵗ Juan Evang.ª, Santiago el Mayor y la Madalena, y dichas figuras van al Remate del ornamento de marmol de quatro depositos, dos Apoyadores para Rejas, y una losa para poner en tierra sobre la Boveda, y toda esta obra de marmol embotido de piedras de diversos colores, conforme los disignos hechos y firmados ante mi el ynfraescrito not° y escriv°., entre el Sr. Sancho de Solerçano Mogroneso Mayordomo Mayor de Sua Ex.ª, del Sr. Bartoloméro Pichati Ingeniero Mayor por Su Mag.ᵈ en este Reyno, del dicho Cav. Cosme, la qual obra se obliga de hazerla dentro de Seys meses, enpenzando a correr desde el primer de Deçiembre primero venidero deste año, cunplideros en fin de Mayo del año venidero 1634, la qual obra promete haçer a contentamiento y gusto de Su Ex.ª y satisfaçion del dicho Ingeniero Mayor, y entregarla aqui en Napoles, y esto por preçio cantidad de Cinco mill ducados napolitanos, de los quales en nuestra presencia el dicho Cavallero recive de Su ex.ª por mano del dicho Sr. Mayordomo ducados Dos mill trecientos y ochenta y seys en tantas doblas, etc.

10. Prota-Giurleo, 1957, p. 148.

11. Brown and Elliott, 1980, p. 268. fn. 41.

12. Trapier, 1952 pp. 73, 116; fig. 67, p. 106; and fn. 63, p. 277. Actually, the subject is the patron saint of Naples protecting the city from an earthquake following volcanic activity in Mount Vesuvius on December 15, 1631. The Count of Monterrey led a procession seeking the aid of Saint Januarius in petitioning Heaven to spare the city. The eruption proved minor, and special ceremonies of thanksgiving were observed.

13. Another version, also signed and dated 1637, in the Harrach Collection in Vienna, was characterized by Mayer (1923, p. 89) as a ''hard, carelessly executed work copied after a Ribera-like painting.'' Recent efforts have been made to re-establish the autograph status of the picture (Spinosa, 1978, no. 106; Munich and Vienna, 1982, no. 74). Both it and an unsigned version (Prado 1070) are inferior in design and execution to the Kress painting. The condition of these works, however, precludes subtle judgments of connoisseurship.

14. The photograph reproduced by Spinosa (no. 190) is of a copy after the Salamanca painting and not the picture formerly in Madrid. Trapier reproduces the right painting (fig. 128).

15. Celano, 1692 (Chiarini ed. 1854), IV, 662-678. Trapier, 1952, pp. 241-242, refers to Celano's account of the *Immaculate Conception* in the Palace in Naples and adds that a contemporary diary of 1647 mentions that a picture of the subject "recently" finished by Ribera had been painted for the royal chapel during the Revolt of Masaniello, but she failed to connect this painting with the one in Santa Isabel in Madrid.

PROVENANCE: Thought to have been in the *clausura* of the Convent of the Augustinian Nuns, Salamanca, donated by Manuel de Fonseca y Zúñiga, 6th Count of Monterrey; José Marqués de Salamanca y Mayol; sale, Paris, June 4-6, 1867, p. 20, cat. no. 26; presumably bought in and resold in Paris, Hôtel Drouot, Collection Salamanca, January 25-26, 1875, pp. 22-23; private collection, Paris, 1934; Baron Thyssen-Bornemiza, Schloss Rohoncz, Lugano; Rudolph Heinemann, New York; with M. Knoedler and Co., Inc., New York; Kress acquisition 1957; Museum of Fine Arts, Houston, Texas 1958-1961; Columbia Museum of Art, no. K2160.

BIBLIOGRAPHY: Tormo, 1916, p. 28; Mayer, 1928, pp. 88, 203 (as a lost painting); Mayer, 1934; Heinemann, 1937, I, 129, no. 351 and II, pl. 238; Darby, 1942, pp. 223-229; Sarthou Carreres, 1953, illus. p. 21; Daulte, 1950, illus.; Gaya Nuño, 1958, no. 2320; Columbia (Contini-Bonacossi), 1962, pp. 128-129, illus. p. 127; Eisler, 1977, pp. 207-209, fig. 2; Spinosa, 1978, p. 110, no. 107, illus.

23

23

Venus Discovering the Dead Adonis
Canvas, 179 x 262 cm (70½ x 103⅜ in)
Signed, bottom left: *Jusepe de Ribera, español Valenciano / ,F, 1637*
Galleria Corsini, Rome

Subjects taken from classical mythology occur with relative infrequency in
Ribera's oeuvre. One of the earliest of these is the *Drunken Silenus* (cat. no. 6),
signed and dated 1626, which was perhaps painted for the Flemish merchant
Gaspar Roomer (d. 1674), who resided in Naples.[1] Most of the known
examples of Ribera's classical subjects, however, were painted during the reign
of the Count of Monterrey as Viceroy of Naples (May 19, 1631-November 12,
1637). Indeed, Monterrey commissioned from the artist a version of *Venus and
Adonis,* which was first recorded in the inventory of his estate in 1653. That
painting, which measured 2½ x 3 *varas,* was similar in size to the Corsini
painting, the only signed example known to have survived.[2]

In this painting Ribera illustrates one of the more popular and familiar themes
from Ovid's *Metamorphoses.* The goddess Venus (Aphrodite) rushes onto the
scene to discover the body of her mortal lover, the beautiful youth Adonis, lying
on the ground. Around his loins is wrapped the magic girdle of love, by means
of which Venus inspired his passion. The outline of his red drapery continues
a line which begins with the horizon, rising diagonally from the lower left
toward the upper right, and incorporates Adonis in a sculptural sense, tying
him to the earth. Venus's outstretched arms and billowing garments reiterate
the diagonal of the landscape, but as she bounds over the clouds, the energies
of her figure produce a forward thrust uniting her with Adonis. The physical
and psychological focal point of the design is at the place where Venus's pale
foot seems to hover above his legs which are silhouetted against the evening sky.

Although Venus had warned Adonis to avoid the wild beasts in the forest, he
could not resist the thrill of the chase. During the hunt, Adonis was fatally
gored by a ferocious boar, routed from its lair by his dogs. Venus, coming to
investigate his absence, suddenly realizes that Adonis is dead. A cry of
anguish is unable to escape from her parted lips, and her eyes gleam with
alarm and tears. Beside the lifeless Adonis lies his hunting spear partially
hidden by a shadow, and his dog approaches hesitatingly to sniff at his
upturned hand. At Venus's side, one of her doves turns back as if to watch the
unfolding tragedy. The rhythms of light and dark, solid form and ethereal
atmosphere, build in alternating patterns of point and counterpoint, adding to
the excitement of the story. The urgency implied by the figure of Venus
heightens for us the anticipation of her discovery, and we become caught up in
the structural energies as well as the emotional dynamics of this drama.

Parallels to Hellenistic sculptural reliefs are suggested by both the emotion of
her face and the urgent movement of her garlanded tresses and her draperies.
Such parallels do not imply that Ribera relied on any specific source, as he

Figure 164
attributed to Ribera. *Venus and Adonis,* 1630s,
Cleveland Museum of Art, Cleveland

did in the case of the *Triumph of Bacchus* (cat. nos. 9, 10), but simply that his approach to the composition was very much conditioned by his experience of antique narrative art.

A large, dramatic painting of the *Death of Adonis* (fig. 164), in the Cleveland Art Museum since 1966, is not signed, and the attribution to Ribera has been questioned.[3] Although this painting has features that generally resemble Ribera's art, the dynamics of the design and its relationship to antique art are different than the Corsini work.

Chenault (1971) draws attention to an anonymous French poem of about 1300 which symbolically compares the death of Adonis to that of Christ. In 1623, the famous Italian poet Giovanni Battista Marino published a poem entitled *Adone,* in which he descrbed Adonis's mortal wound as being on his right side, as was Christ's, and not in the groin, as Ovid's text states. In 1634, Francisco de Quevedo published in Madrid his successful Spanish translation of Francis de Sales' *Introduction to the Devout Life* (1608), in which parallels are also drawn between Adonis and Christ, and Venus and the Virgin Mary.[4] The Death of Adonis was obviously seen as the pagan antetype of the Pietà. In the Corsini painting, the wound is barely visible along Adonis's right side just above the red drapery.

Such parallels between Christian imagery and classical mythology can be expanded to include another of Ribera's great subjects taken from Ovid's *Metamorphoses, Apollo Flaying Marsyas,* known in versions in Naples (fig. 165) and Brussels (fig. 166), both signed and dated 1637. These paintings share many stylistic features with the *Venus and Adonis;* moreover, since early Christian times, Christ has frequently been interpreted as a "new" Apollo.[5]

Several versions of the subject *Venus and Adonis* are mentioned in documents of the seventeenth century:

1. According to his expense records, Jerónimo Villanueva, an Aragonese bureaucrat hand-picked by the Count-Duke of Olivares and appointed in 1627 to manage Philip IV's secret expense account, bought from Rodrigo de Tapia a painting of *Venus and Adonis* by Ribera for the Buen Retiro Palace sometime before June 29, 1634.[6]

2. The inventory of the paintings in the estate of the Count of Monterrey, drawn up in April 1653, includes a *Venus and Adonis* (no. 4), measuring 2½ x 3 *varas,* and a *Monstrous Boy* (no. 186), both by Ribera. The *Venus and Adonis* was given one of the highest valuations. Monterrey's widow died in December 1654; her heir was her nephew Don Luis Méndez de Haro, the Marquis of Carpio (d. 1661). The Count of Monterrey's title and probably his estate, however, passed to Doña Inéz Francisca de Zúñiga, the Count's nearest descendant on the male line of the family, who became the 7th Countess of Monterrey. Luis de Haro was appointed interim governor of the Buen Retiro Palace in 1648 and became Philip IV's favorite and principal minister. He was succeeded in the post of Governor of the Buen Retiro Palace by at least 1654, by his son Gaspar,

Figure 165
Ribera. *Apollo Flaying Marsyas,* 1637, Museo
Nazionale di San Martino, Naples   (Alinari)

Figure 166
Ribera. *Apollo Flaying Marsyas,* 1637, Musées Royaux
des Beaux-Arts de Belgique, Brussels

who had been created Marquis of Eliche in 1647. Another of Luis's sons, Juan Domingo de Haro y Guzmán, married in 1652 his distant cousin, the Monterrey heiress, Inéz Francisca de Zúñiga, thereby uniting both branches of the family. In a letter dated April 1656, the Marquis of Eliche writes to sell the paintings of *Venus and Adonis* and the *Monstrous Boy* for ''urgent needs created by the high costs of the Buen Retiro Palace.''[7] The *Venus and Adonis* was sent to someone named Pasca in 1656 to be sold for 4,400 reales.[8] This was surely not the same painting bought for the Buen Retiro in 1634, as assumed by Trapier and Spinosa. Instead, it is likely that Eliche was disposing of paintings owned by members of his family in order to meet the demands placed on him by the King to help meet royal expenses.

3. A large canvas of *Venus and Adonis* by Ribera is listed in the dowry contract of September 21, 1677, of Micaela Zapata Chacón in Madrid at the time of her marriage to the Marquis of Mortara.[9]

4. Trapier, apparently confused, says that there was a *Venus and Adonis* in the inventory of ''the Count-Duke,'' which the Marquis of Eliche wished to sell in 1656. Spinosa, evidently relying on Trapier, refers to such a work in an inventory of the ''Olivares family.'' No such document is known to this author, but in 1656, the holder of the title of Count-Duke of Olivares was the first Count-Duke's nephew, Luis Méndez de Haro, the Marquis of Carpio.[10]

5. Chenault convincingly posits that a painting identified as *Perseus* by Ribera in the 1686 and 1700 inventories of the Alcázar of Madrid is actually a *Venus and Adonis,* since the description says ''he is dead and a weeping goddess places a garland of flowers on his head.''[11].

These five separate items may, in fact, refer only to three different paintings. Trapier's reference (no. 4) is possibly the painting (no. 2) originally in the collection of the Count of Monterrey, having passed to his heirs after 1653. The painting (no. 5) listed in the inventories of the Alcázar in Madrid is almost certainly the work (no. 1) bought by the Crown in 1634, and transferred from the Palace of the Buen Retiro, since by 1700 it no longer appears in the Retiro inventories. Since no further documents pertain to the Alcázar version, the painting presumably was destroyed in the fire of 1734. Only two of these paintings (nos. 2 and 3), are likely to have survived beyond that date. Although not mentioned in an inventory earlier than 1826, the Corsini painting can be either of these versions or yet another one not mentioned in any known document.

NOTES

1. Palomino, 1715-1724, III, 311; Ceci, 1920, pp. 160-164; Trapier, 1952, pp. 36-38. According to old accounts. Roomer's vast collections were housed in several palaces, including the Palazzo Monteoliveto in which eight works by Ribera were listed as having been seen by Giulio Cesare Capaccio sometime around 1630. These included seven religious paintings and an *Apollo Flaying Marsyas.*

2. Although Spinosa, 1978, p. 109, says that the painting was in the Corsini collection since the seventeenth century, Alba Costamagna, Rome (Palazzo Barberini), 1982, pp. 79-80, says that there is no reference to the painting in

eighteenth-century lists (such as Vasi, Magnan, De la Lande, Venuti, etc.) and it is not mentioned in *Descrizione della Pitture. sculture e architetture esposte al pubblico in Roma, opera cominciata dall'abato Filippo Tito da Città di Castello con l'aggiunta di quanto è stato fatto di nuovo fino all'anno presente, in Roma 1763,* pp. 36-37. The Corsini inventory is found in A.S.R, Notai Capitolini, Officio 8, Not. Bartolomeo Giuseppe Offredi, Vol. 545. These documents are soon to be published.

3. Francis, 1966, pp. 339-347; Chenault, 1971, pp. 68-69; Causa, 1972, fig. 282; Spinosa, 1978, p. 137, no. 386; Brown and Elliott, 1980, p. 269, fn. 56; Cleveland, 1982, no. 222, pp. 507-509. Chenault accepts the Cleveland painting as autograph. The purpose of her article is to present iconographic sources for this subject. She stresses how different the Cleveland painting is from the one in the Corsini collection in composition, design, handling of paint, color, iconography, and psychology. She dates the Cleveland paintings slightly later than the Corsini work. A date is not suggested in the Cleveland catalogue entry. Spinosa rejects this painting from the canon of Ribera's autograph works; Brown and Elliott relegate it to "the workshop or a follower."

4. Quevedo y Villegas, ed. 1961, I, 1675.

5. Wind, 1958, pp. 49, 142-146; Kitzinger, 1964, p. 4; Panofsky, 1974, pp. 257-265; Stott, 1982, pp. 370-388. One of the earliest references to Christ as Apollo/Helios is found in a mosaic in the cemetery under Saint Peter's, Rome (Grabar, 1968, fig. 74, p. 80).

6. Domínquez Bordona, 1932, p. 84; Chenault, 1971, p. 76; Spinosa, 1978, p. 110, no. 105c. Brown and Elliott, 1980, p. 120 and p. 269. fn. 56, were the first to cite the document with the details of this purchase (BNM Ms 7797, fol. 119).

7. Trapier, 1952, p. 236; Pérez Sánchez, 1977, pp. 423, 427, 451; Spinosa, 1978, pp. 109-110, no. 105c; Brown and Elliott, 1980, p. 219; Cleveland, 1982, p. 507. Professor Marcus Burke has generously given of his time and knowledge in tracing this complicated Olivares-Monterrey-Carpio-Eliche lineage. All the titles came together with Catalina de Haro y Guzmán, 8th Countess of Monterrey, who married the 10th Duke of Alba in 1710.

8. Cleveland, 1982, p. 507. The reference for this letter is: Duque de Berwick y de Alba, *Discursos leidos ante la Real Academia de Bellas Artes de San Fernando en la recepción pública del Excmo. Sr. Duque de Berwick y de Alba.* Madrid, 1924, p. 92.

9. Trapier, 1952, p. 236, gives the marriage date as 1677; Spinosa, 1978, pp. 109-110, no. 105a mistakenly gives it as 1634. Micaela Zapata Chacón was the daughter of the Count of Casarrubies. The exact date is given in Cleveland, 1982, p. 507.

10. Trapier, 1952, p. 236; Spinosa, 1978, p. 110. The first Count-Duke of Olivares died on July 22, 1645.

11. Chenault, 1971. p. 76; Bottineau, 1958, p. 325, no. 886; Trapier, 1952, p. 236; Cleveland, 1982, p. 509, which also gives the measurements for the Alcázar painting as 209 x 292 cm.

PROVENANCE: First recorded in the Palazzo Corsini, Rome, in an inventory of 1826.

EXHIBITIONS: Rome (di Carpegna and Lavagnino), 1958, pp. 29-30, no. 39, illus.; Rome (Palazzo Barberini), 1982, pp. 79-80, no. 30. illus.

BIBLIOGRAPHY: Barbier, 1870, p. 384, no. 53; Solvay, 1887, p. 148; Justi, 1889, I, 326; Mayer, 1908, p. 102; Longhi, 1915, p. 132; Paris, 1921, p. 438; Mayer, 1923, pp. 103-104, 197; Hermanin, 1924, p. 64; Delogu, 1928, p. 149; De Rinaldis, 1932, p. 17; Bottari, 1943, p. 384; Golzio, 1950, p. 530; Trapier, 1952, pp. 130-131, fig. 81; Pigler, 1956, II, 246, illus.; Gaya Nuño, 1958, no. 2315, fig. 134; Francis, 1966, pp. 339-347, illus.; Spinosa, 1978, pp. 109-110, no. 105, illus.

24 *see color plate*

Figure 167
The Count of Monterrey, 1631, from Parrino, *Teatro eroico de' Vicere di Napoli,* 1692

24
Knight of Santiago
Canvas, 146 x 107 cm (57½ x 42 in)
Painted in the mid-1630s
Meadows Museum, Southern Methodist University, Dallas, Texas

This arresting and quite well-preserved painting reveals Ribera's accomplishment as a portraitist. Despite what might be several clues to the identity of the sitter, no convincing identification has yet been made. There is some circumstantial evidence that tempts one to think that he might be Don Manuel de Fonseca y Zúñiga, 6th Count of Monterrey, Viceroy of Naples from 1631 until 1637 and Ribera's greatest patron,[1] but the physical resemblance, based on current evidence, is not conclusive. Another possible identity has been proposed in the past, however, which can definitely be disproved.

In 1854, when the portrait was on loan to the Museo Nacional de la Trinidad in Madrid from the collection of the Infante Don Sebastián Gabriel de Borbón y Braganza, it was described by Mesonero Romano as "Portrait of a Girón with doublet and eyeglasses, celebrated picture by Ribera."[2] This self-confident statement would appear to suggest that the sitter was a member of the Girón family, that of the Dukes of Osuna. Evidently predicating himself on this, Spinosa said that the picture passed from the collection of the Dukes of Osuna to that of the Infante Don Sebastián Gabriel perhaps in the early nineteenth century.[3] The very early Osuna provenance, in fact, appears to be spurious.

That the sitter is a Knight of the Order of Santiago, as Monterrey was, is evident from the gold pendant of a cockel shell with a red cross suspended from a gold chain around his neck. That he is a Captain General of the armed forces is evident from the buff leather doublet and black steel collar plate, the sword at his left side, the baton of command held in his right hand, and the red sash identified with partisans of the Spanish in the Thirty Years War. The *golilla,* or stiff white coller, was *de rigeur* at the Spanish court after 1623 and remained in fashion until after Ribera's death. The black-rimmed spectacles are similar to those observed in other portraits of the period (fig. 3).[4]

An engraving of scant artistic merit (fig. 167) conveys a likeness of the Count of Monterrey as he appeared at the beginning of his reign in 1631.[5] In comparison to Ribera's portrait, it is not difficult to imagine that the sitter in the painting is the same person perhaps five years older, a little heavier, a little balder, and wearing glasses. Comparison must also be made, however, with the marble effigy of the Count commissioned from Giuliano Finelli for the Augustinian Convent at Salamanca (see cat. no. 22, fig. 159). The result of that comparison does not particularly favor such an identification.

Regardless of who the sitter in the portrait may be, what must be the earliest reference to the painting, until now overlooked in the literature on Ribera, occurs in the archives of the Dukes of Alba in Madrid. In 1802, following the death of the childless Doña María Teresa Cayetana de Silva y Toledo, 13th Duchess of Alba, the estates and titles of the Duchess, including the vast collection of paintings that by then had subsumed the fabled collections of Monterrey, Carpio, and Eliche (see cat. no. 23), were to pass to Don Carlos Miguel Fitz-James Stuart y Silva, Duke of Berwick and Liria. To avert a complete loss, the other heirs of the Duchess filed a lawsuit against the Duke of Berwick seeking to retain those paintings which had been part of the collections of the Marquis of Carpio (d. 1661) and his son the Marquis of Eliche (d. 1687) and had accrued to the Alba line in 1710 through the marriage of the latter's daughter, Doña Catalina de Haro y Guzmán, 8th Countess of Monterrey, to the 10th Duke of Alba. The suit ended in an agreement whereby the Duchess's heirs were obliged to give to Berwick only thirty-two of the more than five hundred paintings which had that provenance.[6] Barcia published excerpts from a copy of the list drawn up at the time of the suit (preserved in the archive of the Palacio de Liria, Madrid) in which the following entry appears:

> A canvas one and a half *varas* high and scarcely five fourths wide. It is a portrait of a General with his left hand on his sword; in his right hand the baton. He is in armor. It is an original by Josef Ribera, called the Españoleto.[7]

Efforts to locate a description of the same portrait among the seventeenth-century inventories of the Carpio and Eliche collections in the archive of the Liria Palace have produced negative results.[8] Nor does the painting appear in the 1653 inventory, drawn up in Madrid, of the collection of the Count of Monterrey,[9] whence it might also have been adduced to the Alba holdings. Pérez Sánchez, in commenting on the surprisingly few items (265) in the Monterrey inventory, noted that a significant part of the collection was located at the time in other residences of the Count, such as the palace in Salamanca and the castle in Galicia.[10]

While it is impossible at present to document exactly how the painting entered the Alba collection, it appears to be a fact that it was there by 1802 and that it probably got there by descent. In any case, the dispute between the Duchess's heirs and the new Duke was settled in favor of the former; the pictures were subsequently sold, and thus came to an end one of the great family collections of Spanish history. Exactly who owned the painting between 1802 and the time it was acquired by the Infante Don Sebastián Gabriel (before 1841) is not known. It is certainly possible that it was bought from the Duchess's heirs by the Duke of Osuna, thus accounting for the belief expressed by Mesonero Romanos that the sitter was a Girón.

Pictorially, the painting makes an extremely bold impact, with the patterns of bright reds in the table cloth, the sash, and the curtain alternating with the black of the costume and contrasting with the subtly modeled buff doublet. The latter garment adds the appearance of greater weight and girth to the

Figure 168
after Ribera. *A Knight of Santiago,* Private Collection, Madrid

figure than he surely had in actuality. Its golden tone is repeated in the braid and buttons that trim the black sleeves. The highlights on the sash are painted with the virtuoso assurance that characterizes the works of the mid-1630s.

The head is the most remarkable part of the painting. The features of the face are modeled with fairly heavy impasto. The shadows on the right side of the face are indicated by thin glazes that are still completely intact. Ribera's observation and painting of the eyes, seen through the lenses of the eyeglasses, is brilliant, with light glinting off the edges of the lenses and being reflected onto the cheeks adjacent to the shadows cast by the heavy frames. A tiny gold earring is in the sitter's left earlobe.

In the collection of Manuel González in Madrid is a copy of this picture which also belonged to the Infante Don Sebastián in the nineteenth century (fig. 168). Spinosa discusses its "Giordanesque" qualities. It appears rather to be a spiritless nineteenth-century copy, no doubt commissioned by the Infante himself.

NOTES

1. See cat. no. 22, note 4, for the identification of Monterrey as the 6th Count and not the 7th, as previous literature indicates.

2. Cited by Spinosa, 1978, p. 114, no. 134.

3. Spinosa, 1978, p. 114. Don Pedro Girón, 4th Duke of Osuna (b. 1579), was Viceroy of Naples from 1616 until 1620. He died in a Madrid prison in 1624, which effectively eliminates any possibility that he sat for this portrait.

4. As in the *Portrait of Francisco de Quevedo* (fig. 3) once attributed to Velázquez: cf. López-Rey, 1963, no. 532.

5. Parrino, 1692.

6. Barcia, 1911, pp. xii-xiii.

7. Barcia, 1911, p. 249. This reference was kindly pointed out by Professor Jonathan Brown.

8. Both William Jordan and J. M. Pita Andrade have searched for such evidence.

9. Pérez Sánchez, 1970, pp. 418-459.

10. Pérez Sánchez, 1970, pp. 421-422.

PROVENANCE: María Teresa Cayetana de Silva, 13th Duchess of Alba (1762-1802); Infante don Sebastián Gabriel de Borbón y Braganza (1811-1875); exhibited with his collection 1841 at the Museo Nacional de la Trinidad, Madrid, where it was described again in 1854 as "Portrait of a Girón with doublet and eyeglasses, celebrated painting by Ribera;" exhibited in 1876 with other works belonging to Borbón y Braganza, Pau, France; recorded in his will on November 1, 1887; Duke of Osuna; Marchioness of Villafranca; her sale, Christie's, London, July 17, 1925, lot 152; with P. Jackson Higgs, New York, until 1927; Count Allesandro Contini-Bonacossi, Florence and Rome, (d. 1955); his daughter, Anna Maria Pappi; with Colnaghi and Co., London and Richard L. Feigen, Co., New York; Meadows Museum, 1977, no. 77.2.

EXHIBITIONS: Pau, 1876; Rome, 1930, no. 53; San José (Mosby), 1978, no. 42, illus.

BIBLIOGRAPHY: Pau, 1876; Barcia, 1911, p. 249; Frankfurter, 1930, illus. p. 43; Longhi and Mayer, 1930, no. 53, pl. XLVI; Mayer, 1930, illus. p. 35; Pantorba, 1949, pp. 25, 33; Gaya Nuño, 1958, no. 2367; "New Acquisitions," 1977, p. 57; Spinosa, 1978, pp. 113-114, no. 134, illus.

25 *see color plate*

25

Portrait of a Jesuit

Canvas, 195 x 110 cm (76¾ x 43¾ in)

Signed, bottom left: *Jusepe de Ribera español valenciano / ,F, 1638*

Museo Poldi-Pezzoli, Milan

This accomplished portrait, one of the few in Ribera's oeuvre, places him among the first rank of portrait painters of the seventeenth century. The identity of the elderly Jesuit priest is not known, but the presence of the lion beside him has led to the generally held though probably mistaken belief that he is a missionary (Trapier, Spinosa). The presence of the beast in the painting is certainly emblematic; the priest and the lion are shown as if walking together, the man's hand resting gently on the furry head. In Christian iconography, the lion is commonly employed as the symbol of Christ.[1] He is also the attribute of the Evangelist Mark, whose Gospel recounts most fully the Resurrection of Christ, and in paintings, the lion frequently accompanies or symbolizes the Evangelist. It is most probable that the lion in this portrait is used symbolically, and his presence is doubly appropriate here, signifying both Christ and the Society of Jesus.

The Jesuit order was in a period of great ascendancy in the seventeenth century. The founder of the order, Ignatius of Loyola, and his most influential follower, Francis Xavier, were canonized on May 22, 1622, along with Philip Neri and the mystic Teresa of Avila. By 1638, Jesuits were at the tip of Africa, in Southeast Asia, and in China. In Italy and Spain they built and decorated churches from the late sixteenth through the eighteenth centuries. By 1750, the Jesuit Order was among the largest landholders in Naples.

Although at present no known documentation identifies the sitter of this portrait, a passage from De Dominici perhaps provides a clue about this impressive Jesuit:

> And because the confessor of the Viceroy was at that time a father of the Society of Jesus, who lived in the new Collegio of Saint Francis Xavier, in the church of which he had already begun to officiate; therefore, Jusepe [de Ribera] at the request of this father, painted *Saint Anthony of Padua*, which now we see in one of the chapels, and since in the famous church of the Gesù Nuovo the large chapel of Saint Ignatius was adorned with marble, he himself felt it necessary to embellish with pictures the area above the altar, [and so] with this aim, three pictures were ordered from Ribera. . . .[2]

In the early 1640s, Ribera painted three scenes from the life of Saint Ignatius. These canvases were incorporated into a large marble altar ensemble built in the left transept of the Gesù Nuovo in Naples about 1640-1643 by Cosimo Fanzago and dedicated to Saint Ignatius.[3] When the church was struck by bombs in World War II, the paintings were severely damaged, and only two were able to be restored and returned to their original positions: *Pope Paul III*

Figure 169
Ribera. *Pope Paul III Approving the Rule of the Jesuit Order,* early 1640s, Gesù Nuovo, Naples

Approving the Rule of the Jesuit Order (fig. 169) and *Saint Ignatius in Glory* (fig. 170). The third canvas, *Saint Ignatius Writing the Rules of the Society of Jesus,* remains in storage at the Capodimonte Museum.

The four paintings mentioned by De Dominici are the only works known to have been painted by Ribera for the Jesuits. Because of this fact and the artist's close association with the Count of Monterrey, to whom the Jesuit father ministered as confessor, the possibility arises that this portrait may represent the Count's confessor. Perhaps in part because of the portrait, Ribera eventually received the commission of the paintings for the church of Saint Francis Xavier and the Gesù Nuovo. Further research may discover the name of Monterrey's confessor and allow us to determine the merit of this suggested identification.

The sitter's benign character and gentle countenance are sympathetically and forcefully revealed. In contrast to the loose and monochromatic brushwork used to define the face, mane, clawed foot, and switching tail of the lion, the face and hands of the Jesuit are brushed with rich, creamy pigments built from the deep shadows under the chin and along the left side of the face to the heavy impasto of the areas that catch the brightest light. The subtlety of the artist's rendering of light upon form creates the most remarkable sense of the quickness of the human face. The backlighting over the sitter's left shoulder causes the silhouette of his black robe to stand out incisively, the tension of its contour strongly suggesting the form of the body beneath it. The inky blackness of the folds and the crisp white collar and cuffs create a monumental stability and an elegant accent that give life to the image and heighten our appreciation of the sensitive face that confronts us.

Several writers have spoken of a perceived resemblance to the portraits of Velázquez or the monks of Zurbarán. Certainly the chromatic range of blacks and tawny browns suggests some of the portraits of the former, but beyond this correspondence, which reflects the Spanish fashion then dominating Naples, the painting has little stylistic connection with the court painter of Philip IV and even less with Zurbarán.

Figure 170
Ribera. *Saint Ignatius in Glory,* early 1640s, Gesù
Nuovo, Naples

NOTES

1. Ferguson, 1971, p. 21; in Medieval natural histories, lions were thought to be born dead, coming to life after three days when breathed upon by their sire. Because of this lore, they became associated with the Resurrection as symbols of Christ.

2. De Dominici, 1742-1744, III, 5.

3. These paintings, regardless of their very damaged condition, may never have had the mastery of technique expected from Ribera. Spinosa, 1978, pp. 119-129, nos. 176, 177, 178, suggests that studio assistance may account for this quality; nevertheless, details that appear upon close examination as awkwardness of technique and abbreviated modeling become legible with clarity and definition when the paintings are seen in their actual location.

PROVENANCE: Count Carlo Castelbarco; sale Count Castelbarco, Paris, May 2-6, 1870, lot 30; Museo Poldi-Pezzoli, 1881, no. 95.

EXHIBITIONS: Florence and Milan (Longhi), 1951, no. 82, p. 82, pl. 104; Bordeaux (Martín-Méry), 1955, p. 32, no. 52.

BIBLIOGRAPHY: Milan (Morassi), [n.d.], p. 25, no. 95; Mayer, 1923, pp. 129, 200; Pillement, 1929, pl. 39; Morassi, 1936, p. 6; Milan (Wittgens), 1937, no. 95; Mayer, 1947, p. 300; Trapier, 1952, pp 159-162, fig. 112; Lafuente Ferrari, 1953, p. 262; Milan (Berenson), 1955, no. 95; Ainaud de Lasarte, 1955-1956, pp. 115-119; Gaya Nuño, 1958, no. 2359, fig. 140; Spinosa, 1978, pp. 113-114, no. 133, illus.

26 *see color plate*

26

Portrait of a Musician

Canvas, 77.2 x 62.5 cm (30⅜ x 24⅝ in)
Signed, center right: *Jusepe de Ribera / ,F, 1638*
The Toledo Museum of Art
Gift of Edward Drummond Libbey, Toledo, Ohio

That the sitter of this portrait is a musician is confirmed by the roll of paper he holds in his right hand, which represents several lines of musical notation, and by the baton used to beat time, which is held by his unseen left hand. It was proposed by Prota-Giurleo in 1960 that the sitter was Giovani Maria Trabaci (b. ca. 1575), who became choirmaster and organist of the Royal Chapel in 1604, positions which he held until his death in 1647.[1] While this idea has gained some currency, the sitter would appear to be only in his thirties, or forties at the most. Trabaci would have been over sixty in the year this portrait was done. Therefore, while this musician may well have been one who served at the court, he was not likely Trabaci.[2]

The black of the sitter's jacket is somewhat sunken and flat, but his face and hands reveal the unmistakable finesse of Ribera's brush. The creamy flesh tones of the face are fluidly applied, with the shadows along the side of the nose and under the eyebrows achieved with thin glazes. The tip of the nose is brought into relief by a fleck of white. The large, brown eyes with heavy lids are outlined in delicate pink and black. A few lashes were added with individual, light strokes. The black beard, hair and mustache are deftly painted and evoke a wispy texture. The backlighting at the right accents the soft silhouette of the hair as opposed to the sharp outline of the shoulder and helps to give relief to the figure. All told, the artist has created a sensitive likeness of an alert and intelligent young man.

NOTES

1. The date of 1604 is given in the Toledo Museum of Art catalogue, 1976, p. 141. Spinosa, 1978, p. 133, places Trabaci's years of service as 1601-1647.

2. A list of the various music masters serving the Court is given by Prota-Giurleo, 1960, pp. 191-195.

PROVENANCE: Augustus III, Elector of Saxony and King of Poland (reigned 1733-1763); given to the Potocki family, Poland; Count Gregory Stroganoff, Rome, by 1908; with Sangiorgi, Rome; Edward Drummond Libbey, 1925; gift to the Toledo Museum of Art, 1925, no. 26.61.

EXHIBITIONS: New York (Burroughs), 1928, no. 54, illus; Toledo (Gudiol), 1941, p. 86, no. 54, illus.; Oberlin, 1957, no. 5, illus.; Sarasota (Gilbert), 1961, no. 11, illus.; Indianapolis and Providence (Carter and Peat), 1963, no. 65, illus.

BIBLIOGRAPHY: Mayer, 1908, pp. 124-125, pl. XXVII and 1923, pp. 127-128, pl. XXXIII; Muñoz, 1912, II, 107, pl. LXXXII; Mayer, 1929, p. 149; Kapterewa, 1956, pp. 39-40, pl. 23; Gaya Nuño, 1958, no. 2348; Kubler and Soria, 1959, p. 241; Prota-Giurleo, 1960, pp. 190-191, illus.; Toledo, 1976, pp. 138, 141, illus.; Spinosa, 1978, p. 113, no. 124, illus.

27 *see color plate*

27

Jacob with the Flock of Laban

Canvas, 132 x 180 cm (52 x 45¾ in)

Signed, on the rock, lower right: *Jusepe de Ribera español / academico Romano / , F, 1638*

The Trustees of The National Gallery, London

Extensive conservation treatment carried out in 1970 has made it easier to appreciate the great invention of this composition, albeit with the distortions and losses that have been sustained over time. In the comprehensive entry in the catalogue of the London National Gallery, Maclaren and Braham discuss this painting in relation to two known copies (see fig. 174).[1] With losses amounting to about 30 inches (76 cm) from the left and 6 inches (15 cm) from the right and the top, the space now occupied by Jacob is considerably reduced and cramped. The motif of a figure placed in front of a massive tree trunk is one used frequently by Ribera, but shifted to the extreme right in this composition, the left half of the picture was given an unusual openness, with an expanse of blue sky. In this regard, it was a compositional as well as a thematic counterpart to the magnificent *Dream of Jacob* (Prado 1117) (fig. 171), signed and dated 1639.

The story of Jacob, the younger son of Isaac and Rebekah, is told in Genesis, Chapters XXVIII-XXX. After deceiving Isaac into blessing him as the first born instead of his brother Esau, who rightfully deserved the blessing (fig. 172), Jacob left his homeland of Canaan to find a wife among his mother's people in Pandan-aram, Syria. There he met his uncle, Laban, who had two daughters, Leah and Rachel. Jacob pledged seven years of labor as a shepherd of Laban's flock to win Rachel as his wife; the morning after the marriage, though, he found that Laban had substituted his older daughter Leah, since it was the custom that the first born be the first to marry. Jacob complained to Laban who then gave him the hand of Rachel in return for Jacob's pledge of seven more years of work. When the years had passed, Jacob, wishing to return to Canaan, asked Laban for, and received his promise of, the spotted sheep in recompense for the fourteen years' labor during which the flocks had multiplied greatly. Looking out for himself, Jacob took rods from green poplar, hazel, and chestnut trees, peeled them in streaks, and placed them near the water when the strongest animals came to drink and to mate. With this example of spottedness before their eyes, they conceived, and their offspring were abundant, sturdy, and spotted. For six more years, Jacob remained in Syria, tending the flock and making ready for his eventual departure with the entire spotted flock. This story was cited by Saint Francis de Sales in his *Introduction to the Devout Life* (1608, translated into Spanish by Quevedo in 1634) as an example of the benefit which the scriptures (spotted as the rods) can be in one's life if they are kept ever-present as an example.[2] Lope de Vega had also turned the story of Jacob's life into a Baroque vision of human destiny in his play *The Trials of Jacob (Dreams there are that are real).*[3]

Figure 171
Ribera. *Dream of Jacob,* 1639, Museo del Prado, Madrid

Figure 172
Ribera. *Isaac Blessing Jacob,* 1637, Museo del Prado, Madrid

The story of Jacob is meant as a source of inspiration, and Ribera has made it humane and accessible by emphasizing the affectionate relationship that exists between the shepherd and his sheep. Jacob looks toward Heaven for strength. Ribera has captured the determination as well as the gentleness of his character, which emphasizes the scriptural message of patience and industry. He painted an earlier version of this subject, a splendid canvas signed and dated 1632, which is now at El Escorial (fig. 173); in keeping with its earlier date, the contrast of light and shade is more dramatic, heightening the impact of its naturalism. The differences in the two paintings illustrate well the change in the artist's style that occurred in the late 1630s.

Figure 173
Ribera. *Jacob with the Flock,* 1632, Monastery of San Lorenzo, El Escorial

Figure 174
after Ribera. *Jacob with the Flock,* Museo Cerralbo, Madrid

As Maclaren and Braham have shown, radiographic studies reveal that Ribera at first began to model the head of Jacob slightly to the left and that the lamb on his lap was added after the brown robe had been painted. The original appearance of the composition is seen in a copy now in the Cerralbo Museum in Madrid (fig. 174). The reduction appears to have been made in two stages, the first of them not long after the picture was painted. The fragment of a shepherdess's staff projecting into the sky at the extreme left margin appears to be part of an old addition to the painting (believed not to be by Ribera) made at the time it was first reduced. A copy located near Genoa (Spinosa, no. 130a) shows the narrowed composition with the addition of this female figure. A further reduction of the present canvas almost entirely excised that figure from view.

NOTES

1. London. (Maclaren and Braham), 1970 pp. 94-96.

2. Quevedo y Villegas, 1961, I, 1675.

3. Vega Carpio, 1893, III, 253-264.

PROVENANCE: In an anonymous sale (by White), London, April 17, 1806, lot 42; bought by N. W. Ridley Colborne (later Lord Colborne); Lord Colborne Bequest, 1854; The National Gallery, London (cat. no. 244).

EXHIBITIONS: British Institution, 1829, no. 110 and 1847, no. 124.

BIBLIOGRAPHY: Waagen, 1854, p. 241; Mayer, 923, p. 81; London, 1929, p. 308, no. 244; Pantorba, 1946, pl. XLVI; London (Maclaren), 1952, pp. 57-58, no. 244; Gaya Nuño, 1958, no. 2438; Spinosa, 1978, pp. 113-114, no. 130, illus.

28

Figure 175
Ribera. *Christ of Derision,* 1632-1634, Atheneum, Helsinki

Figure 176
Ribera. *Mater Dolorosa,* 1638, Gemäldegalerie, Kassel

Figure 177
Titian. *Mater Dolorosa,* ca. 1555, Museo del Prado, Madrid

28
Christ of Derision

Canvas, 76 x 64 cm (30 x 25 in)
Signed, center left: *Jusepe de Ribera español / ,F, 1638*
Bob Jones University Collection of Sacred Art
Greenville, South Carolina

This solitary, bust-length figure of Christ crowned with a wreath of thorns is cast in a bright light against a shadowy background. Partially draped in a scarlet robe put on him in derision by Pilate's soldiers, Christ holds in his right hand a broken flogging-reed, a mock-symbol of power. This is the ''Man of Sorrows,'' suffering humiliation and torment from his persecutors who jeer: ''Hail, King of the Jews'' (Mark XV:15ff).

The *Christ of Derision,* or *Christ Mocked,* is a subtly different subject from an *Ecce Homo,* an episode which comes later in the Passion when Christ is presented to the crowd (John XIX:4,5). In two examples among his early works (Gerolomini, Naples, and the Real Academia, Madrid), Ribera portrayed Christ with his hands tied, looking worn and oppressed. The full-length figures in the composition in the Brera (fig. 13) are engaged in the actual crowning with thorns. Both of these compositional types are well-known from the masterpieces of Titian.

Ribera painted several versions of this particular interpretation; the painting catalogued here is unquestionably the finest, although the one in Helsinki (fig. 175) is noteworthy. The subject of Christ as the ''Man of Sorrows'' is often paired with a *Mater Dolorosa.* An unusually moving work by Ribera, also signed in 1638, is the painting now in the Gemäldegalerie in Kassel (fig. 176). Although these two paintings are almost identical in size, the brushwork of the *Mater Dolorosa* is more vigorous and the paint is richer, with heavy impasto and subtle color variations. Both paintings are related to famous examples of the subjects by Titian, especially the Kassel composition with the *Mater Dolorosa* (fig. 177) of ca. 1555 in the Prado (443).

PROVENANCE: With E. and A. Silberman Galleries, New York; Bob Jones University, 1952, no. 205.

EXHIBITIONS: New York, 1955, no. 20, p. 32, illus.; Indianapolis (Carter and Peat), 1963, no. 64

BIBLIOGRAPHY: Greenville, 1954, p. 126, illus. p. 127; Gaya Nuño, 1958, no. 2346; Kerrigan, 1960, pp. 352-361, illus. p. 355; Greenville (Marlier and Gudiol), 1961, II, 346, illus. p. 347; Spinosa, 1972, pp. 112-113, no. 123, illus.

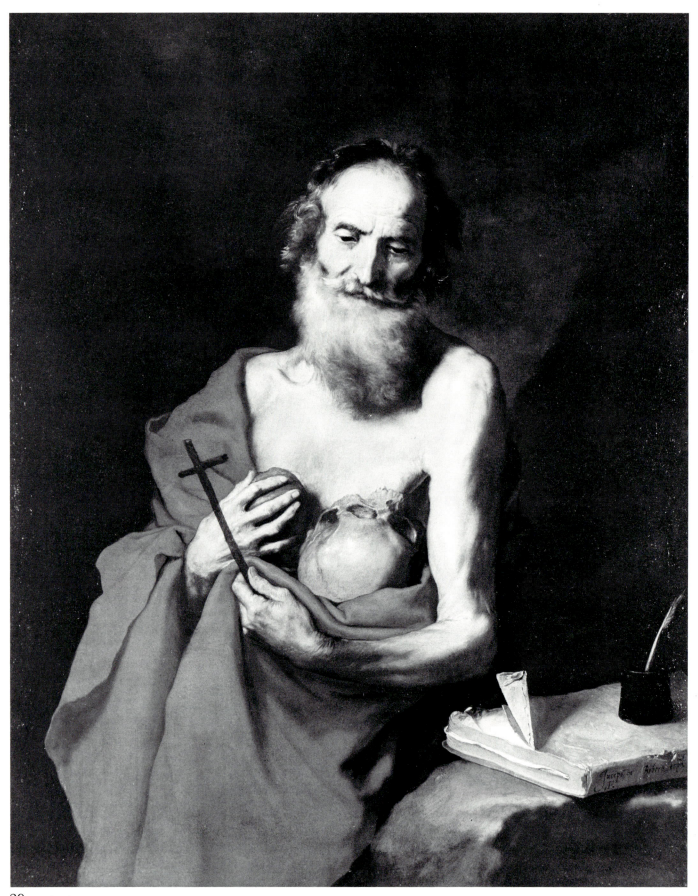

29 *see color plate*

29

Saint Jerome

Canvas, 128.9 x 100.6 cm (50¾ x 39⅝ in)

Signed, on spine of the book, lower right: *Jusepe de Ribera espa*^{ñol} / ,*F,*

Painted ca. 1638-1640

Cleveland Museum of Art, Mr. and Mrs. William H. Marlatt Fund, Cleveland, Ohio

The Cleveland *Saint Jerome* is one of the most beautiful of Ribera's paintings of the saint as a penitent (see cat. no. 7). As Spear indicates, the influence of the Bolognese school, especially that of Guido Reni and Guercino, is noticeable in the painting.[1] The isolation of the figure against a dark background and the naturalism of the form link it to the artist's roots in the art of Caravaggio, but the overall effect has been softened considerably by the impact of Bolognese art. The richly textured impasto retains the imprint of the brush which skillfully details the anatomy of muscle and bone. The result is a vivid presence of the figure; we can readily understand Pacheco's praise of Ribera above all others—even Guido Reni—for his ability to make figures seem to be alive.[2]

In this painting, Ribera has expanded upon an earlier technique in the modeling of the head and hands. In his works before the mid-1630s, he modeled forms with a dark-to-light value scheme, with paint applied heavily in a wet-on-wet procedure. Under the neo-Venetian influence of the later 1630s, he began to refine these surfaces, adding touches of color applied with small, fine brushes in order to give further accent to the flesh. Tiny brushstrokes highlight the surface of the mustache and beard. Along the brow, and especially around the eyes and on the cheeks, Ribera has placed the smallest touches of soft pink, rose, and amber. The resultant tonal variety gives luster to the flesh. These qualities are also apparent in such paintings from the late 1630s as the *Moses* (fig. 27) at the Certosa di San Martino, dated 1638, and the *Saint Jerome,* dated 1640, at the Fogg Art Museum (cat. no. 32).

NOTES

1. Cleveland (Spear), 1971, pp. 154-155, no. 57.

2. Pacheco, ed. 1956, II, 13.

PROVENANCE: Private collection, Italy (?); with F. Kleinberger and Co., New York; Cleveland Museum of Art, Mr. and Mrs. William H. Marlatt Fund, 1961, no. 61.219.

EXHIBITIONS: Cleveland, 1961, no. 68, illus; Indianapolis and Providence (Carter and Peat), 1963, no. 68, pl. 68; Jacksonville, 1965, no. 31, illus.; Cleveland (Spear), 1971, p. 154-155, no. 57, illus.

BIBLIOGRAPHY: Francis, 1966, pp. 339-340, fig. 2; Cleveland, 1978, p. 151, illus.; Spinosa, 1978, pp. 120-121, no. 187, illus.; Cleveland, 1982, pp. 504-506, no. 221, illus.

30 *see color plate*

30

The Martyrdom of Saint Bartholomew
Canvas, 205 x 154 cm (80¾ x 60⅝ in)
Painted ca. 1638-1640
Trafalgar Galleries, London

This large painting with its full-length, life-size figure has only recently been published. Eric Young suggests that a passage from De Dominici may refer to the picture:

> In the Gallery of His Serene Highness the Duke of Modena there are two paintings of ordinary size, in one of which is portrayed the *Martyrdom of Saint Sebastian,* and in the other that of *Saint Bartholomew.* In Genoa, in the house of Spinola, there is a *Saint Jerome* made at the request of Filippo Spinola, and in the house of Felice Pinelli, a painting of 10 palmi and 8 of the Martyrdom of *Saint Bartholomew* of another invention.[1]

Young proposes a date of 1648-1650 for this painting, finding ''the serenity of the saint'' and ''the simplicity of the composition'' significantly different from a large painting representing the martyrdom of a saint traditionally identified as Bartholomew in the Prado.[2] Spinosa also dates this London *Martyrdom of Saint Bartholomew* to the last years of Ribera's life; however, he suggests that studio collaboration may account for the unusual modeling of the boy with the knife in the background.[3] Such attempts to date the painting toward the end of Ribera's career are not unreasonable.

In referring to the Pinelli painting as being ''di altra invenzione'' (''of another invention''), De Dominici may have been intending to distinguish it from the *Saint Jerome* in the Spinola collection. Perhaps he also meant to distinguish it from the more familiar compositional format that Ribera used for some of his earlier martyrdoms, such as the *Martyrdom of Saint Bartholomew* (fig. 12) of about 1615-1616 in the Galleria Pallavicini, Rome, and the *Martyrdom of Saint Lawrence* (fig. 17) of about 1620. To be sure, the painting exhibited here is different from these early works.

In contrast to the crowded and rather mannered composition and the stark naturalism of the early *Martyrdom of Saint Bartholomew* in Rome, the London *Martyrdom* is a work of some subtlety. The weight of the semi-nude figure is suspended from the wrists, creating a strong diagonal that counteracts the rising diagonal formed by the horizon line. The figure forcefully projects from the shadows in dramatic isolation against the dark, silvery background. The landscape elements of clouds, mountains, rocks, and trees are lightly sketched. Half shadows as veils of changing light create subtle modulations in the background; as a result, attention is concentrated on the stark reality of the hanging body of Saint Bartholomew.

Ribera's use of the brush in modeling the figure is more fluid than the deliberate technique of his earlier paintings, and is similar to the method found in the two *Saint Jeromes* exhibited here (cat. nos. 29, 32), especially the example from the Fogg Art Museum. In defining the torso, arms, and legs, Ribera swept his brush in broad, curving strokes along the contours of bony protuberances and firm muscle. The top of the head and the brow have been realized with rich texturing of impasto, as in the earlier *God the Father* (cat. no. 13), but the face is painted more freely with a palette that ranges from hot, sunburnt pink along the nose and cheeks, to the palest highlights on the prominences of nose and brow. Touches of deep red in the lines of the brow, around the eyes, and on the cheekbones further accent the forms. The fluffy beard is painted in a broad range of grays and whites with the illusion of hair produced by the actual bristles of the brush itself leaving their marks in the wet paint. The figure of the boy, which is reminiscent of the similar one in the etching of 1624 (fig. 67), is more thinly painted than we might expect, but it is meant to be partially hidden in the shadows. It is possible that the thin earth pigments with which it is painted have sunk, as sometimes occurs in dark areas, and the face has been purposefully subdued by glazes.

A similar range of surfaces and textures is found in the paintings of *Moses* (fig. 27) and *Elijah* (fig. 28), painted in 1638 and placed at the back of the nave at the Certosa di San Martino. Although the face of Elijah is painted in darker tones than that of Moses, the modeling in both is heightened by the addition of small, carefully placed, fine strokes of red and pink which emphasize the textures of the flesh. These characteristics are shared with the figures of the Old Testament *Prophets,* also of 1638 and in the nave at San Martino.

The Gospel of Saint John (I:44-51) relates that the Apostles Philip and Nathaniel came together in Christ; whereas, the other three Gospel writers refer to Philip and Bartholomew. No other certain facts of Bartholomew's existence are known, and the many accounts of his travels in far distant lands are unsubstantiated. Even the story of his martyrdom may not be true, but it had great appeal to seventeenth-century artists and for Counter Reformation imagery. Following the extensive missions in the Near East, Bartholomew is supposed to have gone to Greater Armenia, preaching and converting with extraordinary zeal. There he was captured by barbarians, flayed, and then beheaded at the command of King Astyages. The broken antique head, therefore, has a double meaning. It refers to the idols Saint Bartholomew cast down and also represents the ultimate form of his martyrdom.

NOTES

1. De Dominici, 1742-1744, III, 16. 10 *palmi* 8 would be approximately two meters. Young's catalogue entry is found in London, *In the Light of Caravaggio,* 1976, pp. 43-44.

2. Darby claimed in 1953 that the Prado painting represents the *Martyrdom of Saint Philip,* not that of Saint Bartholomew, an idea with which Spinosa concurs (1978, p. 117, no. 152). The work is signed and dated, the date being alternatively read as 1630 or 1639. Young accepts the earlier date, Trapier equivocates, and Spinosa qualifies the latter reading with a question mark, but places it in the chronology with other works of 1638 to 1640. I agree with the later dating.

3. Spinosa, 1978, p. 123, no. 200.

PROVENANCE: Carlo del Chiano, Florence, 1839; Prince Demidoff, San Donato, 1839; Sale Demidoff, Paris, 3-4 March 1870, no. 200; Monsieur André Marie, Président du Conseil des Ministres, Paris, until late 1975.

BIBLIOGRAPHY: London, *In the Light of Caravaggio,* 1976, pp. 43-44; Spinosa, 1978, p. 123, no. 200, illus.

31

31
Saint John the Baptist
Canvas, 129 x 181 cm (71 x 51 in)
Signed, on rock under the Saint's right foot: *Josephus de Ribera Hispanus Valentin. . ./ Setaben. . ./ Romano Academic. . ./ faciebat*
Painted ca. 1638-1640
Collection of the North Carolina Museum of Art (Original State Appropriation), Raleigh, North Carolina

Saint John the Baptist was particularly important as a subject in art during the Counter Reformation, as were Saint Sebastian and Saint Jerome. Caravaggio painted the subject numerous times; outstanding among his versions is the deeply brooding, melancholy adolescent now in Kansas City (fig. 178), which was painted about 1604-1605. Images of the young Saint John in the desert also appear frequently in Ribera's oeuvre; two are signed and dated 1638 (Madrid, Real Monasterio de la Encarnación, and Barcelona, Private Collection, (fig. 179)). These, along with the undated versions in Poznán (fig. 180) (National Museum) and Madrid (fig. 35) (Prado 1108), seem to date securely from the period of the most intense Bolognese influence upon Ribera's style.[1] The Raleigh painting, although generally dated from about the same time, exhibits some differences from these other works.

The painting by Ribera now in Raleigh is the version nearest to Caravaggio in terms of its intense chiaroscuro; however, the gentleness of the figure and the lighter chromatic range indicate Ribera's freedom from this important early influence. Caravaggio's moody young Saint John the Baptist seems to reveal a deeper, more troubled psychology than Ribera's. The latter's younger boy is free of self-doubts; he seems certain of his mission as he points to the symbolic lamb. His shepherd's staff is the traditional, long, reed Cross which stands out as a solitary form against the sky at the upper right, a suggestion of the future Calvary.

The figure and the very strong contrast of light and shade in this work resemble some of the artist's early paintings. The pose that Ribera has used for Saint John is reminiscent of the one he developed for the Cogolludo *Preparation of Christ for the Cross* (fig. 19) as well as for figures in his etchings. What differentiates this from earlier works is the more certain command of the brush resulting in a subtler modeling of form and gradation of light. The paint surface has been abraded, especially in the dark earth tones, while the areas that contain lead white, the flesh and drapery, are better preserved.

Ribera rarely signed his name in Latin. The inscription on this painting (published here for the first time) is much the same as the ones which appear on the *Drunken Silenus* (cat. no. 6), the *Saint Jerome and the Angel* (fig. 124) in the Hermitage, and, in a more abbreviated form, the *Saint Jerome and the Angel of Judgment* (cat. no. 7). "Hispanus" identifies Ribera as a Spaniard, "Valentin" from Valencia, and "Setaben" as from Játiva, the old Roman name for the

Figure 178
Caravaggio. *Saint John the Baptist,* 1603-1604, William
Rockhill Nelson Gallery of Art, Kansas City

Figure 179
Ribera. *Saint John the Baptist,* 1638, Private
Collection, Barcelona

Figure 180
Ribera. *Saint John the Baptist,* ca. 1638, National
Museum, Poznán

Figure 181
Guido Reni. *Saint John the Baptist in the Wilderness,*
1640-1642, Dulwich College Picture Gallery, London

city of Ribera's birth. Unfortunately, no date has been discovered on this painting. With the exception of the long inscription in Latin which was used on the *Magdalena Ventura* (cat. no. 11), Ribera did not frequently use a Latinized form for his signature, especially one of this expanded format.

In many ways this painting is like the two masterpieces from 1626; however, Bolognese qualities are apparent. The light and silvery tones never approach those of Guido Reni's late *Saint John the Baptist in the Wilderness* (fig. 181) of ca. 1640-1642, now at Dulwich College, but the indications of the style are there. The condition of the Raleigh painting makes dating rather difficult. All the darks have been abraded and are exaggerated by restorations. The figure has also suffered, and the once rich impasto and brushwork are flattened.

NOTE

1. Spinosa, 1978, p. 17, no. 163 (illustration misnumbered as 164).

PROVENANCE: A. W. Leatham, London; North Carolina Museum of Art, 1952, no. 52.9.183.

EXHIBITIONS: London, 1913-1914, no. 185; Oberlin, 1957, p. 75, no. 6, illus.

BIBLIOGRAPHY: Mayer, 1923, p. 23; Valentiner, 1956, no. 217, p. 85; Gaya Nuño, 1958, no. 2416; Spinosa, 1978, p. 117, no. 163, illus.

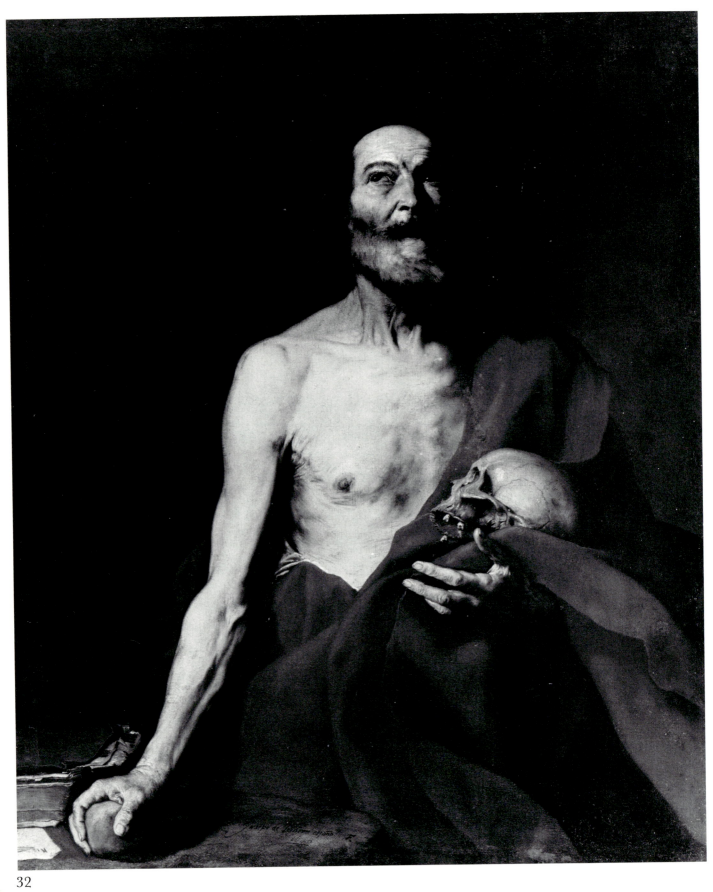

32

32
Saint Jerome

Canvas, 120 x 100 cm (49 x 38⅝ in)
Signed, on the stone, bottom center: *Jusepe de Ribera español , F, / 1640*
The Fogg Art Museum, Harvard University
Cambridge, Massachusetts

The *Saint Jerome* in the Fogg Art Museum and the similar composition in the Louvre are both signed and dated 1640, but the dates of both have sometimes been misread as 1648.[1] The Fogg painting is the finer and better preserved work. It shows the saint in a more frontal, rigid pose than the Cleveland version (cat. no. 29). Saint Jerome's arm is stiff as he clutches the rock of penitence with which he will beat his breast. Beside his fist on the stone ledge are two dog-eared volumes—beautifully painted still-life details placed parallel to the picture plane, unlike the Cleveland version in which the oblique angle of the book adds to the unquiet of the composition. Saint Jerome's left hand, while helping to support the human skull resting in the folds of a red robe, gestures rhetorically in an apparent comment on the brevity of life. (See cat. no. 7 for further details of Jerome's life and the cult of his veneration.)

The surface of this painting is slightly altered by the pattern of the coarsely woven Neapolitan canvas which has generally been impressed into the paint film, but this is a common condition with Ribera's paintings and appreciation of the painting's great finesse is effectively unimpaired. The modeling of the body is extremely subtle, and delicate strokes of the brush have been employed to define the features of the aging torso.

NOTE

1. Spinosa, 1978, pp. 122-123, nos. 197 and 198; Paris (Brejon and Thiébaut), 1981, II, 122, M.N.R. 329. The reading of the date on the Fogg painting as 1640 has been confirmed by that museum's conservation laboratory.

PROVENANCE: Collection Pourtalès, Paris, 1865; Baron Léon Bussières, Paris; Arthur Sachs; gift to the Fogg Art Museum, 1920, no. 1920.7.

EXHIBITIONS: New York (Burroughs), 1928, no. 51, illus. I; Hartford, 1930, no. 45; Iowa State University, 1936; Toledo (Gudiol), 1941, no. 55, illus. p. 88; New York (Durlacher Bros.), 1945; Winnepeg (Eastman), 1951, no. 29; Winnepeg (Eckhardt), 1955, p. 10, no. 4; Oberlin, 1957, p. 75, no. 7, illus.; Sarasota (Gilbert), 1961, no. 12; Indianapolis and Providence (Carter and Peat), 1963, no 67.

BIBLIOGRAPHY: Mayer, 1908, pp. 128, 188; Post, 1922, pp. 15-21, illus.; Gudiol, 1941, p. 18; Darby, 1942, pp. 42-45, fig. 3; Loucheim, 1945, p. 31; Trapier, 1952, p. 169, figs. 116, 117; Ahlborn, 1961, p. 12, illus. p. 13; Spinosa, 1978, pp. 122-123, no. 198, illus.

33 *see color plate*

33

The Clubfooted Boy (Le pied bot)

Canvas, 164 x 92 cm (64⅝ x 36¼ in)
Signed, foreground, bottom right: *Jusepe de Ribera español / ,F, 1642*
Musée du Louvre, Paris

The *Clubfooted Boy,* perhaps Ribera's most famous single painting, was probably commissioned from the artist by Don Ramiro Felipe de Guzmán, Duke of Medina de las Torres and Viceroy of Naples from 1637 to 1644, and his wife.[1]

Many writers have attempted to relate the painting to the tradition of portraits of dwarfs and jesters manifest in various parts of Europe in the sixteenth and seventeenth centuries, which achieved its most brilliant expression in the works of Velázquez.[2] Even within the context of Ribera's own oeuvre, however, the painting sets itself apart from that tradition. Baticle suggested that the *Clubfooted Boy* might be the pendant to the *Dwarf with a Dog* (fig. 182), formerly in the Lederer Collection in Vienna.[3] The latter painting does fall within the tradition of court dwarf portraits, but, as Sullivan has shown, the *Clubfooted Boy* has a clear emblematic significance that sets it apart from such pictures.[4] This meaning also distinguishes the painting from another tradition to which it has frequently been related, that of the *scugnizzo,* or street urchin. Although the child who is portrayed in the painting is both a *scugnizzo* and is physically deformed by his clubfoot and his diseased gums, factors that relate him to Ribera's early drawings and prints of grotesque deformities (figs. 62, 64, 65, 66), his function in this painting is to impress upon us a Christian moral.

Held in the boy's left hand is a *cartellino* inscribed with the Latin words: DA MIHI ELIMOSINAM PROPTER AMOREM DEI ("Give me alms for the love of God"). Such an image of Christian charity was not new in Ribera's oeuvre. The *Blind Beggar and His Boy* (cat. no. 12), executed ten years earlier, was an eloquent representation of it. A half-length image of an old man painted in 1640 and now belonging to the Earl of Derby at Knowsley Hall (fig. 183) also shows a beggar holding a *cartellino* with the inscription VA SENOR MIO COMPATISCA LAVE/CCIA Y U E LE CATIVE ESTADE ("O sir, have pity on this old man [who walks the] difficult road").

As Sullivan rightly points out, these paintings are directly related to the reinforced position of the Catholic Church following the Council of Trent on the subject of the performance of good works as a requisite for salvation. They reflect the belief in man's responsibility for his own destiny in opposition to the Protestant concept of predestination. Sullivan also cites significant parallels with the writings of Saint Francis de Sales and Pierre de Besse, prominent ecclesiast at the court of Louis XIII, whose *Le Démocrite Chrétien* (1615) refers to the laugh as the most Christian of facial expressions because it shows indifference to the trials of earthly existence (see. cat. no. 16).

Figure 182
Ribera. *Dwarf with a Dog,* 1643, ex-Collection
Lederer, Vienna

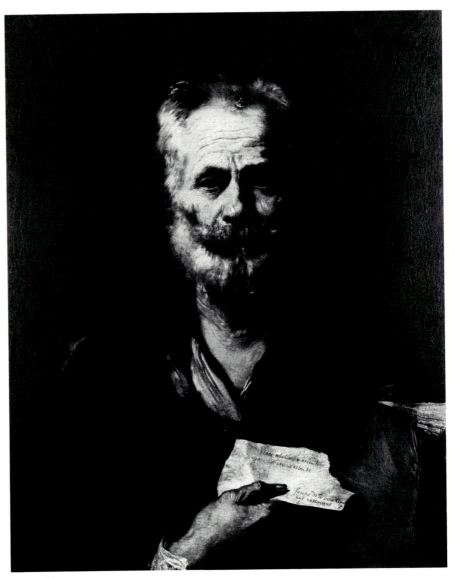

Figure 183
Ribera. *Old Mendicant,* 1640, Collection the Earl of
Derby, Knowsley

In this heroic image of a young cripple, the boy smiles radiantly in complete acceptance of his poverty and of his lot in life as a beggar, for he knows that he will be the instrument by which grace and salvation will come to some generous soul. Appearing to tower above his deformed foot, the smiling boy confidently arches his back and carries his crutch over his shoulder as a soldier carries a musket. It is an image of happiness and an image of triumph—the triumph of poverty.[5]

NOTES

1. Paris (Baticle), 1963, no. 72, pp. 193-195. Baticle was the first to publish this information from an old label on the back of painting: ''Ce tableau sort de la galerie des princes de Stigliano pour lesquels il avait été peint par Ribera,'' As Baticle pointed out, the Duke of Medina de las Torres took as his second wife Ana Carafa Aldobrandini, Princess of Stigliano, in 1637. The inscription, no doubt written many generations later, seems to support the hypothesis, favored by Baticle, that the painting remained in Italy after the Duke's return to Spain and descended through his wife's family.

2. Sullivan, 1977-78, p. 17, reviews this aspect of the literature on the painting.

3. Paris (Baticle), 1963, p. 193.

4. Sullivan, 1977-78, pp. 17-21.

5. Sullivan, 1977-78, p. 20.

PROVENANCE: The Duke and Duchess of Medina de las Torres; Princes of Stigliano, Naples; Dr. Louis La Caze bequest to the Musée du Louvre, 1869, no. 1725.

EXHIBITIONS: Paris, 1849, no. 36; Aix, 1941, p. 203; Montauban, 1942, no. 26; Paris (Baticle), 1963, no. 72; Tokyo, 1966, no. 32, illus.

BIBLIOGRAPHY: MacFall, [n.d.], illus. between pp. 138-139; Raffaelli, [n.d.]; Mantz, 1870, p. 406; Paris (Reiset), 1870, no. 32; Lafond, 1902, pp. 217-227; Paris (Ricci), 1913, no. 1725; Mayer, 1923, pp. 145-146; Paris (Hautecouer), 1926, II, no. 1725; Paris (Nicolle), 1929, pp. 7-8; Ratouis de Limay, 1938, p. 80; Mayer, 1947, p. 300; Sérullaz, 1947, p. 305; Pantorba, 1949, pl. XIX; Trapier, 1952, p. 174, fig. 122; Domínquez, 1953, pp. 80-84; Lafuente Ferrari, 1953, p. 266; Krafft, 1957; Gaya Nuño, 1958, no. 2375, fig. 141; Waterhouse, 1962, p. 178, fig. 153; López-Rey, 1963, p. 335; Paris (Huyghe), 1963, no. 44; Cuoco, 1968; Beguin, 1969, p. 14, no. 2; Constans, 1969, illus. p. 126; Paris (Laclotte), 1970, p. 115; Causa, 1972, p. 927; Spinosa, 1978, pp. 118-119, no. 174, illus.; Sullivan, 1977-1978, pp. 17-21; Chennevieres, 1979, p. 121; Paris (Brejon de Lavergnée and Thiébaut), 1981, p. 122, illus.

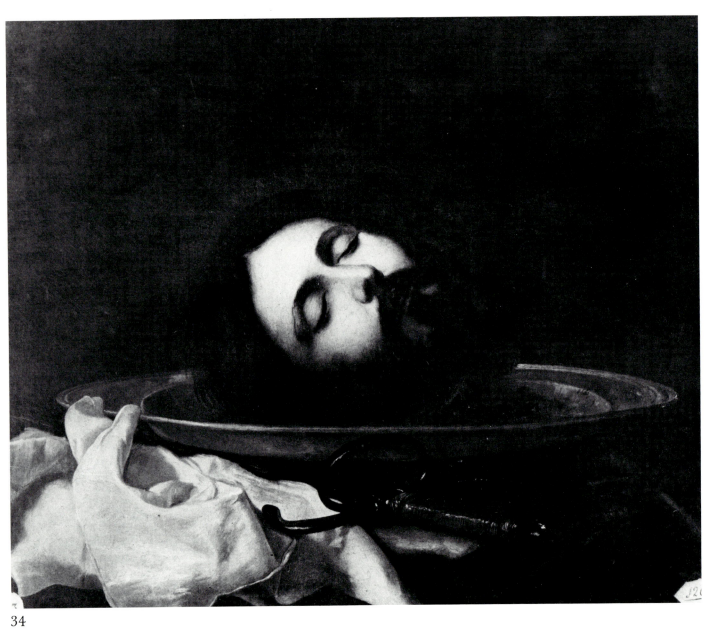

34

Figure 184
Guercino. *Veronica's Veil and the Head of John the Baptist,*
The Art Museum, Princeton University

34

Head of Saint John the Baptist

Canvas, 62 x 73 cm (24⅜ x 28¾ in)

Signed, lower right: *Jusepe de Ribera ,F, / 1644*

Real Academia de Bellas Artes de San Fernando, Madrid

This painting addresses the extremely important issue in Roman Catholicism of the efficacy of relics. Isabel Combs Stuebe has traced the history of the veneration of the head of John the Baptist in the West from the time the relic was brought to Amiens in 1206 from Constantinople, where it had been from the fourth century until the city fell to the Fourth Crusade in 1204.[1] A long tradition of its miraculous healing powers led to its use as a symbol for societies devoted to the sick and infirm. During the Counter Reformation in Spain, one such organization, the Cofradía de San Juan Degollado, founded in Málaga in 1593, also gave aid to the imprisoned. The head of John the Baptist on a charger was also used as a traditional reference to the Holy Eucharist.[2] In a remarkable drawing by Guercino (fig. 184) now in the Princeton University Art Museum, the Head of John the Baptist on a charger is linked with the visage of Christ on Veronica's Veil. The method of depiction was prescribed by Francisco Pacheco in his *Arte de la Pintura* (Seville, 1649), and as Stuebe indicates, his ideas were based on the compositional format established by Leonardo da Vinci about 1506[3] and elaborated by Andrea Solario shortly thereafter.[4] Artists in the seventeenth century also follow this design; an important example for the transition to the Baroque is the painting by Domenichino (fig. 185), now in the Academia de San Fernando, Madrid, painted in the 1630s.[5] Valdés Leal's treatment of the subject, dating from 1658 (Córdoba, Monastery of the Carmelitas Calzados), is very similar to that of Ribera.[6]

This is the earliest of three known versions of the subject painted by Ribera and is perhaps the one inventoried at El Escorial in December 1700.[7] A composition dated 1647, in reverse and with some variation, is in the Museo Civico Gaetano Filangieri, Naples (fig. 186).[8] The third painting, which differs only slightly from the Naples version, is privately owned in Milan.[9] Other versions of the subject are recorded in documents but cannot today be associated with any known paintings.[10]

Despite the potential inherent in the subject for nightmarish gore, Ribera achieves a subtle balance between graphic representation and spiritual transposition. The Baptist's face is serene; his dark beard, continuing the curving lines of his hair, enframes the face. The focus of attention is thus drawn away from the severed neck and concentrates on the idealized and reposeful features. The head lies on the metal charger beside the hilt of the great sword used to accomplish the act of sacrifice. The bloody blade is concealed by a luminous white cloth at the left. In the shadows at the right is a small reed cross. The darkness of the ambiance holds these objects in absolute stillness, and, somehow, the bright illumination seems to convey their miraculous power.

Figure 185
Domenichino. *Head of Saint John the Baptist,* 1630s,
Real Academia de Bellas Artes de San Fernando,
Madrid

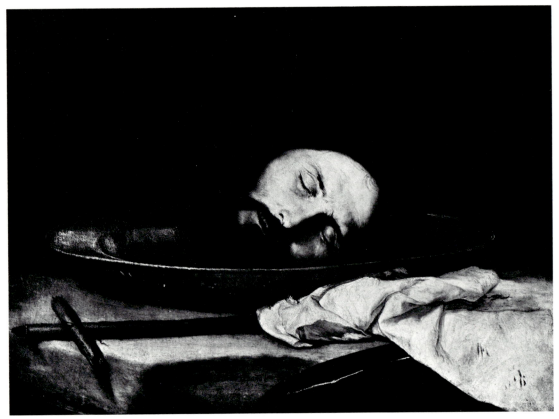

Figure 186
Ribera. *Head of Saint John the Baptist,* 1647, Museo
Civico Gaetano Filangieri, Naples   (Alinari)

The surface of this painting has been badly abraded. Although its state of preservation is less good than the Naples version, its intrinsic qualities are of the same high order.

NOTES

1. Steube, 1968-1969, pp. 1-16.

2. Steube, 1968-1969, pp. 6-7.

3. Copy after Leonardo da Vinci, *Head of Saint John the Baptist.* Collection Albizzi, Domenico di Fiesole; Steube, 1968-1969, fig. 11, see also p. 10.

4. Andrea Solario, *Head of Saint John the Baptist.* Louvre, Paris; Steube, 1968-1969, fig. 9.

5. Pérez Sánchez, 1965, p. 125; 1970, pp. 216-217; no. 64. Spear, 1968, p. 16, fig. 15, pl. 19a.

6. Steube, 1968-1969, fig. 13; Trapier, 1960, fig. 48.

7. Archivo de Palacio, Madrid, Registro 242, fol. 123v-124v.

8. Spinosa, 1978, p. 122, no. 191.

9. Spinosa, 1978, p. 122, no. 191a.

10. These include 1) Collection of the Elector of Brandenburg in 1672, authenticated by Rembrandt's brother-in-law, Gerrit Uylenburgh (Trapier, 1952, p. 249); 2) Alcázar of Madrid in 1686 (Trapier, 1952, pp. 237-238); 3) in the collection of the Count of Pineda in 1697 (Trapier, 1952, p. 283, n. 195); 4) Collection of the Count of Monterrey in 1653 (Pérez Sánchez, 1970, p. 432, no. 36).

PROVENANCE: El Escorial (Inventory of 1700); Real Academia de Bellas Artes de San Fernando, Madrid.

BIBLIOGRAPHY: Ximénez, 1764; Mayer, 1923, p. 198; Madrid (Labrada), 1965, no. 630, p. 72; Spinosa, 1978, p. 121, no. 185, illus.

35

35

Madonna and Child

Canvas, 69.8 x 60 cm (27 ½ x 23 ⅝ in)
Signed, lower center left: *Jusepe de Ribe^{ra} / español acade / mico Roma^{no} / , F, 164(?)*
Philadelphia Museum of Art: William L. Elkins Collection
Philadelphia, Pennsylvania

As noted by Trapier and others, the pose of this small devotional image calls to mind the works of Raphael; Justi saw the source as the *Madonna della Sedia*, and Darby the *Madonna del Popolo*.[1] Indeed, toward the middle of the seventeenth century, there was a renewed interest in such images of maternal affection which had been developed to a high level of sophistication in the High Renaissance. Ribera depicted the Madonna and Child on few other occasions, whereas many painters of a younger generation would make something of a specialty of the subject in the second half of the century.

Spinosa has noted the close relationship between the figure of the Virgin in this painting and her counterpart in the *Mystical Marriage of Saint Catherine of Alexandria* of 1648 in the Metropolitan Museum of Art (cat. no. 36). To understand the relationship of the two paintings it would help to know the exact date of the Philadelphia painting; previous readings favored various dates, with 1648 as the most likely.[2] Recent microscopic examination by the staff of the Philadelphia Museum has suggested 1646.

While the inclination of the Virgin's head is similar to that in the figure in the Metropolitan painting and the faces of the two Marys conform to a single idealized type, the relationship of the figures of the Madonna and Christ Child in each case is completely different. In the affectionate embrace of the two forms, the analogy to Raphael is manifest.

As Trapier pointed out, it is likely that this painting has been reduced somewhat at the bottom, if not on all sides.

NOTES

1. Trapier, 1952, pp. 180-181, fig. 123.

2. Spinosa, 1978, pp. 121-122, no. 195.

PROVENANCE: Princess of Fondi, Naples, as of 1877 (?); George Donaldson, since 1895; William L. Elkins, Philadelphia; gift to Philadelphia Museum of Art, no. E. 24.3.54.

EXHIBITIONS: Naples, 1877; London, 1895-1896, no. 55-1, illus. p. 11; Bordeaux, 1955, no. 48; Buffalo, 1957; Oberlin, 1957, p. 75, no. 8.

BIBLIOGRAPHY: Sedelmeyer, 1896, no. 76; Philadelphia, 1900, no. 120, illus.; Darby, 1946, p. 155, fig. 1; Trapier, 1952, pp. 179-182, fig. 123; Gaya Nuño, 1958, no. 2379; Spinosa, 1978, pp. 121-122, no. 195, illus.

36 *see color plate*

36

The Mystical Marriage of Saint Catherine of Alexandria
Canvas, 209.6 x 154.3 cm (82½ x 60¾ in)
Signed, on stone ledge seat, lower right: *Jusepe de Ribera español / accademico R.o.^{no} / , F, 1648*
Lent by The Metropolitan Museum of Art
Samuel D. Lee Fund, 1934, New York

A unique subject in Ribera's oeuvre, this large work is not only one of his finest late canvases, it is also one of the masterpieces of his entire career. Combining the most refined, classicizing elegance with a hard visual scrutiny, it unites in apparent harmony the two predominant currents in Ribera's art. Ribera has infused the intricate relationships of the forms with simplicity and rhythmic grace, and the pervading mood is one of peace and tranquility.

The theme of the Mystical Marriage of Saint Catherine was a favorite one in the Baroque era. Born in Alexandria, Catherine was the daughter of Costis, half-brother of the Roman Emperor Constantine the Great, who was married to Sabinella, Queen of Egypt. As a child she was known for her intellectual achievements and her pious nature. Eventually, her subjects urged her to marry in order that the royal line be continued, but she demurred, expressing her intention to wait for the most perfect of all men. In a dream, Catherine had a vision of the Virgin holding the Christ Child in her arms; the Virgin asked the Child to take Catherine as his servant, but he averted his head and refused, saying that she was not beautiful enough. Following this, Catherine sought out a hermit in the mountains who instructed her in the Christian faith and baptized her. After her baptism, Christ appeared to her again in a dream and took her as his celestial spouse, placing a ring on her finger which she found on awakening and kept for the rest of her life. Eventually, Catherine was subjected to torture and martyrdom for refusing to renounce her faith and sacrifice to the idols. That well-known episode in her life has also been frequently depicted.

Ribera has skillfully characterized the Christ Child—he is capable of withdrawing his hand and turning away as he did before—in the moment of deciding to favor the beautiful princess. Catherine (fig. 187) kneels in adoration at the feet of the gentle Madonna (fig. 188) who solemnly presents her Child to his spiritual bride. Catherine's elegant, exquisitely modeled hand takes the chubby hand of the Infant and lifts it to her lips. At the moment of mystical union, the Virgin looks knowingly out at the viewer. Saint Joseph also looks into our space but not into our eyes. Saint Anne approaches the Infant Christ with a basket of fruit, holding delicately in her hand a thorny rose, the familiar symbol of Christ's Passion. On the floor, under the projecting stone ledge on which the Virgin is seated, is a wicker sewing basket containing an orange cloth, a white cloth, and a large pillow usually associated with needlework and domestic responsibilities.

Figure 187
Ribera. *Saint Catherine,* (detail of cat. no. 36)

Figure 188
Ribera. *Madonna and Child,* (detail of cat. no. 36)

A recent cleaning undertaken by Mr. John Brealey and the staff of the painting conservation department at the Metropolitan Museum of Art has restored the intensity and radiance of the colors of this painting. The elegant silver gown and white mantle worn by Saint Catherine shimmer with luminous accents applied with a fine brush. Shadows are created with glazes containing traces of deep color—for example, a plum tone on the silver sleeve. Saint Catherine's translucent veil, which has slipped to her shoulders, is painted with a thin film of ochre accented by darker ochre lines along its border. This color reinforces the dominant golden tone of the flowing robe which has a slight damask pattern in the weave and is modeled in deep, sculptural folds. The phenomenal luminous blue of the Virgin's robe is the chromatic climax of the composition.

PROVENANCE: Private collection, Genoa, until 1807/1808; Jean-Baptiste-Pierre Le Brun, Paris, from 1807/1808 to after 1810; Sir Thomas Baring, 2nd Bart., Stratton Park, Southampton, Hampshire, by 1824-d. 1848; Thomas Baring, M.P. for Huntingdon, 1848-d. 1873; Thomas George Baring, 1st Earl of Northbrook, Stratton Park, 1873-d. 1904; Francis George Baring, 2nd Earl of Northbrook, Stratton Park, 1904-1919; sale, 2nd Earl of Northbrook, December 12, 1919, Christie's London, no. 134; with Colnaghi, London, 1919-1921; Henry George Charles Lascelles, Viscount Lascelles, later 6th Earl of Harewood, London, 1921-1934; with Arnold Seligmann, Rey and Co.; Paris and New York, 1934; the Metropolitan Museum of Art, 1934, Samuel D. Lee Fund, no. 34.73.

EXHIBITIONS: London. British Institution, 1828, no. 51; London. Royal Academy, Winter Exhibition, 1872, no. 97; London, 1895-96, no. 61; London. Magnasco Society, 1925; New York, 1940, no. 115; Boston, 1970; New York, 1953, no. 125; New York, 1971, no. 1.

BIBLIOGRAPHY: Le Brun, 1809, II, pp. 18f., pl. 128; Buchanan, 1824, II, 251, 255; Waagen, 1838, III, 39; Waagen, 1854, p. 180; Richter, 1889, pp. 182f., no. 237, illus.; Justi, 1889, p. 320; Woermann, 1890, p. 179; Mayer, 1908, pp. 117-119, pl. XXXIV and 1923, pp. 118f.; Lafond, 1902, p. 69; Mayer, 1922, p. 274, pl. 203; "The Magnasco Society," Apollo, 1925, p. 297, illus. p. 298; "The Metropolitan Museum Buys Well Known Canvas by Ribera," Art News, 1934, p. 12; Wehle, 1934, pp. 119-122; Toledo, Ohio (Gudiol), 1941, p. 86, illus. pl. 56; Berger, 1943, illus. pp. 20f.; Darby, 1946, pp. 160, 163, 167, 168-170, fig. 4; New York, 1952-1953, p. 230, no. 125, illus. p. 125; Trapier, 1952, pp. 179, 205f., figs. 134-136; Gaya Nuño, 1958, no. 2396, illus. VIII; Kubler and Soria, 1959, p. 242, pl. 126; Waterhouse, 1962, p. 180, fig. 154; Gállego, 1962, p. 107, illus. p. 88; Fahy, 1971, p. 457, illus.; Angulo Iñiquez, 1971, p. 109; Washington, D. C. (Shaw), 1972, p. 70; Haskell, 1976, p. 20, pl. 35; Spinosa, 1978, p. 122, no. 194, illus.

37

37
Saint John the Baptist
Canvas, 73 x 99 cm (28 ¾ x 39 in)
Signed, above sheep's head, lower left: *Jusepe de Ribera / español / ,F, 1650*
The Wellington Museum, Apsley House, London

This painting of *Saint John the Baptist,* once in the Spanish royal collection, was with the plunder captured in the baggage of Joseph Bonaparte after the battle of Vitoria in 1813. It became part of a sizable gift of works of art made by the restored King Ferdinand VII to the Duke of Wellington following the liberation of the Iberian peninsula. During the course of a nineteenth-century restoration, necessitated perhaps because of damage resulting from the military campaign, the size of the painting may have been reduced and its signature and date tampered with. This is the explanation proposed by Spinosa for the observation that the painting's style is at odds with the date of 1650 that is inscribed on it.[1]

The somewhat cramped feeling of the composition may indicate that the painting was once larger. It might even have represented a full-length figure. The modeling of the figure, his sheepskin garment, and the red drapery are similar to those found in the large canvas of the subject in the Convent of the Encarnación in Madrid, signed and dated 1638. The orientation of the figure in the Apsley House *Saint John* is more erect than that in the Encarnación canvas. Both, however, make use of a large tree trunk cutting diagonally across the background landscape. This same feature characterizes the large *Saint John* (Prado no. 1108) (fig. 35), to which Spinosa compares the Apsley House work and which resembles it in other matters of style. It also is a structure and motif used in the London *Jacob and the Flock* (cat. no. 27), which is signed and dated 1638. It is possible that the conception of this painting actually dates from around 1640 rather than 1650.

NOTE

1. Spinosa, 1978, pp. 117-118, no. 164 (illustration misnumbered as 163).

PROVENANCE: In 1789, in the Oratory, Royal Palace, Madrid; captured by the Duke of Wellington after the Battle of Vitoria in the baggage of Joseph Bonaparte; the Duke offered to return it with other captured booty to the Spanish Royal Collections, but Ferdinand VII presented it to the Duke; Dukes of Wellington, Apsley House, London, no. 115; in 1947, Apsley House and part of the contents, including this painting, were presented by the 7th Duke of Wellington to the British Nation; Wellington Museum, Apsley House, no. 1627.

BIBLIOGRAPHY: London (The Wellington Museum), [n.d.], I, xiv-xv, 108-109, no. 115; Mayer, 1923, p. 198; London, 1952; pp. 3, 28-29, and supplement, p. vi, no. 1627; Gaya Nuño, 1958, no. 2400; London (Gibbs-Smith, C.H. and H.V.T. Percival), 1964, p. 45, no. 1627; Spinosa, 1978, pp. 117-118, no. 164, illus.

38 *see color plate*

38

Saint Sebastian

Canvas, 121 x 100 cm (47⅝ x 39⅜ in)
Signed, on rock, lower left: *Jusepe de Ribera / ,F, 1651*
Museo e Gallerie Nazionali di Capodimonte, Naples

The subject of Saint Sebastian has always provided artists with the opportunity and challenge of representing the almost nude male body. With the advent of the Renaissance and its embrace of the antique canon of ideal beauty, pictures and statues of Saint Sebastian became a measure of an artist's command of classical formal language. Because of the Counter Reformation's stress on martyred saints and Sebastian's special position as the saint invoked against the plague (believed in ancient times to be brought on by Apollo's arrows), the subject was in demand by Ribera's clients. He painted it several times—from the early picture at Osuna (cat. no. 4) to this last one dated the year before his death. In making it something of a specialty, adapting it to the advantages of his own naturalistic style, he realized some of the most theatrical paintings of his career and some of the most breathtaking images of martyrdom painted in the Baroque era.

Sebastian was born in Narbonne, the son of a noble Roman family from Milan, and was a member of the Praetorian Guard under the Emperor Diocletian (A.D. 284-305). The young man served the emperor with honor and distinction, but he was a clandestine Christian in this reign of severe persecution. When Sebastian's faith was revealed, Diocletian, with deep regret, ordered him to be bound to a stake and shot to death with arrows. Later, Irene, widow of the martyred Saint Castulus, went to obtain Sebastian's body, only to discover that he was still alive. Upon regaining his health, Sebastian returned to the palace to plead for the Christian cause. The emperor, an avowed enemy of Christianity, ordered him to be clubbed to death and his body to be thrown into the sewer of Rome.[1]

Saint Sebastian seems to have occupied Ribera's thoughts frequently in the decade of the 1620s when he produced at least six drawings of the saint in various poses (fig. 52) and an etching (fig. 50) which Brown dates to ca. 1620.[2]

The grand composition of *Saint Sebastian Cured by Saint Irene* in Leningrad is signed and dated 1628 (fig. 189) and represents a tremendous advance over the rather stiff version at Osuna. Left for dead, the limp body of the young man, his head thrown back, hangs heavily from his wrist, which is still tied to a tree. The attendant figures of Irene and her servant are barely visible in the shadows, while the blazing light drenches the body of the martyr in the foreground. Eight years later, Ribera created another masterpiece in the large, single-figure composition of *Saint Sebastian* formerly in the Kaiser Friedrich Museum in Berlin, which was tragically destroyed in World War II (fig. 190).

One of the most dramatic paintings of Ribera's entire oeuvre, there is an almost uncomfortable and rather morbid sensuousness about this athletic figure tied by the wrists, fainting, and near death.

The half-length *Saint Sebastian* today in the Museo di Capodimonte was painted for the Certosa di San Martino where it accompanied a *Saint Jerome,* also dated 1651 (fig. 47). Trapier stated that both paintings may be associated with works of those subjects, mentioned in a document of 1638 as pictures for which the monks owed the artist money.[3] However, the document she refers to is an undated summary statement written after 1651 incorporating all of the work done by Ribera for the Certosa. Following a suit filed by the Ribera heirs against the Certosa on December 12, 1652, the monks drew up a counter statement in which they summarized the commission awarded to the painter by Giovanni Battista Pisante, Prior of the Certosa (d. 1638). The *Saint Jerome* (fig. 47) and the *Saint Sebastian* are recorded as part of this same large commission for which Ribera had received satisfactory payment before his death.[4] Although perhaps begun as early as 1638, both paintings, like the massive *Communion of the Apostles (Institution of the Holy Eucharist)* (fig. 49), may have remained unfinished until 1651. To be sure, the design of this *Saint Sebastian,* with its strong diagonal orientation and atmospheric openness, relates to other compositions from the late 1630s and early 1640s. Because the painting bears the date of 1651, however, it is not possible to know just how much of the work he actually did at an earlier date.[5]

The saint's form is mostly silhouetted against the dark form of the tree trunk. The modeling of his body is extremely subtle, and the sense of space is enhanced by the gradual transition between the darks of the shadows, which never completely "devour" the form, and the lights of the sky. The clear blue of the sky provides a chromatic balance to the warmth of the flesh tones. The white of his loincloth is beautifully handled, and the bark of the tree stump in the right foreground adds visual and textural interest.

Figure 190
Ribera. *Saint Sebastian,* 1636, [destroyed] Kaiser
Friedrich Museum, Berlin

NOTES

1. Butler, 1981, I, 128-130.

2. Brown, 1973, etching no. 1; drawings nos. 6, 10, 12, 13, 17, 19; see also Brown, 1972, pp. 2-7.

3. Trapier, 1952, p. 225.

4. Faraglia, 1892, pp. 675-676. The history is found in Archivio di Stato, *Monasteri soppressi,* 2142, f. 40; Conti del Giuseppe di Ribera P. Horo. Published in Faraglia, 892, p. 670.

5. As regards the signature, it is curious that the ''6'' of the date is reversed— something that occurs on no other painting by Ribera.

PROVENANCE: Painted for the Certosa di San Martino, Naples, removed in 1806; Pinacoteca del Museo Nazionale, Naples; Museo e Gallerie Nazionali di Capodimonte.

BIBLIOGRAPHY: Mayer, 1923, pp. 163-164; Naples (De Rinaldis), 1928, p. 266, no. 312; Trapier, 1952, pp. 225-227, fig. 149; Brin, 1957, pp. 382-384, illus.; Gaya Nuño, 1958, no. 2408; Naples (Molajoli), 1964, p. 52, fig. 69; Causa, 1972, p. 283, illus.; Spinosa, 1978, pp. 123-124, no. 203, illus.

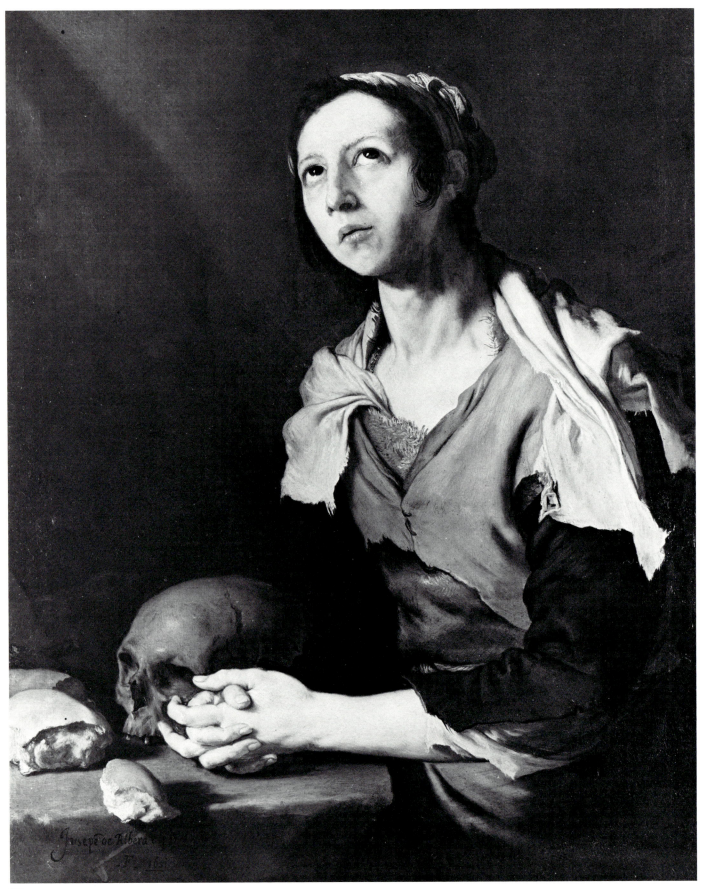

39

39

Saint Mary of Egypt

Canvas, 88 x 71 cm (34 ⅝ x 27 ⅞ in)
Signed, lower right on stone ledge: *Jusepe de Ribera español / ,F, 1651*
Museo Civico Gaetano Filangieri, Naples

During the fifth century, disciples of the ascetic Saint Cyriacus discovered a
naked old woman living in the desert. A legend soon formed around the simple
story she told them. At the age of twelve, Mary, as she was called, ran away
from her parents and went to Alexandria where she lived as a prostitute for
seventeen years. One day, hearing about a pilgrimage to Jerusalem, she decided
to follow along for the adventure of the journey. When her fellow pilgrims
entered a church at Jerusalem for the feast of the Holy Cross, Mary's way was
barred by a supernatural force. Shocked and overcome by remorse for her life
of sin, she vowed to reform her ways and asked an image of the Virgin to
sustain her in her pledge to spend the remainder of her life in penance. She
heard a voice which said, ''Go across the River Jordan and thou shalt find
rest,'' and she crossed over to live in the desert, having bought three loaves of
bread to serve as her only sustenance. More than forty years later, the holy
monk Zosimus found her, and she asked him to bring her communion. The
great width of the river prevented him from reaching her, however. Thereupon,
aided by supernatural powers, she walked across the water to receive the Holy
Eucharist and began to recite the *Nunc dimittis.* A year later, Zosimus returned
at Mary's request so that she might take communion again, but he found her
dead with an inscription written in the sand asking him to bury her body.
Mary of Egypt epitomized the hermit saints who turned their backs on the
decadence of Rome and embraced a life of penance in the early Christian era.
Their examples were paramount among the reverential priorities of the
Counter Reformation Church. Ribera depicted Mary of Egypt on several
occasions.[1]

Ribera has shown Saint Mary as a woman of about thirty years of age, her age
at the time of her conversion, dressed in the ragged clothing of a penitent. Her
hands are clasped, and her gaze directed Heavenward. A skull rests beside her
hands as a reminder of death, and the three crusts of bread which nourished
her in the desert are beautifully modeled by the strong light that falls from the
left. Traditionally, the model for this painting was thought to be Ribera's eldest
daughter Margarita, who was born in 1630. Margarita's husband, Giovanni
Leonardo Sersale held a government appointment in Lecce. When he died
suddenly in September of 1651, Margarita returned to Naples where, in
October, she was delivered of a posthumous child. The child lived only a few
hours. Most likely, the twenty-one year old Margarita, whose beauty was
legendary, did not really pose for this painting.

The *Saint Mary of Egypt* is one of the technical triumphs of Ribera's late career.
The paint surface, which is in superior condition, demonstrates the artist's

secure command of the brush despite his protestations of age and illness in letters written to the monks of the Certosa di San Martino during the summer of 1651. The tight control of the thick, oily paint used for the drapery is reminiscent of the *Philosophers* of the 1630s, especially the Wilton *Democritus* (cat. no. 16). The subtle gradations in the patterns of light and dark are carefully modulated to produce the greatest effect of naturalism. Particularly fine passages occur in the creamy, mellow white of the ragged scarf about Saint Mary's shoulders.

NOTE

1. See Spinosa, 1978, nos. 161, 166.

PROVENANCE: Duke of Miranda, Naples; Museo Civico Gaetano Filangieri, Naples.

EXHIBITIONS: Florence, Palazzo Vecchio, 1911; Florence (Tarchiani), 1922, p. 153, no. 820; Bergamo (Ojetti), 1924, p. 171, illus.; San Casciano Val di Pesa (Nugent), 1930, II, 21-24; Naples, Palazzo Reale, 1954, p. 21, no. 22; Bucharest (Causa and Spinosa), 1972; London (Whitfield and Martineau), 1982, p. 233, no. 130, illus.

BIBLIOGRAPHY: Naples (Filangieri), 1888, p. 308; Frizzoni, 1889, 293-300; Filangieri, 1891, 342; Ceci, 1894, 65-67; Rolfs, 1910, p. 305; Rusconi, 1911, X, 1-32, illus.; Tarchiani, 1911, XI, 77-92; Marangoni, 1922, p. 22; Giglioli, 1922, pp. 201-231; Mayer, 1923, pp. 84-85, 199-200, illus.; Tarchiani, 1927, p. 171, illus.; Born, 1945, XXVII, 213-226; British War Office Reports, 1946, pp. 80-81; Trapier, 1952, pp. 211-212, 215, 217, illus.; Bénézit, 1956 ed., VII, 211; Gaya Nuño, 1958, no. 2409; Naples (Acton), 1961, p. 31; Spinosa, 1978, pp. 124-124, no. 206.

VERSIONS: Museum of Art, Bucharest

BIBLIOGRAPHY

Ahlborn, R. E. "Ribera at Joslyn," *Joslyn Society of Liberal Arts, Annual Report,* Omaha, Nebraska, (1961), pp. 12-13.

Ainaud de Lasarte, Juan. "Ribalta y Caravaggio," *Anales y Boletín de los Museos de Arte de Barcelona,* (1947), pp. 345-413.

Ainaud de Lasarte, Juan. "Pintura española del siglo de oro en Burdeos," *Goya,* 70-72 (1955-1956), pp. 115-119.

Aix. *Caravage et le Caravagisme Européen,* II. 1941.

Angulo Iñiquez, Diego. *"The Blind Old Beggar* by Ribera," *Allen Memorial Art Museum Bulletin,* Oberlin College, 14 (Winter 1957), pp. 59-62.

Angulo Iñiquez, Diego, *Ars Hispaniae, XV: Pintura del Siglo XVII.* Madrid, 1971.

Baccheschi, Edi and Cesare Garboli. *L'Opera completa di Guido Reni.* Milan, 1971.

Baldinucci, Filippo. *Notizie dei professori del disegno.* I, fol. 129, (1681) ed. Florence, 1846.

Barbier de Montault, Xavier. *Les musées et galeries de Rome.* Rome, 1870.

Barcia, Angel M. de, *Catálogo de la colección de pinturas del Excmo. Sr. Duque de Berwick y de Alba.* Madrid, 1911.

Barnard Castle (Ellis, Tony). *Neapolitan Baroque and Rococo Painting.* Bowes Museum, June 1–August 12, 1962.

Barnard Castle (Young, Eric). *Four Centuries of Spanish Painting.* Bowes Museum, 1967.

Baticle, Jeannine and Cristina Marinas. *La Galerie Espagnole de Louis-Philippe au Louvre.* Paris, 1981.

Bazin, Germain. *Trésors de la peinture au Louvre.* Paris, 1957.

Beguin, Sylvie. "Hommage à Louis La Caze,' *Revue du Louvre,* 2 (1969), p. 14.

Bénézit, E. *Dictionnaire critique et documentaire des Peintres, Sculpteurs, Dessinateurs et Graveurs.* Paris, 1956.

Bergamo (Ojetti, U., N. Tarchiarni, and L. Dani). *La pittura italiana del seicento e del settecento all 'mostra di Palazzo Pitti.* Milan, Rome, 1924.

Berger, Klaus. "Courbet in his Century," *Gazette des Beaux-Arts,* ser. 6, 24 (1943), pp. 19-40.

Beroqui, Pedro. *El Museo del Prado. (Notas para su historia).* Madrid, 1933.

"Bibliografía," *Archivo Español de Arte,* 30 (1957), p. 344.

Bissell, R. Ward. *Orazio Gentileschi and the Poetic Tradition in Caravaggesque Painting.* University Park, 1981.

Bodart, Didier. *Louis Finson.* Brussels, 1970.

Bordeaux (Martín-Méry, Gabriele). *L'Age d'or espagnole, La peinture en Espagne et en France autour du Caravagisme.* Musée des Beaux-Arts, 1955.

Born, Wolfgang. "An Unknown Work of Ribera in St. Louis, Missouri: *Christ Crowned with Thorns,* " *Gazette des Beaux-Arts,* 27 (1945), pp. 213-226.

Boschloo, A. W. A. *Annibale Carracci in Bologna, Visible Reality in Art after the Council of Trent.* The Hague, 1974.

Bottari, Giovanni Gaetano and Stefano Ticozzi. *Raccolta di lettere sulla pittura, scultura ed architettura.* Milan, 1822-1825.

Bottari, Stefano. *Storia dell'arte italiana.* II, Milan, 1943.

Bottineau, I. "L'Alcázar de Madrid et l'inventaire de 1686," *Bulletin Hispanique,* 60 (1958), p. 325.

Bousquet, Jacques. *Recherches sur le séjour des peintres francais à Rome au 17 ème.* Montpellier, 1980.

Brin, Irene. "Crónica de Roma: El nuevo museo nacional y las galerias de Capodimonte," *Goya,* 18 (1957), pp. 382-384.

British War Office. *Reports.* 1946.

Brown, Jonathan. "Note on Princeton Drawings 6: Jusepe de Ribera," *Record of The Art Museum, Princeton University,* 31 (1972), pp. 2-7.

Brown, Jonathan. *Jusepe de Ribera: Prints and Drawings.* Princeton, 1973.

Brown, Jonathan. "More Drawings by Jusepe de Ribera," *Master Drawings,* 12 (1974), pp. 367-372.

Brown, Jonathan and J. H. Elliott. *A Palace for a King, The Buen Retiro and the Court of Philip IV.* New Haven, 1980.

Brussels. *Le portrait espagnol du XIVe au XIXe siècle.* Palais des Beaux-Arts, 1970.

Buchanan, William. *Memoirs of Painting.* London, 1824.

Bucharest (Causa, Raffaello and Nicola Spinosa). *Seculul de aur al picturii napolitane.* 1972.

Buck, Richard D. "Oberlin's Ribera: A Case History," *Allen Memorial Art Museum Bulletin,* Oberlin College, 14 (Winter 1957), pp. 62-69.

Buffalo, New York. *Trends in Painting, 1600-1800.* Albright-Knox Gallery, 1957.

Butler, Alban. *Lives of the Saints.* Westminster (Maryland), 1981.

Causa, Raffaello. *Pittura napoletana dal XV al XIX secolo.* Bergamo, 1957.

Causa, Raffaello. *Opere d'arte nel Pio Monte della Misericordia.* Naples, 1970.

Causa, Raffaello. *La pittura del seicento a Napoli dal naturalismo al barocco.* Reprint in *Storia di Napoli,* 5, (1972).

Causa, Raffaello. *L'Arte nella Certosa di San Martino a Napoli.* Naples, 1973.

Cavestany, J. *Floreros y bodegones en la pintura española.* Madrid, 1939-1940.

Ceán-Bermúdez, Juan Augustín. *Diccionario histórico de los más ilustres profesores de las bellas artes en España.* Madrid, 1800.

Ceci, Giuseppe. "La figlia dello Spagnoletto," *Napoli Nobilissima,* 3 (1894), pp. 65-67.

Ceci, Giuseppe. "Scrittori della storia dell'arte napoletana anteriori al de Dominici," *Napoli Nobilissima,* 8 (1899), pp. 163-168.

Ceci, Giuseppe. "Un mercante mecanate del secolo XVII: Gaspare Roomer," *Napoli Nobilissima,* n.s. 1 (1920), pp. 160-164.

Celano, Carlo. *Notizie del bello, dell'antico e del curioso dell città di Napoli.* (1692) ed. Chiarini, G. B., Naples, 1859.

Chenault, Jeanne. "'Ribera in Roman Archives," *The Burlington Magazine,* 111 (September 1969), pp. 561-562.

Chenault, Jeanne. "Ribera, Ovid, and Marino: *Death of Adonis,"* *Paragone,* 259 (1971), pp. 68-67.

Chenault, Jeanne, "Jusepe de Ribera and the Order of Christ: New Documents," *The Burlington Magazine,* 118 (May 1976), pp. 304-307.

Chenault Porter, Jeanne. "Ribera's Assimilation of a Silenus," *Paragone,* 355 (1979), pp. 41-54.

Chennevieres, Philippe de. "Souvenir d'un directeur des Beaux Arts," *L'Artiste 1888-1889,* Paris, 1979.

Cleveland (Spear, Richard). *Caravaggio and His Followers.* Cleveland Museum of Art, October 27, 1971–January 2, 1972.

Cleveland. *Catalogue of Paintings. Part 3: European Paintings, 16th, 17th, and 18th Centuries.* Cleveland Museum of Art, 1982.

Cleveland. *Cleveland Museum of Art Handbook.* 1978.

Cleveland. *Year in Review.* 1961.

Colonna di Stigliani, Ferdinando. "Inventario dei quadri di Casa Colonna, fatto da Luca Giordano," *Napoli Nobilissima,* 4 (1895), pp. 29-32.

Columbia, South Carolina (Contini-Bonacossi, Alessandro). *Art of the Renaissance, from the Samuel H. Kress Collection. The Columbia Museum of Art, Columbia, South Carolina.* 1962.

Coniglio, Giuseppe. *I vicere spagnoli di Napoli.* Naples, 1967.

Constans, Claire. "Catalogue," *Revue du Louvre,* 19 (1969), p. 126.

Cranford Manor. *A Catalogue of the Pictures at Cranford Manor in the Possession of Lord Wimborne.* London, 1888.

Crombie, Theodore. "Naples in the North," *Apollo,* n.s. 77 (1962), p. 396.

Cuoco, Alina and C. Alegret. *Jusepe de Ribera* (Collection *Chefs d'Oeuvre de l'Art).* Paris, 1968.

Czobor, Agnes. *"The Five Senses* by the Antwerp Artist Jacob de Backer," *Nederlands Kunthistorisch Jaarboek,* 23 (1972), pp. 317-327.

D'Afflitto, Luigi. *Guida . . . di Napoli.* Naples, 1834.

D'Amico, Rosa. *Catálogo generale della raccolta di stampe Antiche della Pinacoteca Nazionale di Bologna, Gabinetto delle Stampe. Sezione VII, Incizioni d'invenzione romani e napoletani del XVII secolo.* Bologna, 1978.

Danvila Jaldero, Augusto. "Reseña crítica des las obras de José Ribera, el Spagnoletto," *Revista de España,* 120 (1888), pp. 162-210.

Darby, Delphine Fitz. *Francisco Ribalta and His School.* Cambridge (Massachusetts), 1938.

Darby, Delphine Fitz. "The Magdalene of the Hispanic Society by Jusepe de Ribera," *The Art Quarterly,* 5 (1942), pp. 223-229.

Darby, Delphine Fitz. "In the Train of a Vagrant *Silenus,"* *Art in America,* 31 (1943), pp. 140-150.

Darby, Delphine Fitz. "The Gentle Ribera, Painter of the Madonna and the Holy Family," *Gazette des Beaux-Arts,* ser. 6, 39 (1946), pp. 160-172.

Darby, Delphine Fitz. "Review of Elizabeth DuGué Trapier, *Ribera,"* *The Art Bulletin,* 35 (1953), pp. 68-74.

Darby, Delphine Fitz. "Ribera and the Wise Men," *The Art Bulletin,* 44 (December 1962), pp. 279-307.

Daulte, François. *La Pinacotéque de Villa Favorita. (Formes et Couleurs).* Lausanne, 1950.

De Dominici, Bernardo. *Vite dei pittori, scultori, ed architetti napoletani.* Naples, 1742-1745.

Delogu, Giuseppe. "Riberismo," *L'Arte,* 31 (1928), pp. 148-154.

De Rinaldis, Aldo. *Neapolitan Paintings of the Seicento.* New York, 1929.

De Rinaldis, Aldo. *La Galleria Nazionale d'Arte Antica.* Rome, 1932.

Domínguez, Martín. "El Testamento de Ribera," *Archivo de Arte Valenciano,* 24 (1953), pp. 80-84.

Domínguez Bordona, Jesús. "Noticias para la historia del Buen Retiro," *Revista de la Biblioteca, Archivos y Museos,* 10 (1933), p. 84.

Doria, Gino. *Il Museo e la Certosa di San Martino.* Naples, 1964.

Edinburgh (Waterhouse, Ellis). *Spanish Paintings.* Edinburgh Festival, Arts Council of Great Britain, The National Gallery of Scotland, August 19–September 8, 1951.

Eisler, Colin. *Paintings from the Samuel H. Kress Collection, European Schools, Excluding Italian.* Oxford, 1977.

El Escorial. *Eighth Marvel of the World.* Madrid, 1967.

Fahy, Everett. *"Juan de Pareja* by Diego Velázquez: A History of the Portrait and its Painter," *Metropolitan Museum of Art Bulletin,* 29 (June 1971), p. 457.

Faison, S. Lane. "Baroque and Nineteenth-Century Painting," *Apollo,* 88 (1968), pp. 466-477.

Faraglia, Nunzio Federigo. "Notizie di alcuni artisti che lavorarono nella chiesa di S. Martino e nel tesoro di S. Gennaro," Società di Storia Patria, Naples, *Archivio Storico per le Province Napoletane.* 10 (1885), pp. 435-461.

Faraglia, Nunzio Federigo. "Notizie di alcuni artistici che lavorarono nella chiesa di S. Martino sopra Napoli," Società di Storia Patria, Naples, *Archivio Storico per le Province Napoletane.* 17 (1892), pp. 657-678.

Farmer, David Hugh. *The Oxford Dictionary of Saints.* Oxford, 1978.

Felton, Craig. "The Earliest Paintings of Jusepe de Ribera," *Bulletin of the Wadsworth Atheneum,* ser. 6 (Winter 1969), pp. 2-11.

Felton, Craig. *Jusepe de Ribera, a Catalogue Raisonné.* Ph.D. Dissertation, University of Pittsburgh, 1971.

Felton, Craig. "More Early Paintings by Jusepe de Ribera," *Storia dell'Arte,* 26 (1976), pp. 31-43.

Ferguson, George. *Signs and Symbols of Christian Art.* New York, 1961.

Fernández Bayton, Gloria. *Inventarios reales, Testamentaría del rey Carlos II, 1701-1703.* Madrid, 1975.

Ferrari, Oreste and Giuseppe Scavizzi. *Luca Giordano.* Naples, 1966.

Filangieri e Moncada, Gaetano. "Documenti per la storia, le arti e le industrie dell province napoletane," *Indice degli artefici delle arti maggiori e minori,* Naples, 1891.

Fiordelisi, Alfonso. "La Trinità delle Monache," *Napoli Nobilissima,* 8 (1898), pp. 181-187.

Florence. *Mostra del ritratto italiano dalla fine del secolo XIV all'anno 1861.* Palazzo Vecchio, 1911.

Florence (Ojetti, Ugo and Nello Tarchiani). *Il ritratto italiano dal Caravaggio al Tiepolo alla mostra di Palazzo Vecchio nel MCMXI sotto gli auspici del Comune di Firenze.* 1927.

Florence (Tarchiani, Nello). *Pittura italiana del seicento e del settecento.* 1922.

Florence and Milan (Longhi, Roberto). *Caravaggio e dei Caravaggeschi.* 1951.

Forster-Hahn, Françoise. *Old Master Drawings from the Collection of Kurt Meissner, Zurich.* Stanford, 1969.

Fort Worth. *Kimbell Art Museum. Catalogue of the Collection.* 1972.

Fort Worth. *Kimbell Art Museum. Handbook of the Collection.* 1981.

Francis, Henry. "Jusepe de Ribera: *The Death of Adonis,*" *Cleveland Museum of Art Bulletin,* (November 1966), pp. 339-347.

Frankfurter, Alfred M. "The Spanish Old Masters at Rome," *The Antiquarian,* (August 1930), p. 43.

Frizzoni, G. "Il Museo Filangieri in Napoli," *Archivio Storico dell'Arte,* 2 (1889), pp. 293-300.

Galante, Gennaro Aspreno. *Guida sacra della città di Napoli.* Naples, 1873 (ed. 1967).

Gállego, Julián. *La peinture espagnole.* Paris, 1962.

García Hidalgo, José. *Principios para estudiar el arte de la pintura.* Madrid, 1693. ed. Madrid, 1955.

Gaya Nuño, Juan Antonio. *Historia de los museos de España.* Madrid, 1955.

Gaya Nuño, Juan Antonio. *La pintura española fuera de España.* Madrid, 1958.

Gaya Nuño, Juan Antonio. "Peinture picaresque," *L'Oeil,* 84 (1961), pp. 53-61.

Geneva. *Les chefs-d'oeuvre du Musée du Prado.* Musée d'Art et d'Histoire. June-August 1939.

Gerson, Horst. *Rembrandt Paintings.* Amsterdam, 1968.

Giglioli, Odorado H. "Le mostra d'arte antica a Firenze," *Rassegna d'Arte.* 7-8 (1922), pp. 201-231.

Gilbert, Claire. "Sur une composition retrouvée de Ribera d'après le relief alexandrin dit Visite de Dionysos chez Ikarios," *Revue Archéologique,* 41 (1953), pp. 70-81.

Gnudi, Cesare and Gian Carlo Cavilli. *Guido Reni.* Florence, 1955.

Golzio, Vincenzo. *Storia dell'arte classica e italiana, Il seicento e il settecento.* Turin, 1950.

Gombrich, Ernst. *Art and Illusion. A Study in the Psychology of Pictorial Representation.* Princeton, 1969.

Gudiol, José. "Span of Spanish Painting, 1150-1828," *Art News,* 40 (1941), p. 18.

Grabar, André. *Early Christian Art.* New York, 1968.

Graves, Robert, *The Greek Myths.* New York, 1955.

Greenville, South Carolina. *Bob Jones University Catalogue.* Greenville, 1954.

Greenville, South Carolina (Marlier, Georges and José Gudiol). *Bob Jones University. Catalogue of the Art Collection.* Greenville, 1961.

Harris, Enriqueta. "Exposición de pinturas y dibujos napolitanos en el Museo Bowes de Barnard Castle," *Archivo Español de Arte,* 36 (1963), pp. 131-133.

Hartford. *Exhibition of Italian Paintings of the Sei- and Settecento.* Wadsworth Atheneum, January 22–February 5, 1930.

Hartford. *Harvest of Plenty.* Wadsworth Atheneum, October 24–December 1, 1963.

Hartford. On Loan from Duveen. Wadsworth Atheneum. September 1967.

Haskell, Francis. *Rediscoveries in Art.* London, 1976.

Heinz, Günther. "Realismus und Rhetorik im Werk des Bartolomeo Passarotti," *Jahrbuch der Kunsthistorischen Sammlungen in Wien.* (1972), pp. 153-169.

Hellman, George S. *Original Drawings by the Old Masters. The Collection Formed by Joseph Green Cogswell, 1786-1871.* New York, 1915.

Hermanin, Frederico. "Acquisti dell R. Galleria d'Arte Antica," *Bollettino d'Arte,* 5 (1924-1925), pp. 3-10.

Hibbard, Howard. "Guido Reni's Painting of the *Immaculate Conception,*" *The Metropolitan Museum of Art Bulletin,* (Summer 1969), pp. 19-32.

"High Flavors," *Apollo,* n.s. 96 (Summer 1972), p. 247.

Hodge, Gerald. "Spanish Art: a Contribution to Medicine," *Journal of the American Medical Association,* 209 (1969), p. 1696.

Hoogewerff, G. J. "Hendrick van Somer, Schilder van Amsterdam, Navolger van Ribera," *"Oud-Holland,* (1943), pp. 158-172.

Iconografía Española. Junta de Iconografía Nacional, Madrid [n.d.].

Indianapolis (Carter, David Giles and Wilbur D. Peat). *El Greco to Goya: A Loan Exhibition of Spanish Painting of the 17th and 18th Centuries.* The John Herron Museum of Art, February 10–March 24, 1963.

Indianapolis (Fraser, A. Ian). *A Catalogue of the Clowes Collection.* 1973.

Indianapolis (Janson, Anthony F. with A. Ian Fraser). *100 Masterpieces of Painting. Indianapolis Museum of Art.* 1980.

Iowa State University. *Figure Paintings.* November 5-30, 1936.

Jacksonville, Florida. *700 Years of Spanish Painting.* October 28–November 30, 1965.

Justi, Carl. *Diego Velázquez and His Times.* 1889.

Justi, Carl. "Review of Richter, 1889," *Kunstchronik,* 1 (1890), p. 320.

Kapterewa, T. *Velázquez und die spanische Porträtmalerei.* Leipzig, 1956.

Kerrigan, Anthony. "Sobre las razzias en el arte europeo," *Goya*, 36 (1960), pp. 353-361.

Kitzinger, Ernst. *Early Medieval Art.* Bloomington, 1964.

Konečný, Lubomír. "Another 'Postilla' to the Five Senses by Jusepe de Ribera," *Paragone*, 285 (1973), pp. 85-92.

Konečný, Lubomír. "Shades of Leonardo in an Etching by Jusepe de Ribera," *Gazette des Beaux-Arts*, 95 (1980), pp. 91-95.

Krafft, Jean. "Le rire, harmonie perdue," *Aesculape*, 10 (November 1957).

Kubler, George and Martin Soria. *Art and Architecture in Spain and Portugal.* Baltimore, 1959.

Lafond, Paul. "Des portraits de fous, de nains et de phenomènes en Espagne aux XVe et XVIe siècles," *Revue de l'Arte Ancien et Moderne*, 11 (1902), pp. 217-227.

Lafuente Ferrari, Enrique. *Breve historia de la pintura española.* Madrid, 1953.

Le Brun, Jean-Baptiste-Pierre. *Recueil de graveurs au trait . . .* Paris, 1809.

Loeser, Charles. "I quadri italiani nella galleria di Strasburgo," *Archivio Storico dell'Arte*, ser. 2, 2 (1896), p. 285.

London (Braham, Allan). *El Greco to Goya. The Taste for Spanish Paintings in Britain and Ireland.* The National Gallery, 1981.

London. *Exhibition of Spanish Art.* New Gallery, 1895-1896.

London. *Exhibition of Spanish Painting.* Arts Council of Great Britain, The National Gallery, 1938.

London (Gibbs-Smith, C. H. and H. V. T. Percival). *The Wellington Museum, Apsley House.* 1964.

London. *Illustrated Catalogue of the Exhibition of Spanish Old Masters in Support of the National Gallery Funds and for the Benefit of the Sociedad Española de Amigos del Arte.* Grafton Galleries, October 1913–January 1914.

London. *In the Light of Caravaggio.* Trafalgar Galleries, 1976.

London (Kitson, Michael). *Salvator Rosa.* Hayward Gallery, October 17–December 23, 1973.

London (Maclaren, Neil). *An Exhibition of Spanish Painting.* Arts Council of Great Britain, The National Gallery, 1947.

London (Maclaren, Neil and Allan Braham). *National Gallery Catalogues. The Spanish School.* 1970.

London. *The National Gallery. Catalogue. II.* 1929.

London (Pérez Sánchez, Alfonso E. and Xavier de Salas, catalogue; and Nigel Glendenning, introduction). *The Golden Age of Spanish Painting.* Royal Academy of Arts, January 10–March 14, 1976.

London. *Wellington Museum, Apsley House. Guide.* 1952.

London (Whitfield, Clovis and Jane Martineau). *Painting in Naples 1606-1705 from Caravaggio to Giordano.* Royal Academy of Arts, 1982.

Longhi, Roberto. "Battistello," *L'Arte*, (1915), pp. 58-75, 120-137.

Longhi, Roberto and August L. Mayer. *Gli antichi pittori spagnoli della collezione Contini-Bonacossi.* Rome, 1930.

Longhi, Roberto. "I *Cinque Sensi* del Ribera," *Paragone*, (1966), pp. 74-78.

López Navio, José. "La gran colección de pinturas del Marqués de Leganés," *Analecta Calasanctiana*, Madrid, 1962.

López-Rey, José. "Views and Reflections on the Exhibition 'Trésors de la peinture espagnole' at Paris,' *Gazette des Beaux-Arts*, ser. 6, 24 (1963), pp. 333-334.

López-Rey, José. *Velázquez.* London, 1963.

Los Angeles. *A Decade of Collecting: 1965-1975.* Los Angeles County Museum of Art, April 8–June 29, 1975.

Loucheim, A. B. "St. Jerome, Variations on a Theme," *Art News*, 44 (1945), p. 31.

Lugano (Heinemann, Rudolph). *Stiftung Sammlung Schloss Rohoncz, Lugano-Castagnola, Villa Favorita.* Zurich, 1937.

Lurie, Ann Tzeutschler and Denis Mahon. "Caravaggio's *Crucifixion of Saint Andrew* from Valladolid," *The Bulletin of the Cleveland Museum of Art*, 64 (January 1977), pp. 1-24.

MacFall, Haldane. *The Later Italians and the Genius of Spain.* London, [n.d.]

Madrazo y Kuntz, Pedro de. *Viaje artístico de tres siglos por las colecciones de los reyes de España.* Madrid, 1884.

Madrid (Labrada, Fernando). *Real Academia de Bellas Artes de San Fernando. Catálogo de las pinturas.* 1965.

Madrid (Madrazo, Pedro de). *Catálogo del Museo del Prado.* 1913.

Madrid (Pérez Sánchez, Alfonso E.). Museo del Prado. *Catálogo de dibujos, I. Dibujos españoles siglos XV-XVII.* 1972.

Madrid. *Museo del Prado, Catálogo de las pinturas.* Madrid, 1972.

"The Magnasco Society," *Apollo*, 2, p. 297.

Mancini, Giulio. (1614-1621), ed. Luigi Salerno, *Considerazioni sulla pittura.* Rome, Accademia Nazionale dei Lincei, 1956-1957.

Mantz, Paul. "La collection La Caze au Musée du Louvre," *Gazette des Beaux-Arts*, ser. 2, 3 (1870), pp. 393-406.

Marangoni, M. *Il Caravaggio.* Florence, 1922.

Marangoni, M. *Vita d'Arte.* 1922.

Marini, Maurizio. "Caravaggio 1607: *La negazione di Pietro,*" *Napoli Nobilissima*, 12 (September-October 1973), pp. 189-194.

Martin, John R. *"The Butcher's Shop* of the Carracci," *The Art Bulletin*, 45 (1963), pp. 263-266.

Martínez, José [Jusepe]. *Discursos practicables del nobilísimo arte de la pintura.* Madrid, ed. 1866.

Martínez Ripoll, Antonio. *Catálogo de las pinturas de la antigua colección d'Estoup de Murcia.* Murcia, 1981.

Mateu y Llopis, Felipe. "Un breve comentario paleográfico y onomástico a los documentos biográficos setabenses de Ribera," *Archivo de Arte Valenciano*, 24 (1953), p. 6.

Mayer, August. *Jusepe de Ribera.* Leipzig, 1908.

Mayer, August L. "Notes on Spanish Pictures in American Collections," *Art in America*, 3 (1915), pp. 309-320.

Mayer, August. *Geschichte der Spanische Malerei.* Leipzig, 1922.

Mayer, August. *Jusepe de Ribera, Lo Spagnoletto.* Leipzig, 1923.

Mayer, August. "El *Bacchanal* de Ribera y su origen," *Boletín de la Sociedad Española de Excursiones,* 25 (1927), pp. 159-160.

Mayer, August. "The Contini-Bonacossi Collection of Old Spanish Masters," *Apollo,* 12 (1930), pp. 1-8.

Mayer, August. "Anotaciones a Algunos Cuadros del Museo del Prado," *Boletín de la Sociedad Española de Excursiones,* 42 (1934), pp. 291-299.

Mayer, August. "New Documents and Attributions from the Strasbourg Museum to the Venice Palazzo Ducale," *Gazette des Beaux-Arts,* ser. 6, 27 (1945), pp. 83-92.

Mayer, August. *Historia de la pintura española.* Madrid, 1947.

"The Metropolitan Museum Buys Well Known Canvas by Ribera," *Art News,* 32 (August 18, 1934), p. 12.

Mexico City. *Maestros europeos en las Galerías de San Carlos, México.* Milan, 1963.

Milan (Berenson, Bernard and others). *La Pinacoteca Poldi-Pezzoli.* 1955.

Milan (Morassi, Antonio). *Il Museo Poldi-Pezzoli in Milano.* Rome, [n.d.].

Milan (Wittgens, R.). *Il Museo Poldi-Pezzoli a Milano.* 1937.

Milicua, José. Review of E. DuGué Trapier, *Ribera, Archivo Español de Arte,* 25 (1952), pp. 296-298.

Milicua, José. "El centenario de Ribera: Ribera en Roma, el manuscrito de Mancini," *Archivo Español de Arte,* 25 (1952), pp. 309-322.

Minneapolis. *Treasures from the Allen Memorian Art Museum.* 1966.

Moffitt, John F. "Observations on the *Poet* by Ribera," *Paragone,* 337 (1978), pp. 75-90.

Montauban. *Exposition des chef d'oeuvres espagnoles du musée du Louvre.* Chambre de commerce, 1942.

Morassi, Antonio, *Ribera.* Milan, 1936.

Muller, Priscilla E. "State of Research: Contributions to the Study of Spanish Drawings," *The Art Bulletin,* 58 (1976), pp. 604-611.

Munich and Vienna. *Von Greco bis Goya: Vier Jahrhunderte Spanische Malerei.* Munich, February 20–April 25; Vienna, May 14–July 11, 1982.

Muñoz, Antonio. *Pièces de choix du collection du Comte Grégoire Stroganoff.* Rome, 1912.

Naples (Acton, Francesco). *Il Museo Civico Gaetano Filangieri di Napoli.* 1961.

Naples (Bologna, Ferdinando and Raffaello Causa). *Mostra didattica di Carlo Sellitto, primo Caravaggesco napoletano.* Museo e Gallerie Nazionali di Capodimonte, 1977.

Naples (Causa, Raffaello). *La Madonna nella pittura del '600 a napoli.* Palazzo Reale, 1954.

Naples (De Rinaldis, Aldo). *Pinacoteca del Museo Nazionale di Napoli.* 1928.

Naples (Filangieri, Gaetano). *Catálogo del Museo Filangieri.* 1888.

Naples (Molajoli, Bruno). *Notizie su Capodimonte, Catálogo delle gallerie e del museo.* 1960.

Naples (Ortolani, Sergio). *La mostra della pittura napoletana dei secoli XVII-XVIII-XIX.* 1938.

Naples. *Ribera.* 1877.

"New Acquisitions," *Art Journal,* 37 (Fall 1977), p. 57.

New York. *Art Treasures of the Metropolitan.* The Metropolitan Museum of Art, November 7, 1952–September 7, 1953.

New York (Burroughs, B.). *Exhibition of Spanish Paintings from El Greco to Goya.* Metropolitan Museum of Art, February 17–April 1, 1928.

New York. *Exhibition at Durlacher Brothers.* 1945.

New York. *An Exhibition of Paintings.* E. and A. Silberman Galleries, 1955.

New York. *Masterpieces of Art.* World's Fair, 1940.

New York. *Masterpieces from the Wadsworth Atheneum, Hartford, Connecticut.* Knoedler Galleries, January 21–February 15, 1958.

New York. *The Painter's Light.* The Metropolitan Museum of Art, 1971.

New York (Wehle, Harry B.). *The Metropolitan Museum of Art. A Catalogue of Italian, Spanish and Byzantine Paintings.* 1940.

Nicodemi, Giorgio. "La pinacoteca dell' Arcivescovado di Milano," *Rassegna d'Arte,* 14 (1914), pp. 279-288.

"Noticias de arte," *Goya,* 17 (1957), pp. 339-340.

Oberlin, Ohio. "Exhibition of Paintings and Graphics by Jusepe de Ribera, Catalogue," *Allen Memorial Art Museum Bulletin,* Oberlin College, 14 (Winter 1957), pp. 73-88.

Obuena, José. " 'El Españoleto', Gloria Valenciana," *Archivo Español de Arte,* 24 (1953), pp. 95-97.

Pacelli, Vincenzo. "New Documents Concerning Caravaggio in Naples," *The Burlington Magazine,* 119 (December 1977), pp. 819-827.

Pacelli, Vincenzo. "Caracciolo Studies," *The Burlington Magazine,* 120 (August 1978), pp. 493-496.

Pacheco, Francisco. *Arte de la pintura, su antiguedad, y grandezas.* Seville, 1649, ed. Madrid, 1956.

Palm, Erwin W. "Ein Vergil von Ribera," *Pantheon,* 33 (1975), pp. 23-27.

Palm, Erwin W. "Review of Jonathan Brown, *Jusepe de Ribera: Prints and Drawings,* " *Pantheon,* 33 (1975), pp. 80-81.

Palm Beach, Florida. *Portraits: A Record of Changing Tastes.* Society of the Four Arts, February 1964.

Palomino de Castro y Velasco, Antonio. *El Parnaso español pintoresco laureado.* Madrid, 1724, ed. Madrid, 1947.

Panofsky, Erwin. "Albrecht Dürer and Classical Antiquity," *Meaning in the Visual Arts.* New York, 1974.

Pantorba, Bernardino de. *José de Ribera.* Barcelona, 1946.

Paoletti, John, "The Italian School," *Apollo,* 83 (December 1968), pp. 425-426.

Paris, Pierre. *"L'Arte en Espagne au XVIII siècle,"* in A. Michel *Histoire de l'Arte.* 4, Paris, 21.

Paris (Baticle, Jeannine). *Trésors de la peinture espagnole.* Musée des Arts Décoratifs, 1963.

Paris (Brejon de Lavergnée, Arnauld and Dominique Thiébault). *Catalogue sommaire illustré des peintures du musée du Louvre. II. Italie, Espagne, Allemagne, Grande-Bretagne et divers.* (With Spanish entries by Jeannine Baticle.) 1981.

Paris (Carvallo, J.). *Exposition d'art ancien espagnol. Hôtel Jean Charpentier, Summer 1925.*

Paris. *Exposition du bazar Bonne Nouvelle* (appartenant à Monsieur La Caze). 1849.

Paris (Hautecouer, Louis). *Musée National du Louvre, Catalogue des peintures exposées dans les galeries. Il, Ecole Italienne et Espagnole.* 1926.

Paris (Huyghe, René). *Musée du Louvre.* (Nouvelle edition francaise.) 1963.

Paris (Laclotte, Michel). *Musée du Louvre.* 1970.

Paris (Nicolle, Marcel). *La peinture au Musée du Louvre, école espagnole.* 1929.

Paris (Pérez Sánchez, Alfonso E. and Xavier de Salas). *La peinture espagnole du siècle d'or de Greco à Velázquez.* Petit Palais, April-June 1976.

Paris (Reiset, Frédéric de). *Notice des tableaux légués au musée impérial du Louvre par Louis La Caze.* 1870.

Paris (Ricci, Seymour de). *Description raisonnée des peintures du Louvre, I. Italie et Espagne.* 1913.

Parks, R. *"Ribera's Early Drunken Silenus,"* *Bulletin of the Art Association of Indianapolis,* 1954.

Parrino, Domenico Antonio. *Teatro eroico e politico de'governi de' Vicere del Regno di napoli.* Naples, 1692.

Pasadena, California (Hermann, Frank). *Selected Paintings at The Norton Simon Museum, Pasadena, California.* London and New York, 1980.

Pau. *Catalogue abrégé des tableaux exposés dans les salons de l'ancien asile de Pau, appartenant aux héritiers feu Msr. l'Enfant don Sébastien de Bourbon et Bragance.* September, 1876.

Pepper. D. Stephen. *"Caravaggio riveduto e corretto: la mostra di Cleveland,"* *Arte Illustrata,* 5 (March 1972), p. 178.

Pérez Sánchez, Alfonso E. *Pintura italiana del siglo XVII.* Madrid, 1965.

Pérez Sánchez, Alfonso E. *"Las colecciones de pintura del Conde de Monterrey,"* *Bolétin de la Real Academia de la Historia,* (1970), pp. 417-459.

Pérez Sánchez, Alfonso E. *Pintura italiana del siglo XVII.* Casón del Buen Retiro, Madrid, April–May 1970.

Pérez Sánchez, Alfonso E. *Los Ribera de Osuna.* Seville, 1978.

Philadelphia. *Catalogue of the William L. Elkins Collection.* Paris, 1900.

Pigler, Alois. *Barockthemen.* Budapest-Berlin, 1956.

Pillement, Georges. *Ribera.* Paris, 1929.

Ponz, Antonio. *Viaje de España.* Madrid, 1776.

Posner, Donald. *Annibale Carracci.* London, 1971.

Post, Chandler R. *"Painting of St. Jerome by Ribera,"* *Fogg Art Museum Notes,* 1 (1922), pp. 15-21.

Prohaska, Wolfgang. *"Carlo Sellitto,"* *The Burlington Magazine,* 117 (January 1975), pp. 3-11.

Prohaska, Wolfgang. *"Beiträge zu Giovanni Battista Caracciolo,"* *Jahrbuch der Kunsthistorischen Sammlungen in Wien,* 74 (1978), pp. 153-269.

Prota-Giurleo, Ulisse. *Pittore Napoletani del Seicento.* Naples, 1953.

Prota-Giurleo, Ulisse. *"Giovanni Maria Trabaci e gli organisti della Real Cappella di Palazzo di Napoli,"* *L'Organo,* (December 1960), pp. 190-191.

Quevedo y Villegas, Francisco. *Obras completas, Prosa.* Madrid, 1961.

Raffaelli, Jean Francois. *"Promenades d'un artiste au Musée du Louvre,"* *Annales politiques et littéraires,* Paris, [n.d.].

Raleigh, North Carolina (Valentiner, W. R.). *Catalogue of the Paintings, North Carolina Museum of Art.* 1956.

Ratouis de Limay, Paul. *"Trois collectionneurs du XIXe: Le docteur La Caze,"* *Le Dessin,* (June-July 1938), p. 80.

"Review of Roberto Longhi, I Cinque sensi del Ribera," *Archivo Español de Arte,* 39 (1966), p. 232.

Richmond, Virginia. *Treasures in America.* January 13-March 5, 1961.

Richter, J. P. *Descriptive Catalogue of the Collection of Pictures Belonging to the Earl of Northbrook.* London, 1889.

Rodríquez-Buzón Calle, Manuel. *La Colegiata de Osuna.* (Arte hispalense), Seville, 1982.

Rodríquez Marín, Francisco. *El gran Duque de Osuna.* Madrid, 1920.

Rof, Carvallo J. *Enigmas de la mujer barbuda de Ribera.* Madrid, 1975.

Rogadeo di Torrequadra, Eustachio. *"La quadreria del Principe di Sicilia,"* *Napili Nobilissima,* 7 (1898), pp. 72-75, 107-110.

Rogers, Paul. *"The Blind Man and His Boy,"* *Allen Memorial Art Museum Bulletin,* 14 (Winter 1957), pp. 49-59.

Rolfs, Wilhelm. *Geschichte der Malerei Neapels.* Leipzig, 1910.

Rome. *Gli antichi pittori spagnoli della collezione Contini-Bonacossi.* Galleria Nazionale. May-June 1930.

Rome. *Un' antologia di restauri.* Galleria Nazionale d'Arte Antica, Palazzo Barberini, 1982.

Rome (di Carpegna, Nolfo and Emilio Lavagnino). *Pittori napoletani del '600 e del '700.* Palazzo Barberini, April-May 1958.

Ruffo, Vincenzo. *"Galleria Ruffo nel secolo XVII in Messina,"* Part IV. *"Lettere di Pietro da Cortona, di Ribera lo Spagnoletto, di Artemisia Gentileschi, del cavaliere Massimo Stanzione, di Luca Forte, del Prior di Bagnara,"* *Bollettino d'Arte,* 10 (1916), pp. 44-47.

Ruotolo, R. *Mercanti-collezionisti fiamminghi a Napoli, Gaspare Roomer e i VandenEynden.* Meta di Sorrento, 1982.

Rusconi, A. J. "La Galerie Nationale Romaine Galerie Corsini," *Les Arts*, 1 (1902), pp. 17-30.

Rusconi, A. J. "Exposition des portraits italiens a Florence," *Les Arts*, 10 (1911), pp. 1-32.

Salazar, Lorenzo. "La patria e la famiglia dello Spagnoletto: Nuovi documenti," *Napoli Nobilissima*, 3 (1894), pp. 97-100.

Salazar, Lorenzo. "Salvator Rosa ed i Fracanzano," *Napoli Nobilissima*, 12 (1903), pp. 119-123.

San Casciano Val di Pesa (Nugent, M.). *Alla mostra della pittura italiana del'600 e '700. Note e impressioni*. 1930.

Sandrart, Joachim von. *Academie der Bau-, Bild- und Mahlerey-Kunst von 1675*. (ed. by A. R. Pelzer, Munich, 1925).

San Francisco. On Loan from Norton Simon. De Young Museum, 1968-1970.

San José, Costa Rica (Mosby, Dewey F.). *Cinco siglos de obras maestras de la pintura en colecciones norteamericanas cedidas en préstamo a Costa Rica*. 1978.

Southhampton. *Exhibition*. 1946.

Sarasota, Florida (Gilbert, Creighton). *Baroque Painters of Naples*. The John and Mable Ringling Museum of Art, March 3-April 4, 1961.

Sarnelli, Pompeo. *Guida dei forestieri par Napoli*. Naples, 1697.

Sarthou Carreres, Carlos. *Juan José de Ribera y su arte, el Españoleto y su patria*. Madrid, 1947.

Sarthou Carreres, Carlos. "Juan José de Ribera 'El Espanoleto'," *Archivo de Arte Valenciano*, 24 (1953).

Scannelli, Francesco. *Il microscosmo della pittura*. Cesna, 1657.

Scaramuccia, Luigi. *Le finezze de pennelli italiani*. Pavia, 1674.

Schleier, Erich. "Una Postilla per i *Cinque sensi* del giovane Ribera," *Paragone*, (1968), pp. 79-80.

Schnapper, Antoine. "Les académies peintes et le *Christ en Croix* de David," *La Révue du Louvre*, 24 (1974), pp. 381-392.

Sedelmeyer, Charles. *Third Series of One Hundred Paintings Belonging to the Sedelmeyer Gallery*. Paris, 1896.

Sérullaz, Maurice. *Evolution de la peinture espagnole des origines à nos jours*. (Horizon de France), Paris, 1947.

Sigismondo, Giuseppe. *Descrizione della città di Napoli*. Naples, ed. 1824.

Solvay, Lucien. *L'arte espagnol*. Paris-London, 1887.

Sopher, Marcus S. *Seventeenth-Century Italian Prints*. Stanford, 1978.

Spear, Richard. "Prepatory Drawings by Domenichino," *Master Drawings*, 6 (1968), pp. 111-131.

Spear, Richard. "Unknown Pictures by the Caravaggisti," *Storia dell'Arte*, (1972), pp. 149-161.

Spinazzola, Vittorio. "Note e documenti sulla fondazione, i riordinamenti e gli inventati della R. Pinacoteca del Museo Napoli," *Napoli Nobilissima*, 8 (1898), p. 48.

Spinosa, Nicola. *L'opera completa del Ribera*. Milan, 1978.

Stechow, Wolfgang. "A Note on *The Poet* by Ribera," *Allen Memorial Art Museum Bulletin*, 14 (1957), pp. 60-72.

Stechow, Wolfgang. "Jusepe de Ribera," *Oberlin Alumni Magazine*, (May 1957), pp. 12-13.

Stockholm (Nordenfalk, Carl and others). *Stora Spanska Mästare*. National Museum, December 12, 1959-March 13, 1960.

Stott, Deborah. "Fatte à Sembianza di Pittura: Jacopo Sansovino's Bronze Reliefs in S. Marco," *The Art Bulletin*, 64 (1982), pp. 370-388.

Stoughton, Michael. *Paintings of Giovanni Battista Caracciolo*. Ph.D. Dissertation, The University of Michigan, 1974.

Stoughton, Michael. "Review of Mostra Didattica Carlo Sellitto," *Antologia di Belli Arti*, 1 (1977), pp. 366-369.

Stoughton, Michael. "Giovanni Battista Caracciolo: New Biographical Documents," *The Burlington Magazine*, 120 (April 1978), pp. 204-215.

Stoughton, Michael. "G. B. Caracciolo and His Son, Pompeo: Documents from the Archivio Storico del Banco di Napoli," *Antologia di Belle Arti*, 4 (1980), pp. 187-194.

Strasbourg (Haug, Hans). *Catalogue, Musée des Beaux-Arts, Strasbourg*. 1938.

Strasbourg. *Verzeichnis des Kunstmuseums der Stadt Strasbourg*. 1912.

Strazzullo, Franco. *La Real Cappella del Tesoro di S. Gennaro*. Naples, 1978.

Sullivan, Edward. "Ribera's Clubfooted Boy: Image and Symbol," *Marsyas*, 19 (1977-1978), pp. 17-21.

Tarchiani, Nello. "La mostra del ritratto Italiano dalla fine del secolo XVI all'anno 1861, in Palazzo Vecchio a Firenze," *Rassegna d'Arte*, 11 (1911), pp. 77-92.

Tokyo. *Le grand siècle dans les collections francaises*. National Museum, 1966.

Toledo (Cardona, María de). *Catálogo, Fundación Duque de Lerma, El Hospital de Tavera*. 1951.

Toledo (Pérez Sánchez, Alfonso E.). *El Toledo de El Creco*. Hospital de Tavera/Iglesia de San Pedro Martin. April-June 1982.

Toledo, Ohio (Gudiol, José). *Spanish Painting*. The Toledo Museum of Art, March 16-April 27, 1941.

Toledo, Ohio. *The Toledo Museum of Art, European Paintings*. 1976.

Tormo y Monzó, Elías. *Ribera en El Museo del Prado (El arte en España No. 21)*. Barcelona, [1912].

Tormo y Monzó, Elías. "Varias obras maestros de Ribera, inéditas," *Boletín de la Sociedad Española de Excursiones*, 24 (1916), pp. 11-16.

Tormo y Monzó, Elías. *Los cuadros de Ribera de la colegiata de Osuna y cómo dio principio nuestro pintor a su glorioso nombradía*. Osuna, 1919-1920.

Tormo y Monzó, Elías. *Ribera*. Barcelona, 1922.

Torriti, Piero. *La Galleria del Palazzo Durazzo Pallavicini a Genoa*. Genoa, 1967.

Trapier, Elizabeth DuGué. *Ribera*. New York, 1952.

Trapier, Elizabeth DuGué. *Valdés Leal, Spanish Baroque Painter*. New York, 1960.

Tufari, Raffaele. *La Certosa di S. Martino in Napoli.* Naples, 1854.

Turner, Evan. "Ribera's Philosophers," *Wadsworth Atheneum Bulletin,* (Spring 1958), pp. 5-14.

Vega Carpio, Lope Félix de. *Los trabajos de Jacob (Sueños hay que verdad son). Obras de Lope de Vega.* (Real Academia Española). Madrid, 1893.

Viardot, Louis. *Les Musées d'Allemagne et de la Russie.* Paris, 1844.

Vienna. *Description des tableaux et des pièces de sculpture que renferme la Gallerie de Son Altesse Francois Chef et Prince de la Maison de Liechtenstein.* 1780.

Vienna (Fanti, Vicenzio). *Descrizione completa di tutto ciò che ritrovarsi nella Galleria di pittura e scultura di sua altezza Giuseppe Wenceslas del S.R.I. principe regnante della casa di Liechtenstein.* 1767.

Vienna (Heinz, Günther). *Katalog der Graf Harrach'schen Gemäldegalerie.* 1960.

Vienna (Kronfeld, Adolf). *Führer durch die Fürstliche Liechtensteinsche Gemäldegalerie.* 1927 and 1931.

Viñes, Gonzalo I. "La verdadera partida de bautismo del Españoleto y otros datos de familia," *Archivo de Arte Valenciano,* 9 (1929), pp. 18-24.

Vitzthum, Walter. *Cento disegni napoletani, sec. XVI-XVII.* Florence, 1967.

Vitzthum, Walter and Catherine Monbeig-Goguel. *Le dessin à Naples du XVIe siècle au XVIIIe siècle.* Paris, 1967.

Vitzthum, Walter. "Disegni inediti di Ribera," *Arte Illustrata,* 4 (1971), pp. 74-84.

Volpe, Carlo. "Annotazioni sulla mostra caravaggesca di Cleveland," *Paragone,* 263 (January 1972), pp. 72-73.

Waagen, Gustav F. *Works of Art and Artists in England.* London, 1838.

Waagen, Gustav F. *Treasures of Art in Great Britain.* London, 1854.

Washington, D. C. (Shaw, J. B.). *Old Master Drawings from Christ Church Oxford.* National Gallery of Art, 1972.

Waterhouse, Ellis. *Italian Baroque Painting.* London, 1962.

Wehle, Harry B. "A Painting by Jusepe de Ribera," *The Metropolitan Museum of Art Bulletin,* 29 (1934), pp. 119-122.

Wethey, Harold E. "Spanish Painting at Indianapolis and Providence," *The Burlington Magazine,* 105 (1963), pp. 206-208.

Wethey, Harold E. *Titian: The Religious Paintings.* London, 1969.

Wilton House (Gambarini, C.). *A Description of the Earl of Pembroke's Pictures.* London, 1731.

Wilton House (Pembroke, Sidney, 16th Earl of). *A Catalogue of the Paintings and Drawings in the Collection at Wilton House, Salisbury, Wiltshire.* London, 1968.

Wind, Barry. "Annibale Carracci's 'Scherzo': The Christ Church *Butcher Shop,*" *The Art Bulletin,* 58 (March 1976), pp. 93-96.

Wind, Edgar. *Pagan Mysteries in the Renaissance.* New Haven, 1958.

Winnipeg (Eastman, A. C.). *Favorite Italian and Spanish Masters of the 17th and 18th Centuries (The Baroque Era).* Winnipeg Art Gallery Association, October 24-November 18, 1951.

Winnipeg (Eckhardt, F.). *El Greco to Goya.* Winnipeg Art Gallery Association, April 16-May 5, 1955.

Wittkower, Rudolf. *Art and Architecture in Italy, 1600 to 1750.* Baltimore, 1965.

Woermann, Karl. "Jusepe de Ribera," *Zeitschrift für bildende Kunst,* 1 (1890), pp. 141-150, 177-184.

Wright, Georgia. "Caravaggio's *Entombment* Considered *in situ,*" *The Art Bulletin,* 60 (March 1978), pp. 35-42.

Ximénez, Fr. Andrés. *Descripción del Real Monasterio de San Lorenzo del Escorial.* 1764.